THE MODERN QUR'AN: LESSONS FOR TODAY

THE MODERN QUR'AN: LESSONS FOR TODAY

Ahmed Affi

Copyright © 2016 Ahmed Affi
All rights reserved.

ISBN: 0954567218
ISBN 13: 9780954567217

ACKNOWLEDGEMENT

All praises due to God for His mercy and blessings and for making it possible to complete this book. There are too many individuals to name on this page who have selflessly assisted me in the preparation of this book, but I am especially indebted to Hassan Affi for his invaluable contribution; in particular, for his helpful suggestions, assisting with the research and for typing the complete draft of the book.

The completion of this book would not have been possible without the generous financial contribution of Hussein Affi and Abdullahi Affi, and to my family who have been patient with me during the writing of this book, I also thank you. A special thank you goes to my dearest wife, Fadumo Farah, for her always unwavering support, guidance and encouragement.

CONTENTS

Acknowledgement · v
Glossary ·ix
Introduction ·xiii

Chapter 1   Arabia Before and After Muhammad · · · · · · · · · · · · · · 1
Chapter 2   Prophet Muhammad's Life and Struggles · · · · · · · · · · · 9
Chapter 3   What is the Qur'ān? · 23
Chapter 4   Revelations of the Qur'ān · 41
Chapter 5   Stages of Revelation · 53
Chapter 6   Muhammad in Medina · 59
Chapter 7   Unambiguous Verses and Ambiguous Verses · · · · · · · · 80
Chapter 8   Qur'ānic Oaths · 92
Chapter 9   Mysterious Letters · 104
Chapter 10 Argumentation · 112
Chapter 11 Commanding Right and Forbidding Wrong · · · · · · · · 130
Chapter 12 The Qur'ānic Concept of Justice · · · · · · · · · · · · · · · 149
Chapter 13 Qur'ānic Legislation · 162
Chapter 14 Mecca and Medina Surahs · · · · · · · · · · · · · · · · · · · 191
Chapter 15 The Qur'ān and Other Holy Scriptures · · · · · · · · · · · 204
Chapter 16 Abrogation in the Qur'ān · 219
Chapter 17 Qur'ānic Inimitability · 229
Chapter 18 Qur'ānic Jihad · 244

Chapter 19 Qur'ānic Compilation · 258
Chapter 20 The Aesthetic Power of the Qur'ān · · · · · · · · · · · · · · · 270

　　　　　　Bibliography and Further Reading · · · · · · · · · · · · · · · · 281
　　　　　　Index · 291

GLOSSARY

Companion: a Muslim believed to have met and lived with the Prophet during his lifetime.

Contextualist: the socio-historical context of the Qur'an.

Hadith: sayings and practices of the Prophet Muhammad transmitted through a chain of narrators; the Prophet's normative example.

Hajj: annual pilgrimage to Mecca. Muslims are enjoined to undertake the Hajj once in their lifetime, if they are financially and physically able to do so.

Halal: permissible; in Islamic law what is not prohibited.

Haram: forbidden; in Islamic law that which is prohibited.

Injīl: the Gospel, the scripture bestowed to the Prophet Jesus.

Islam: one who surrenders himself willingly to God, without limiting this term to any specific community.

Ka'ba: the holiest shrine of Islam in Mecca.

Kāfir: those who knowingly deny the prophethood of Muhammad. Concealment of the truth.

Mathal: simile, parable, metaphor, symbol.

Muhkam: inherently clear Qur'anic verses that allow for one definitive interpretation.

Mu'min: a believer; a person of faith.

Mutashābih: verses of the Qur'an that are ambiguous and allow for a range of interpretations and diversity of opinion.

Naskh: abrogation of a text of the Qur'an.

Ramadan: the ninth month of the Islamic lunar calendar; the month of fasting. The Qur'an was first revealed to the Prophet Muhammad during this month.

People of the Book: people who received revelation from God, such as Jews and Christians.

Shari'ah: lit. water source, the path,

Shaikh: old man, leader, religious scholar.

Shi'ah: faction or party, the largest group of Muslims after the Sunnis.

Sīrah: referring to the biography of the Prophet Muhammad.

Sunni: a member of the largest branch of Islam.

Surah: any of the 114 chapters of the Qur'an. Each chapter contains a number of verses.

Textualist: a form of tradition-based tafsir (exegesis) which examines interpretation from a strictly linguistic and/or text based perspective

GLOSSARY

Torah: the scripture revealed to the Prophet Moses.

Ummah: people, community; people sharing a common religion.

Ummiy: gentile, commonly interpreted to mean "unlettered".

INTRODUCTION

AT A TIME when an abundance of information is available online and through other formal and informal channels, why another book about the Qur'ān?

The fact is that an abundance of information does not equate to the quality of that information, and that much of what people think they know about the Qur'ān is simply inaccurate; often grievously so. From the seeds of these inaccuracies greater and greater misapprehensions grow, among Muslims and non-Muslims alike, often with very distressing consequences for everyday life.

From the earliest days of his Call to receive God's word, Muhammad was in no doubt whatsoever that the message he was receiving was a continuation, or even a revival, of the revelations received by the earlier prophets. This is backed up by material from the early Surahs from Mecca, in which the Qur'ān speaks of the "recorded revelations of Abraham and Moses."[1] Reflecting the social composition of Medina, the Qur'ān discusses the Jewish community pragmatically in terms of the political pacts they had made, and the violations they had committed. With respect to Christians, they are discussed in much more theological and religious terms.

Since the earliest days of Islam, Muslims have held the Qur'ān to be the literal divine word of God, revealed to the Prophet Muhammad between 610 and 632 (throughout the book we will refer to a Christian Era (C.E.) timeline, as this is the convention that most readers will be familiar with). In this respect, it goes well beyond the classification of any other religious

---

1 Q. 87:18-9.

document. Moreover, the Qur'an also represents the most comprehensive guide that God has ever sent, or ever will send, to humankind. This means that it both encompasses and goes beyond the earlier revelations provided by Him.[2]

An important feature of the Qur'ān is the fact that it was revealed over a period of slightly more than twenty-two years, taking in the entire period of Muhammad's career as a prophet. Throughout this historic timeframe, many rulings on the correct policies in times of peace and war, on legal issues, and on the correct way to conduct oneself ethically in one's private and public life were made. In this respect, the Qur'ān is markedly different to the other great holy books, the Torah and the Gospel, because it has a strong practical and political dimension and is not just a book about devotion to God, or the correct way in which to worship Him. This is mirrored in the life of Muhammad, who dedicated himself to helping his followers to work on their own moral improvement, individually and collectively, rather than devoting themselves to focusing on the personal, private and metaphysical aspects of divinity. In God's words, and through the example of His prophet, Muhammad, we can see that He wishes humans to do good and avoid evil,[3] and that He encourages His people to strive towards the creation of a society that is both just and compassionate.[4]

Today, it is painfully clear that God's vision of a society run along lines of justice and compassion remains no more than a vision. The current reality is that increasing numbers of people express hatred and contempt of Islam and Islamic civilisation, a dismal situation that was predicted by Muhammad himself, when he said, "There will be a time when your religion will be like a hot piece of coal in the palm of your hand; you will not be able to hold it."

This book has been written to address the confusion and misapprehensions that are so often a feature of discussions about the Qur'ān. It will

---

2 Q. 12:111; 10:37; 6:114.
3 Q. 9:112.
4 Q. 55:9.

INTRODUCTION

help those who seek the truth to understand the Qur'ān (and thus Islam) better by exploring its origins, development, composition and philosophy, and why it occupies such a central position in Muslims' lives. In so doing, it addresses the current lack of a single, simple text that discusses all of the central elements of Qur'ānic studies. Until now, anyone looking for a good basic text to learn about the central tenets and history of Islam actually had to pore over countless heavy tomes by learned Islamic scholars in order to gain access to information on all the central topics. This book thoroughly examines and critiques all the major issues in the field of Qur'ānic studies, uniting them in a single volume that will be accessible to most readers. Among other things, it elucidates the early history of Islam, the nature of revelation, similarities and differences between the Qur'ān and other holy scriptures, and how legal and moral rulings were revealed and propounded to the people. It also addresses, face-on, some of the more contentious issues in Islam today, such as the concept of jihad, or holy war, and Muslims' belief in the Qur'ān's inimitability. In order to make this complex material as digestible as possible, it has been written with the average lay reader, with no knowledge of Qur'ānic studies or of Arabic, in mind, using language that is clear and concise, and avoiding jargon and exclusive terminology as far as possible.

Critics of Islam often ask why, if the Qur'ān urges people to live according to its values of compassion and tolerance, Islam is often associated with violence towards non-Muslims, and poor treatment of the weaker people in society. The awful truth is that both Muslims and non-Muslims frequently quote passages from the Qur'ān to, respectively, justify this behaviour and accuse Islam of being inherently violent. Both choose to ignore the fact that the Qur'ān's verses must be understood in the social and political context of seventh century Arabia, when they were revealed.

How do we reconcile the Qur'ān's timeless nature with the statement that its Surahs need to be understood within this context? We need to understand that the *moral* value of a Surah never changes, even if the specifics of a ruling may no longer apply. Understanding how this works in practice means having a good knowledge of Muhammad's life, both in Mecca and in Medina, and of the spiritual, social, economic, political and legal climate of the day, along with the associated norms, laws, customs, manners, institutions and values of the region. This means knowing many details about how early Muslims and their contemporaries lived, including the types of homes they had, how they dressed, how they ate, and how society was organised, including details of family structure, social hierarchy, taboos and rites of passage. All of this is important because it is essential to understanding the Qur'ān's context, and also because the Qur'ān itself refers to all of these aspects of life frequently. Throughout the Qur'ān there is frequent reference to the cultural, moral world of Arabia at the time of Muhammad, and to the norms and values of the people who lived there.

Because the pagan Arabs of Mecca and Medina engaged in commerce and social interactions with other communities, they were already familiar with the idea of the one true God, and their many social interactions had led to a rich exchange of legends, myths, ideas, stories about historical figures, images and rituals, all of which the Qur'ān used to bring its message home to them. Whether these narratives came from Biblical, folkloric, or other sources, they were relevant and accessible to the Arabian people of the time. The Qur'ān also integrated some of the pre-Islamic values and norms of the day into the new religion. What could be demonstrated to be important and as bringing a positive value into the new faith was retained, and what was indecent and inappropriate was rejected. Some of these values and norms were context-specific. For example, in those days thieves, men and women alike, were punished by having their hands amputated. When the Qur'ān ruled that this custom was legitimate, it was in the context of the seventh century, when there was no central judicial system, no prisons, and no system of social welfare. As we have all these things today, this punishment is no longer fitting, although the precept of punishment for wrong-doing, with the potential for redemption, remains (this and many other topics are discussed in detail in the chapters that follow).

INTRODUCTION

The Qur'ān was revolutionary in many ways, including the manner in which it directly addressed the appalling situation in which so many Arabian women lived in the seventh century, quite literally treated like chattel. It discusses their suffering and makes rulings that are designed to alleviate it. It also looks at the situations endured by other vulnerable elements in society, such as slaves and the poor. Filtered through Muhammad's mind and experience, the Qur'ān reveals God's response to the question of how to deal, on a moral level, with the many issues present in Arabian society. In the early Surahs in particular, which were revealed when Muhammad was in Mecca, the Qur'ān unequivocally stresses the importance of dealing with the problems of polytheism, the exploitation of the poor, malpractices in trade, and general irresponsibility. To combat these social handicaps and crimes, the Qur'ān reveals a unique, supreme God to whom everyone is responsible for their actions, and God's wish that they should work earnestly towards the elimination of gross socioeconomic inequity.

Qur'ānic theology, and its moral and legal teachings, also explore the area of politics in the historic and social context of the Meccans' rejection of Muhammad's message, his rebuttal, and the lengthy to-and-fro that followed. Later, in Medina, in the context of opposition from the Jewish community and, to a lesser extent, the Christian community, the Qur'ān again incorporates elements of these historic events in its teaching. We can describe the Qur'ān's approach to the Jews and Christians of the day as "ambivalent". On the one hand, they are respected as the "People of the Book" who share much with Islam, while on the other, their moral and spiritual conduct are discussed in some detail, and often with reference to their shortcomings. Muhammad's own attitude towards Jews and Christians was clearly influenced by the social, political and theological environment of the day. Nonetheless, when the Qur'ān deals with these realities, it is within the logic of its own faith and worldview. For instance, the Qur'ān states:

Hence, who could be more wicked than those who bar the mention of God's name from (any of) His houses of worship and strive for their ruin, (although) they have no right to enter them save in fear of God. For them, in this world, there is ignominy in store; and for them, in the life to come, awesome suffering.[5]

One of the basic principles of Islam is that every faith in which belief in the one true God is a central element must be respected, even when one stridently disagrees with many of its principles. For this reason, all Muslims are bound by God to both honour and protect any house of worship dedicated to Him, regardless of whether it is a mosque, church, or synagogue. The Qur'ān also rules that it is sacrilegious for any Muslim to try to stop the followers of another faith from worshipping God according to their own traditions and norms. For example, consider Muhammad's treatment of a group of Christians who travelled to Medina from their home area. Far from being disrespected, he granted them free access to his mosque, and his full permission to engage in worship there, despite their belief in Jesus as "the son of God" and Mary as "the mother of God"; both concepts that are anathema to Islam.

Islam came into being at a time when increasing numbers of Arabs had realised that their pagan ways of worship were futile, and had started looking for meaning and truth. While many of them were familiar with the concept of monotheism because of their contact with Jews and Christians, few were attracted to these faiths because of the two groups' constant bickering; "the Jews assert 'the Christians have no valid ground for their beliefs', while the Christians assert, 'the Jews have no valid ground for their beliefs', and both quote the divine writ."[6] In the Qur'ān, God revealed what was true within Judaism and Christianity, and what was false. Indeed, throughout the Qur'ān God makes it clear that there is a great deal of truth in all of the faiths that have their origin in divine revelation, and

---

5 Q. 2:114.
6 Q. 2:113.

INTRODUCTION

that the differences that have arisen in them subsequently have resulted from a combination of wishful thinking[7] and the gradual corruption of God's original message.[8]

Like Christianity, Islam teaches the essential equality of all human beings. However, the Qur'ān is unique for the supreme importance placed on reason and argument in its pages, both of which qualities cannot be separated from its structure. These qualities have had an unparalleled influence on the development of Islamic scholarship, internalising the approach and integrating it into all their work.

Using a wide range of inspirations, the Qur'ān often points out its use of metaphors and analogy specifically, and uses dramatic language to point to the contrasts between heaven and hell, this world and the afterlife, believers and disbelievers, and so forth. The way in which the Qur'ān addresses people directly is noteworthy, as is its use of language that generalises (i.e. "those who believe" or "those who deny the truth") which underlines its messages' universal importance and applicability.

This book draws together some of the finest research and thought in the field of Qur'ānic studies, and presents it in a series of chapters that focus on some of the trickier issues in the Qur'ān, bringing clarity to complex matters and inviting the reader to think about what the revelations bestowed upon Muhammad all those years ago might mean for them.

Chapter One starts with some sociological and historical background. Seventh century Arabia was very, very different to today's world anywhere on the globe, and knowing a little about what life was like back then for Muhammad and his peers helps to set the scene. Chapter Two explores what we know of the life of Muhammad, both before and after he started to receive revelations from God. Chapter Three examines the essential nature of the Qur'ān, while Chapter Four looks at how the revelations were received, and what the impact of them was. Chapter Five explores the various stages of revelation, and the implication of each stage for the nature and

---

7 Q. 2:111.
8 Q. 22: 67-9.

style of the revelation. Chapter Six provides more historical background by exploring Muhammad's life in Medina, and the growth and establishment of Islam in the region from this point on. At this point in the book we begin to turn towards more complex matters, and to explore some of the trickier, and at times contentious, elements of the Qur'ān. In Chapter Seven we look at the ambiguous and unambiguous verses, and strive to understand the implications of each, and how we can apply them to our own lives and decision-making. In Chapter Eight we explore how the pre-Islamic tradition of oaths and oath-making found new life in the Qur'ān, with many implications for how it was received and written down. In Chapter Nine we examine the so-called "mysterious letters" of the Qur'ān, which have puzzled Islamic scholars through the ages, and in Chapter Ten, we look at the range of exciting and inventive ways in which the Qur'ān uses the art of argumentation to engage the listener or reader with his or her own intellect. In Chapter Eleven we explore the sacred trust given to all Muslims to command right and forbid wrong, and also look at the various categories of people who are implied in these commands. In Chapter Twelve, we look at justice as it is described and codified in the Qur'ān, and at the implications for our complex modern world. In Chapter Thirteen, we look at legislative matters, and explore which issues the Qur'ān legislates around and which (equally importantly) it does not. Chapter Fourteen examines the differences between the Surahs received in Mecca, when Muhammad and his followers lived a precarious existence in a hostile environment, and those received in Medina, where they were finally able to start establishing themselves as a community. Chapter Fifteen looks at the relationship between the Qur'ān and the other holy books of revelation, the Torah and the Gospel, and explores the relationship between the two while, on a related matter, Chapter Sixteen looks at abrogation in the Qur'ān, what it truly means, and how misapprehensions in this area have led to dilemmas and issues with very serious consequences. Chapter Seventeen explores how the Qur'ān, which was received and written down at a specific point in history, is nonetheless inimitable, timeless and eternally valid. Chapter Eighteen

INTRODUCTION

examines a term that is well-known but (lamentably) little understood; Islamic jihad. Chapter Nineteen explores the way in which the Qur'ān was compiled and how this impacts on our study of it today, and Chapter Twenty brings our volume to a close with an exploration of the important aesthetic qualities of the Holy Book.

While these chapters can be read sequentially, each can also be read as a separate article to enhance your experience of getting to know the Qur'ān better in the way that suits you best. This book has been written with recourse to the work of many of the finest scholars in the field of Islamic studies, and it is my hope that it will be a launch-pad that will encourage you to get to know this field in ever greater depth.

Throughout this book, my goal has been to bring a better knowledge of the Qur'ān, with much clarity, to the lay reader. An often-repeated criticism of the Qur'an is that is outdated and out of touch with present realities, but looking at it closely, it is perfectly clear that it is a "living book" that can easily be adapted to the modern world and our complex needs, so long as its messages are understood in the proper context.

As we go through our lives, striving to do the will of God, we can put ourselves in a position to assess our current reality and change it to whatever extent seems necessary. In this way, we can reconfigure our priorities in line with an understanding of the Qur'ān's relevance in the current context.

From start to finish, this book maintains a focus on the central message of the Qur'ān which is that we, as human beings, must stand together. We are all equal, and we are all equally responsible for striving to understand one another, for respectfully accepting our differences and for ensuring that if we must compete with one another, it should be only to see who can excel in doing good.

CHAPTER 1

ARABIA BEFORE AND AFTER MUHAMMAD

IN ORDER TO understand the rapid spread of Islam in the Arabian Peninsula, and the dramatic religious, social and cultural changes that occurred in that area subsequently, it is important to know at least a little about the social and historical circumstances of the seventh century, when Muhammad first brought his message to the inhabitants of this part of the world.[1]

When Muhammad started preaching to the Arabs, Arab society was hugely different to today. Although much of what today is considered the Middle East fell under the rule of one of two great empires – the Byzantine Empire (which was then largely Christian) and the Sassanid (Persian) Empire (which was then largely Zoroastrian)[2] – the area that first witnessed the adoption and spread of Islam, the Arabian Peninsula, was characterised by a very particular sort of society, influenced by the local climate, history and social norms, that had contact with these two imperial superpowers only at the very fringes of its territory, and that was uniquely adapted to living in that challenging environment.

Arab peoples filled the Arabian Peninsula and the Syrian Desert, united by a common language. Most were nomadic pastoralists, who earned their living in the hot, arid climate by shepherding their animals from one area to the next, setting up camp wherever they found themselves in their quest for pasture and water. In these long-ago days there was as yet

---

1 Saeed, 2008 (b), 36.
2 Saeed, 2008 (b), 36.

no concept of nationhood, and identity was forged primarily by family and tribal links, by the nomadic lifestyle and dependence on livestock, and by linguistic ties. This nomadism, too, would have tended to inhibit the development of mutually incomprehensible dialects or languages. By moving around, and frequently coming into contact with other groups, the Arabic language remained a common currency that brought together a large, shifting group of people.[3]

At this point in Arab social development, political organisation was strictly along tribal and family lines, with no centralised authority whatsoever. At various periods in the past there had been attempts to establish kingdoms, but these had not generally impacted on the wider group, being restricted to the peripheral areas of the Arab territories and generally under the auspices of foreign powers. For instance, Petra, a Nabatean kingdom, which was subsumed by the Roman Empire in 106 AD, and Palmyra in the third century, were Arab states that demonstrated heavy influence from Greek and Roman culture. They derived funds from the fact that they lay on important caravan routes,[4] as well as contact via these merchants with the outside world. There were also small settled communities in towns such as Mecca and Medina, which are discussed below.

Despite the presence of these atypical centralised settlements, most Arabs' experience of life was one in which their primary loyalties lay with their immediate family, relatives, and the people with whom they travelled and raised their tents as they moved from one location to the next. Tribal identities, while certainly important, came a far second to these much more immediate interests.

In the context of these scattered, mobile communities, policing or law enforcement on a centralised basis were impossible. Law and order – necessary in every society – took the form of retaliation for crimes and offenses, backed up by the dense network of kinship ties that everyone

---

3 Kennedy, 2004, 16.
4 Kennedy, 2004, 16.

enjoyed. If someone was murdered, or if his property was stolen, his entire kinship network was morally bound to extract retribution or compensation on his behalf. This system applied both to the large nomadic population and the smaller settled ones. In these distant times, it meant that anyone was ready, at any moment, to defend not just himself, but anyone from his entire kinship network. Women, too, were often involved in defending temporary camps, raiding, or exacting retribution in one way or another. The result was an entire population, male and female, young and old, with finely-honed military skills.[5] Conversely, in many other areas in Europe and Asia at this time, the settlement pattern and local cultures created a situation whereby most civilians lived and invested their labour in one area, and military activities were the business of specialist soldiers, and not the general population.

Beyond the immediacy of one's camp group and kinship network, tribes were led by chiefs. A good chief had a reputation for hospitality that was not exactly disinterested; welcoming strangers into the group meant that information about good lands for grazing, the location and state of other nomadic groups, and general news, were made available.[6] Chiefs also played a certain role in social organisation. Although they could not perform edicts or give rulings, they could offer judgements in the case of disagreements within the tribe. Beyond the social pressure of general opinion, there was no way for these to be enforced.

Although this picture of Arab society may give a superficial impression of primitivism and a degree of chaos, this was far from the truth. For many centuries, the entire Arabian Peninsula had been an immensely important conduit for trade, with multiple and complex impacts on the people who lived there. Goods had been transported across the region from the area bordering the Indian Ocean to feed the vast Roman Empire; spices, perfumes and other expensive products. Goods from the southern part of the Arabian Peninsula were also greatly prized in classical times. These

---

5 Kennedy, 2004, 18.
6 Kennedy, 2004, 19-21.

included frankincense and myrrh, which were important to the Romans for religious and ritual purposes, including funeral rites.[7]

As stated above, urban settlements were the exception rather than the norm in a society dominated by nomadic pastoralists. Mecca stands out as a particularly interesting case. Although it was still quite a small town in the seventh century, the people of Mecca were entrenched in the streets of their urban settlement. Mecca had developed around a reliable source of water, the ZamZam well, which was widely – and understandably, in the demanding desert environment – considered to be miraculous.[8] The tribal affiliation of the Meccans was Quraysh, with several clans of the tribe represented in the town. Local society was stratified; some families enjoyed great wealth and influence, while others were relatively poor and marginalised.[9] The town's economy had two main pillars; the substantial caravan trade, and income from the many pilgrims who visited. Because of its strategic location, and its reliable source of water, traders and merchants carrying valuable products from east to west, and vice versa, regularly stopped off at Mecca. Jewish and Christian pilgrims visited a site, the Ka'ba, said to have been built by the prophet Abraham and his son Ishmael, and they needed accommodation and food too.

As in the case of their nomadic brethren, there was no centralised authority in Mecca, but the community was loosely ruled by a consortium of influential elders, who used a system of consultation, and everyone could count on the support of their clan and kin network in times of difficulty and strife.[10] Members of the settled community of Mecca also formed alliances with diverse nomadic groups; the area surrounding the town was heavily populated by nomads, and also experienced considerable caravan traffic. The land surrounding Mecca was

---

7   Kennedy, 2004, 22-3.
8   Saeed, 2008, 4.
9   Saeed, 2008, 4.
10 Saeed, 2008, 4.

arid, and there was no possibility of developing any meaningful form of agriculture, while pastoral nomads had to move often to secure sufficient pasture for their livestock, which were mostly camels and goats, and to gain access to the always-precious water. As resources were frequently scarce, raids and violence broke out regularly, and these alliances proved very necessary to protect both people and the goods they were travelling with. However, the strong principles of mutual care that were central to the way of life of nomadic Arabs were less in evidence in Mecca, where vulnerable members of society, such as the elderly or the disabled, were sometimes left to fend for themselves,[11] in the broad context of a community that tended to be rather fatalistic, with the sense that there was little one could do to improve or change the situation. Literacy was not completely unknown, but it was very rare. The education system, such as it was, was devoted to teaching young people the skills they needed to survive in their difficult circumstances. As in many other preliterate societies, however, language and its inventive and creative use were very much prized, and those who could express themselves with great eloquence were hugely admired.[12]

Medina, the other major urban settlement, had quite a different character to Mecca. It had developed around the Yathrib oasis, and was populated by a number of tribal Arab communities which practiced a combination of nomadic pastoralism and settled agriculture, as well as some Jewish tribes. Arabs and Jews alike tended to become involved in conflict with other tribes that sometimes escalated to war, and a series of complex alliances and networks had developed as a result.[13]

Prior to Muhammad, the Arabs had no real centralised system of belief. Instead, small groups had their own ideas about spirituality and ethics, and pagan gods were recognised in a system that involved the provision of sacrifices and gifts in the hope of obtaining favour rather than

---

11 Saeed, 2008, 5.
12 Saeed, 2008 (b), 37.
13 Saeed, 2008, 5.

anything resembling theology as we know it from the great monotheistic faiths. Those who lived in the urban centre of Mecca had come into contact with the idea of monotheism, and a very small number worshipped a single deity and backed away from the worship of idols, but this minority practice posed no threat to the variety of figures in the loose Arab pantheon of gods. Most people worshipped a range of local deities, often somewhat half-heartedly, and had no concept of an afterlife.[14] Some communities were familiar to an extent with Christianity, which was spreading through the region, and there were also various Jewish tribes scattered about the area.

Various factors facilitated the spread of Islam throughout the Arabian territories. Perhaps most significantly, the presence of a common language across a huge territory helped to form the basis of the growth of a wider identity, and would contribute to the rapid spread of Islam among these scattered peoples; although there must have been some dialectal differences, the fact that everyone spoke essentially the same vernacular would make it easier for Muhammad to spread his message, and for those who received it to share his teachings with everyone they met. Moreover, the nomadism that was the norm throughout the region, along with a culture of hospitality and a traditional respect for the oratorical arts, facilitated the spread of new ideas. As the Islamic faith grew in outreach, it was not a question of whole tribes converting to Muhammad's message *en masse*, but of individual people, their families, and those they travelled and worked with, finding resonance with his words, one by one.

In fact, certain political factors had enormous implications for the spread of Islam throughout the region. The Byzantine and Sassanid (Persian) empires, which each bordered the Arabian territories, had long been locked in a bitter struggle. In the early seventh century, the Sassanid Empire conquered an area that corresponds today to parts of Syria and Anatolia, which lay near the Byzantine Empire. They took Damascus in

---

14 Saeed, 2008, 5.

613, Jerusalem in 614, and Egypt in 615-6, while also attempting to take over Constantinople. At the time, it appeared that the Byzantine Empire was about to fall. This was bad news not just for the Byzantines, who were primarily Christians, but also for the nascent Muslim community; both Christians and Muslims were monotheists who worshipped the same One God, while the Sassanids were pagans, who observed many deities. In this context, Muhammad received a revelation that foretold Byzantine victory within a few years. This revelation, recorded in the Qur'ān, states:

> Defeated have been the Byzantine. In the lands close by (that is, the areas corresponding to the parts of Syria and Anatolia, mentioned above), yet it is they who, notwithstanding this their defeat, shall be victorious, within a few years, for God rests all power of decision, first and last. And on that day will the believers rejoice.[15]

This revelation was initially greeted with great scepticism and even derision by the Sassanids, but within six or seven years things started to change, and it became clear that Muhammad was correct. Emperor Heraclitus of the Byzantine Empire managed to defeat the Sassanids and they were forced to retreat from Asia Minor. By 624, he had invaded their territory, and by 626, the Sassanid army was destroyed. In the process, both empires had devoted massive resources and time to their struggle, resulting in the weakening of their hold throughout the region, which facilitated the spread and eventual dominance of Islam not just in its birthplace in the Arabian Peninsula, but throughout a wider area encompassing what today is considered the Middle East.[16]

As Islam spread, so did the influence of the Arab peoples. Arab power grew, and Arabs moved into areas previously administered by the Byzantine Empire and other territories. These were areas that had, because of the declining imperial powers, already experienced dramatic social change even

---

15 Qur'ān, 30:1-4.
16 Asad, 2003, 617, note 2.

before Islamic peoples arrived, becoming more pastoral and more dependent on local, rather than centralised, civic structures – like the communities of the Arabian Peninsula. In the context of a time of rapid social change, Muslim Arabs influenced shifts and trends that were already taking place.[17]

---

17 Kennedy, 2004, 22-4.

CHAPTER 2

PROPHET MUHAMMAD'S LIFE AND STRUGGLES

MUHAMMAD WAS BORN in around 570 to a Meccan clan, the Hashim, which belonged, like so many, to the Quraysh tribe which dominated Mecca, and from which the local leadership came.

The Hashim clan claimed descent from a man named Hashim, who was in his time a very important member of the Quraysh. History links him with the opening of the trade route across Arabia to Syria (so important to the financial well-being of Mecca and all her residents), and he was also known to have been involved in providing both pilgrims and the permanent residents of Mecca with food and water.

After Hashim's death, the clan lost status steadily, although his son did feature as a spokesperson of the Quraysh tribe, and was also involved in works surrounding the reopening of the "miraculous" ZamZam well, to which Mecca owed its very existence. Over the next couple of generations, the clan gradually lost power, until it was no longer among the most influential or wealthy clans of Mecca.[1] While certainly still respectable at the time of Muhammad's birth, the Hashim were no longer a well-to-do family.

Muhammad did not have an easy start to life: His father, Abdullah, died before he was born while on a trading expedition to Syria,[2] leaving him under the supervision of his mother, Amina, and his grandfather,

---

1 Kennedy, 2004, 29.
2 Kennedy, 2004, 30.

Abdul Muttalib. His very early childhood was not spent primarily with his mother but, as was traditional at the time, in the care of a Bedouin woman. She served as wet nurse to him when he was a baby, and raised him among her people; apparently the Bedouin were initially reluctant to take in the fatherless child, with no economic prospects in evidence.[3] Amina died when her son was just six years old. After his mother's unfortunate death, Muhammad was cared for by his grandfather, who in turn died when he was eight. At this stage, Muhammad's uncle, Abu Talib, who was then the leader of the Hashim clan, became his guardian.

This was a time when Mecca in general was becoming increasingly important and prosperous, and the young Muhammad would have been keenly aware of the centrality of international trade to the well-being of the town where he lived. At the same time, this growth in wealth appears to have stoked nascent social tensions in the area; something else of which he must have been aware.[4] Beyond that, little is known of the details of how Muhammad spent his childhood and youth. One can imagine that life must sometimes have been hard for an orphaned child in the often very harsh atmosphere of Mecca, even with the protection of his uncle. Did he miss his mother, or pine for the maternal embraces of the woman who had nursed him at her breast and cared for him throughout his early childhood? History simply does not relate and the answers are left to our imagination.

Muhammad had largely grown up and come of age in Arabia's most important business and religious centre,[5] so it is unsurprising that he was drawn to a career in trade.[6] By the time he had reached his twenties, Muhammad was working as a trader in the employ of a woman, a wealthy widow named Khadija. Despite the age difference (she was fifteen years older than him), when she saw how honest, hard-working and

---

3   Kennedy, 2004, 30.
4   Kennedy, 2004, 30.
5   Gabriel, 2007, 54.
6   Kennedy, 2004, 30.

reliable he was, Khadija proposed marriage to Muhammad. He accepted, and they were married for twenty-five years. Throughout their marriage, which seems to have been a happy relationship characterised by mutual respect and support, the couple lived in Mecca. As well as companionship and love, this marriage provided Muhammad with a degree of financial security, and he occupied a more important position in Meccan society than might have been expected for someone from a clan that had lost so much in the preceding years. As further testimony to the happiness of their union, Muhammad and Khadija had a number of children, including their daughter Fatima. Fatima's children would go on to be hugely important to Islam.[7]

Muhammad became quite well-known locally as a businessman, and as someone who could intervene in conflicts to help people to successfully reach a peaceful solution. In all of this, he was greatly supported by his wife. Although we don't know much about the apparently relatively uneventful years of their marriage, history relates that Muhammad was recognised as someone with a particularly fine-tuned sense of what was right and ethical, and that he had developed the habit of retreating to a cave outside Mecca, known as Hira, for the purpose of deep thought and self-examination.

It was in the cave of Hira, in around 610, when he was about forty years old, that Muhammad first received his call to testify for God.[8] This took the form of the first revelation recorded in the Qur'ān, and is considered to mark the beginning of his prophethood.

As discussed in Chapter One, at this time most of the people in the Arabian territories were pagans and polytheists, although Christianity and Judaism were minority practices, especially in the areas that had been influenced by the Byzantine Empire. We have also considered the fact that many people were at least aware of the existence of monotheistic religions, probably because of conversations and debates with the many people who

---

7   Kennedy, 2004, 30.
8   Rahman, 1979, 11.

regularly crossed the Arabian Peninsula in caravans with precious goods, and stopped off in Mecca and Medina to rest on their way from Yemen to Syria,[9] to eat and restock their food and water reserves.[10] There may also have been a certain amount of proselytising on the part of Christians who sought to increase their numbers.[11] Pilgrims visited the Ka'ba in Mecca in large numbers once a year and the monotheistic views of these Christians and Jews had mingled with local ideas of polytheism.

The annual pilgrimage to Ka'ba, known as the Hajj, saw people from all over the Arabian territories attending the Ka'ba to worship, providing Mecca with one of its most important sources of income. To service the pilgrims' many needs after their long, tiring journeys, markets were set up all around the town that provided the pilgrims with their requirements, and the Meccans with a wonderful opportunity to make money. In a community that was often beset with conflict, the fact that acts of violence were explicitly banned during these markets must also have been attractive, providing everyone with some respite from the tensions that were such a frequent feature of life in the area.

The Qur'ān itself provides some information about the beliefs held in the area before Islam. It mentions the belief in a supreme god called Allah, alongside the worship of statues, celestial bodies including the sun and the moon, and assorted minor deities thought to have the ability to intercede with Allah. Different people gave different aspects of the local belief system their own emphasis.

Muhammad taught that there was just one true God, who had created the world and everything and everyone in it. In this context, worshipping a wide range of idols and pagan gods was an offence to God. Particularly noteworthy is the fact that Muhammad's idea of monotheism was intrinsically interlinked with the idea that all humans were born equal, and that

---

9   Haleem, 2010, xii.
10 Rahman, 1989, 152-3.
11 Rahman, 1989, 152.

social and economic justice were an essential element of faith.[12] Although a number of Meccans were at least nominally monotheistic, there is no compelling evidence to suggest that the "One God" they worshipped was the same "One God" as Muhammad's, and there is certainly no evidence to indicate that it had any connection with the idea that society should be reformed, or that efforts should be made to make it more fair and just.

In fact, while Muhammad's revelations about the nature of a One True God are certainly important, and fundamental to an understanding of Islam, his messages about social justice and support for the poor and weak were just as important, and possibly even more revolutionary.[13] His message was one that was hard for people from a tribal society, in which certain groups and clans enjoyed higher status and privilege simply because of who they were, to understand: that, to God, we are all the same; we are all part of humanity.

While it may be true to say that the peoples of Arabia had already started to experience a degree of religious turmoil, Muhammad's message was unprecedented, and cannot be considered as an offshoot of any other locally emergent ideas.[14] Moreover, even before he started to receive revelations from God, Muhammad had been deeply concerned with matters of social justice, and with the ultimate purpose and meaning of humanity; it was for this reason that he had so often felt the need to retreat to his cave to engage in deep contemplation.

It is important to note that, despite these periodic immersions in nature, Muhammad was very much an urban man. He had grown up and spent his adult life thus far in the bustling atmosphere of a busy town located on important trade and pilgrimage routes that linked Arabia with the rest of the known world. From childhood, he had been surrounded by commerce and by hordes of people. He had married a woman who was herself embedded in local commerce. It would be a mistake to imagine

---

12 Rahman, 1979, 11-2.
13 Rahman, 1979, 11.
14 Rahman, 1979, 11.

that Islam emerged from the pastoral, nomadic culture of so much of the Arabian Peninsula; rather, Muhammad and his revelations were born of the mercantile, urban and sophisticated (by the standards of the day) culture in which he had been brought up.[15]

Together with his revelations, the Prophet was instructed to spread the word to all, and he obeyed this instruction. The Prophet's detractors, having heard his call to worship one God, retorted by asking if he really claimed that all the creative powers and qualities he described could truly exist in just one God.[16] Very quickly, the Meccans, and in particular those in positions of power, rejected everything he was saying, less because of concerns about any challenge to their religious beliefs than because of fears that the fundamental nature of their society and their business interests would be challenged, and that they would lose access to the power and authority they enjoyed. For wealthy people in positions of prestige, the idea that the poor and weak were as beloved by God as they were was difficult to countenance. Some of them attempted to dismiss Muhammad's words as essentially recycled elements from the Jewish and Christian traditions,[17] with the implication that as they had seen no need to convert to either of those faiths, nor were they likely to change their minds in response to Muhammad's words.

As Muhammad continued to receive revelations, he preached against usury (interest-bearing loans), and in favour of supporting the poor and seeing them as equals in the eyes of God. This raised the ire of many listeners considerably, and some influential Meccans went so far as to accuse him of being mad, possessed, or a magician. They sneered at him, saying that no real prophet would be seen in the market place, where ordinary people did their shopping and attended to their everyday affairs, and that Muhammad was not important or noble enough to have been chosen by God. If God *really* wanted a prophet, they said, why this relatively humble

---

15 Rahman, 1979, 12.
16 Q. 38:5.
17 Rahman, 1989, 152.

man, an ordinary small merchant, rather than an important person with means at his disposal? Like them, he had to eat and to go to the marketplace to buy his food, so how could that be?[18] For proof, Muhammad's critics demanded that he bring an angel with him to show that he was really communicating with God. In response, the Qur'ān retorted that if angels had lived on earth, an angel-prophet would have been sent.[19] Muhammad's detractors even arranged a visit to Medina to consult some members of the Jewish community living there on how best to overcome Muhammad in the context of a religious argument. They knew that the Jews, like the emergent Muslim community, were monotheists and that, like them, they had a special holy book. The members of the Quraysh who made this trip felt that the Jews might be able to help them understand Muhammad and his message, which was so foreign to them. Maybe, they hoped, the Jews would be in a position to help them understand what he was preaching about, and what the significance of it for them was.

In the face of all this opposition, Muhammad's own faith and message became increasingly clearly defined.[20] When Muhammad's detractors asked, "Why was this Qur'ān not sent down upon some big man in the two cities?"[21] the Qur'ān replied saying both, "Do they distribute the mercy of your Lord?"[22] and, "God knows where to put His messengership."[23]

As well as preaching belief in the One True God, Muhammad also taught that the world would one day end with a last judgement, when everyone who had ever lived would be brought before God and judged according to how they had spent their days. Faithful believers who had been good and virtuous would be rewarded by spending eternity in heaven, and those who did not believe, or who were insufficiently pious and good-living, would suffer forever in hell. As there was no local concept of an

---

18 Q. 25:7.
19 Q. 17:95.
20 Rahman, 1979, 14-5.
21 Q. 43:31.
22 Q. 43:32.
23 Q. 6:124.

afterlife, these ideas were completely new, and very challenging for people to take on board. Many Meccans strongly rejected Muhammad's statement that there was an afterlife into which they would be reborn, and they were also very angry at his statement that those who did not believe could never enter heaven; this implied that their own ancestors, whom they revered and to whom they ascribed all their most prized qualities, were burning in hell! For a lineage-based society, this was shocking indeed.[24] They rejected the idea that the dead could be returned to life. The Qur'ān responded with arguments from nature and in particular from embryology.[25]

The good will Muhammad had enjoyed as a respected local businessman was soon threatened, and the few followers he had initially attracted with his dramatic revelations were all subjected to ridicule, which escalated to conflict and even persecution. Aghast at the thought that Muhammad's teachings might spread and threaten their positions, wealthy Meccans put up an all-out, concentrated, sustained opposition to the spread of Islam. They found it very hard to accept the basic doctrine Muhammad taught; that God was one, the creator of humankind and the natural world. The idea that worshipping many pagan deities affronted God was anathema to them, coming as they did from a polytheistic, pagan tradition. They did this, after all, and they took personally Muhammad's remarks that they should stop. In the context of rejecting his doctrine, they pointed out that the Christians believed in the Trinity,[26] and claimed that this meant that they worshipped three deities, not one. The Qur'ān, however, stated that the Heavens and Earth would have collapsed if they had been created and governed by more than one god[27] and asserted in response to the belief that God has daughters or a son: "He begets not, and neither is He begotten, and there is nothing that could be compared with Him".

---

24 Dammen McAuliffe, 2006, 25.
25 Haleem, 2010, 5; Q. 36:76-83; 56:47-96.
26 Q. 38:7.
27 Q. 21:23; 23:91.

However, for those who listened to Muhammad, and found resonance in his message, it does seem likely that the fact that they had come across other religions, notably Judaism and Christianity, was important. Although Muhammad's teachings are not directly related to the aforementioned religions in a simple linear way, the fact that they were aware of other people with diverse beliefs, and that at least some of them had become interested in religious dialogue, suggests that some people were receptive to hearing new ideas, and prepared to at least consider the notion that everything they had believed before might be wrong.[28]

New Muslims were persecuted and sometimes even tortured, although there was no systematic approach to this ill-treatment; it was more a case of society reacting to change at individual and family level, and mostly rejecting it on an essentially visceral level. Some converts were persecuted by their own families, and those who came from the poorest classes, including widows, orphans and slaves, were the most likely to suffer as a result of their faith, as they had no one to support them.[29]

As well as being horrified by Muhammad's threat to their traditional religious practices and polytheistic faith, the Meccans worried that the very nature of their society was being challenged. Whereas their community was full of interest groups involved in commerce and politics, Muhammad's teachings emphasised social justice, and became incrementally more concerned with the idea that usury should be condemned, as it resulted in the exploitation of the poor by the wealthy. The idea that the wealthy should go to lengths to provide the poor with support purely for the sake of doing God's work was also anathema. The people of Mecca now boycotted not just Muhammad, but everyone who was related to him, whether or not they subscribed to his revelations.[30]

As it became steadily more apparent that Muhammad's message was gaining traction, those who did not like to see his success became

---

28   Rahman, 1989, 153.
29   Gabriel, 2007, 60-1.
30   Haleem, 2010, xii.

increasingly anxious, perhaps partly because of his accusations that they committed fraud in work, took advantage of the poor, and worshipped idols. Attempts were made to persuade Abu Talib, Muhammad's uncle, to step in and stop him from preaching, or at least to announce in public that Muhammad was no longer under his protection. However, this failed, and the number of converts to Islam continued to grow, now including Abu Bakr and Abu 'Cubaida ibn Jarrah, who were prominent local citizens. Abu Talib, who never accepted Islam himself, is to be commended for the steadfast way in which he refused to denounce his nephew,[31] despite their obvious differences and his apparent reluctance to take his revelations seriously.

A number of local leaders from the Quraysh tribe held a meeting to come up with a plan to derail Muhammad's growing success. They launched a propaganda campaign against him during an annual pilgrimage to the Hajj, with the unintended effect of making many who might not otherwise have heard of him aware of Muhammad and his message.

By the time he had been preaching for five years, Muhammad sent some of his followers, in particular those who were relatively weak and defenceless, to safety with the king of Abyssinia (today known as Ethiopia), who was a Christian, and who would provide a refuge to these worshippers of the one true God. The new Muslims who stayed behind continued to suffer.

The fact that Islam was gradually becoming a faith of important local people, as well as of the poor and dispossessed, gave the movement increasing strength, and fresh impetus to Muhammad's mission. Members of the Meccan community, including representatives of the local Jewish groups, periodically tried to debate Muhammad, but they were never able to silence him, and the movement that they all wanted to see wither continued to grow. With growing awareness that there was nothing they could do to stop it, some wealthy Meccans eventually decided that they too might follow Muhammad, but they balked at being associated with the many poor,

---

31 Rahman, 1979, 11.

"unimportant" people he counted among his followers. Were they suffering from a collective guilty conscience, because the Qur'ān accused them of worshipping idols, engaging in fraudulent activities, and exploiting the poor? Certainly, all of these activities were regular features of life in Mecca. They asked Muhammad to disown Muslims from the lower classes, but he refused to do so.[32] They asked Muhammad's uncle, Abu Talib, to cease protecting him and to hand him over, but Abu Talib refused,[33] upon which a boycott of all the Hashim was instigated. But Abu Talib was getting older; when he died, and when Muhammad's wife Khadija passed away at around the same time, Muhammad lost his primary sources of practical and emotional support.

Those Muslims who remained in Mecca while their peers sought succour in Abyssinia suffered terrible persecution.[34] Over the next six years, Muhammad and the few followers who remained suffered dreadfully. However, even while the poorest Muslims were immigrating to Abyssinia, a small number of influential Meccans converted to Islam. One was Umar ibn al-Khattab, who had initially been hostile to Muhammad, and had even threatened to kill him, and another was Hamza ibn Adbul-Muttalib, Muhammad's own uncle. With these important men now featuring among the converts, the small but growing Muslim community started to garner the strength it needed to stand up to the largely hostile Quraysh tribe.[35]

Spurned, the leaders of the Quraysh got together to come up with a new plan and decided to embark on a concerted effort to denounce Muhammad in the public realm, and bring him to disgrace. However, their efforts to harm the prophet and his mission backfired spectacularly; rather than harming him, their propaganda had the effect of introducing him and his ideas to all the Arab peoples, including the people of Medina, Arabia's second most important urban centre.

---

32 Q. 6:52.
33 Q. 18:28; 6:52-54.
34 Haleem, 2010, xii.
35 Rahman, 1989, 157.

As his situation deteriorated further, Muhammad began to search for support outside Mecca, with little success until he encountered a group from Medina at a trade fair near Mecca. Impressed with his teachings and thinking that he could serve as arbiter for Medina's own bitter internal feuds, they returned the following year and made an agreement to welcome and support Muhammad. Some time thereafter, in 622, Muhammad and his supporters in Mecca immigrated to Medina, and established themselves there. The Hijra, as this emigration is called, marked the beginning of the Muslim community as an autonomous political community, and the year in which it took place was subsequently adopted by Muslims as the first year of the Islamic calendar.

Medina had quite a different character to Mecca. Whereas Mecca was a cosmopolitan town by the standards of the day, with a constant stream of visitors and a big annual influx of pilgrims, Medina experienced less trade, but had a more diverse settled population, with a fairly substantial Jewish community, as well as a relatively large population of Christians.[36] Scholars of the Qur'ān note that there are certain stylistic differences between the elements that were received by Muhammad in Mecca, and those recorded in Medina, reflecting the differences in the populations with which he was communicating.[37]

To comfort Muhammad, in the face of the many difficulties he had encountered and was continuing to deal with, the Qur'ān recounts the various ways in which earlier prophets had suffered, just like him. For example, it says:

> If they call thee (Muhammad) a liar, so too before them the people of Noah called him a liar, as did 'Ad and Thamud, and the people of Abraham, the people of Lot, and the people of Madyan. Moses

---

36 Rahman, 1989, 153.
37 Rahman, 1989, 161.

also they called a liar. And I indulged the unbelievers, then I seized them, and how (terrible) was My retribution.[38]

One revelation states "nothing is said to you but what was said indeed to the apostles before you."[39] This refers to the Prophet's opponents, who said that he himself had invented what he claimed to be a divine revelation, and their demands that he should enact miracles in order to prove that he was really a prophet of God. All the earlier prophets had also had to deal with such accusations and scorn.[40] The Qur'ān records: "And so they assert, (Muhammad himself) has invented this (Qur'ān)." In response, Muhammad was told to, "Say (unto them) "produce, then, ten Surahs of similar merit, invented (by yourselves), and (to this end) call to your aid whomever you can, other than God, if what you say is true".[41] When they failed to produce the ten Surahs, they were then asked to produce a Surah of a similar merit. He was also instructed to: "...Say (unto them): "Produce, then, a Surah of similar merit; and (to this end) call to your aid whomever you can, other than God, if what you say is true",[42] and "If they (whom you have called to your aid) are not able to help you, then know that (this Qur'ān) has been bestowed from on high out of God's wisdom alone, and that there is no deity save Him. Will you, then, surrender yourselves unto Him?"[43] Furthermore, he was told, "And (so, O Prophet), if they give thee the lie, say: "To me (shall be accounted) my doings, and to you, your doings: you are not accountable for what I am doing, and I am not accountable for whatever you do".[44]

It is clear that Muhammad, the prophet, refuted the unfounded allegations that he was the author of the Qur'ān, rather than God. After all,

---

38 Q. 22:42-4.
39 Q. 41:43; Rubin, 2006, 245.
40 Asad, 2003, 736.
41 Q. 11:13.
42 Q. 10:38.
43 Q. 11:14.
44 Q. 10:41.

he was an ordinary, illiterate man. Given this fact, how could someone like him produce such extraordinary work, when even learned, wealthy, and influential members of the higher social classes were unable to do anything of the sort? The verse cited above, as noted by Asad[45] serves to point out that the failure of anyone else in Mecca to produce something comparable with the Qur'ān illustrates the false idea that the Qur'ān could possibly be anything other than the divine word of God, which will remain unalterable until the end of time. Muhammad and, by extension, anyone who reads or listens to the Qur'ān, is thus reminded that Muhammad was simply called by God to spread the message of the Qur'ān, with no remit to convert listeners into accepting it. In this capacity, when he encountered people who opposed his message, he told them that each of us is responsible for our own actions. Ultimately, God is the only arbiter of the truth.

Needless to say, the Qur'ān rejected all the charges against it and the prophet, saying: "is this sorcery or is it, rather, the case that you are blind";[46] "your companion is not possessed - he has seen him (the agent of Revelation) on the clear horizon, who is not niggardly of giving news of the Unseen. Nor is this (the Qur'ān) the word of Satan the outcast – so where are you going? This is but a Reminder to the world".[47]

The early years of Islam were difficult ones for Muhammad and for all of his followers, but more quickly than anyone could initially have imagined, Islam spread, and the number of followers grew steadily.

---

45 2003.
46 Q. 52:15.
47 Q. 81:22-27.

CHAPTER 3

WHAT IS THE QUR'ĀN?

PUT SIMPLY, THE Qur'ān is the last Holy Book among other holy books, such as the Torah and the Gospel, that were sent to God's prophets as a series of revelations at various points in history.

The Qur'ān was not sent to Muhammad as a single book, or revealed in just one session, but as a series of revelations that refer to events taking place in Arabia and in Muhammad's life, while (more significantly) presenting a message that is timeless in its relevance and importance. Using the terminology of the day, the Qur'ān describes itself as being on a Preserved Tablet[1] and as a Protected Book,[2] which are both terms that highlight its unique qualities.

The revelations contained within the Qur'ān initially came to Muhammad during his periods of self-imposed isolation in the cave of Hira in the outskirts of Mecca. For many years, he had gone there to meditate and contemplate, away from the chaos of the city, but he had never done anything specific to invite God's intervention, and could never have imagined that he would be called to serve as a prophet of God. At first, when the revelations started to come, he was resistant, and even frightened by the momentous responsibility he was being asked to assume.

Muhammad's wife, Khadija, was the first to recognise his prophecy, and she comforted and reassured him, becoming the first to recognise her husband as a prophet of God and therefore the first believer. After this, Muhammad received revelations regularly, and emerged from each episode

---

1 Q. 85:21-22.
2 Q. 56:77-78.

with the information recorded indelibly in his brain.[3] The original, therefore, is with God and cannot be lost or damaged through the carelessness or malice of man.

The Qur'ān, as we know it on earth, takes the form of a document composed of revelations that were received by Muhammad and memorised and written down by his followers, with the final edited version emerging after Muhammad's death in 632.[4] Its basic doctrines are that God, the creator of the universe, is one, incomparable and alone in His divinity, and that worshipping a wide range of pagan deities, as the people of Mecca did at the time, is anathema to Him; that the world will end with a final judgement when everyone who has ever lived is brought before God and judged by Him, with virtuous true believers rewarded, and those who did not believe, or who lived unrighteous lives, punished for all eternity.[5] The Qur'ān warns listeners against ignoring its message until it is too late and reminds them, "… it is God Who has with Himself the supreme reward."[6] It is invariably unequivocal in stressing its huge importance as the final Word of God.

In terms of structure, the Qur'ān is divided into 114 chapters, known as Surahs, which are of very unequal lengths; some are immensely short, and others very long. Those that were received and written down in Mecca tend to be the shortest and the most succinct. As Muhammad's life as a prophet continued, the Surahs become progressively longer. The earliest are intense, and deep, with extraordinary "psychological moment", with "the character of brief but violent volcanic eruptions."[7] One can sense the tension and strain Muhammad experienced as the information was forced into his consciousness during his periods of contemplation in the cave. Surahs can be defined as a set of verses that, together, deal with a specific theme in an orderly and logical way, containing a preface, a central theme

---

3 Donner, 2006, 25.
4 Donner, 2006, 25.
5 Donner, 2006, 25.
6 Gwynne, 2009, 211.
7 Rahman, 1979, 30.

and a conclusion; at least three verses. By and large, in the Qur'ān the shorter the Surah, the more profound and meaningful it is.[8]

The Qur'ān begins with a simple prayer for guidance "Guide us on the straight way"[9], followed by the declaration that, "This is the book in which there is no doubt, a guidance to the God-fearing."[10] The Qur'ān's primary role, therefore, is to bring the faithful closer to God by revealing His truth through the medium of human speech, in a way that ordinary people can understand, and so that they can then integrate His message into their daily lives. Together, these messages from God constitute His moral law for humanity, and it is humankind's responsibility to submit to this law, and to endeavour to live at all times in a manner consistent with it. This submission is what is meant by the term *islam*, from which the name of Muslims' faith comes from.

After Muhammad and his followers went to Medina, the style of the Qur'ān starts to change. The Surahs tend to become longer, it becomes more fluent and easier to read, and there are many more instructions about how to create, organise and manage the emerging Muslim state, including some about the proper way to manage legal issues and live in an orderly, communal way.

Comparison is one of the many tools the Qur'ān uses to argue points, and it does so in a range of ways, including similarity, analogy, parable and degree.[11] This technique is particularly noteworthy when the Qur'ān discusses legal matters.

All Muslims accept that the Qur'ān is the word of God, and they hold the book in great awe and consider it miraculous, because it provides Humanity with God's final Word. It is all this, but it is not just a Holy Book, but also a guide to how to live in both the spiritual and the practical sense. It discusses where humankind ultimately comes from, the nature of

---

8 Farahi, 2013, 57.
9 Q. 1:6-7.
10 Q. 2:2.
11 Gwynne, 2009, 110.

God, the proper conduct for Muslims in public and in private, and it urges humankind to do good and stay away from evil deeds, while always being mindful that, whatever their activity, they are (or should be) acting in the service of God.

While the Qur'ān does contain instructions for legal and civic matters, its primary importance is as a guide for teaching people the correct moral attitude towards one another and towards God. In all arenas of life, including politics, religious life, and interactions between people, everything should be done in the spirit of service to God.[12] In order to achieve this, it is necessary to strive for balance between all of the crucial aspects of life; for instance, to find a balance between pride and hopelessness, and between understanding the fear of God and the mercy of God. As Rahman says, the Qur'ān strives to help people to release the greatest amount of "creative moral energy" possible.[13]

In all this, the Qur'ān's purpose is to make known to people the nature of their relationship with God and the universe, and to bring them to an awareness of a higher consciousness and means of communicating with God, enriching their lives and making it easier for them to make wise and Godly choices.

God's relationship with humankind is described as a Covenant, which refers to the obligations, social and spiritual, including those towards other human beings, which arise from faith in God.[14] God had already entered into Covenant with humanity before, but this had not been a great success. Humankind's failure to properly recall and observe the terms of the Covenant resulted in its lapsing over time. The Qur'ān states: "We had already extended the Covenant to Adam before, but he forgot, and We found no firm resolve in him."[15] Adam was misled and disobeyed God.[16] Being merciful, God punished Adam temporarily, and continued to offer

---

12 Rahman, 1979, 241.
13 Rahman, 1979, 241.
14 Asad, 2003, 363.
15 Q. 20:115.
16 Q. 20:121.

him guidance. Those who keep the Covenant with God are rewarded with "blessings, prosperity, power and heaven."[17]

In the Qur'ān, references to God "speaking" and man "answering" refers to God's creative acts and humankind's response to it.[18] The Qur'ān states that, "they who are true to their bond with God and never break their Covenant[19] are true believers. Thus, the intended audience for the Qur'ān is not a "chosen people" that is exclusive in any way (unlike the clear tribal identity of many religious faiths at the time, in which one had to be born into a particular faith, which was identified with the ethnic group, and to which one could not convert), but *anyone* who observes God's law – any of the descendants of Adam.[20] This is made clear in the following verses:

> And whenever thy Sustainer brings forth their offspring from the loins of the children of Adam. He calls upon them to bear witness about themselves: "Am I not your Sustainer?"-to which they answer; "Yes, indeed, we do bear witness thereto" (of this We remind you) lest you say on the Day of Resurrection." "Verily, we were unaware of this."[21]

According to the Qur'ān, babies are born with the natural ability to perceive God, a quality known as "fitrah," and this instinctive ability makes every mentally fit human being "bear witness about himself" before God. However, the ability to perceive God can be adversely affected by excessive self-indulgence or environmental influences. As each of us moves through life, the decisions we take and the actions we make can, if they are not Godly, have the effect of blunting our ability to perceive our Creator.

The Qur'ān casts a wide net in seeking inspiration, and making points that can be accessed and understood. To make its message clear, it uses a

---

17 Gwynne, 2009, 5.
18 Asad, 2003, 230, note 139.
19 Q. 13:20.
20 Gwynne, 2009, 8.
21 Q. 7:172.

diverse range of examples and parables from the natural world and from society. For example, hypocrites are compared to travellers who lose their fire[22] and to those caught in a storm;[23] those who break their oath are compared to a woman who unravels her own spinning;[24] polytheists to a man serving many masters who disagree with one another;[25] charity to a seed,[26] and good and evil words to good and evil trees.[27]

In this generous usage of examples from the natural world, the Qur'ān is dramatically different to other documents that seek to explain the condition of humanity. Socrates, for example, believed that human beings should be considered completely separately to the natural world.[28] The Qur'ān, however, takes a much broader, more holistic view, and frequently draws the reader's attention to the world around him. It references the changing winds, shifts between day and night, the clouds, the stars in the sky, and the planets in space. Even the ordinary little honeybee gets a mention.[29]

Plato, Socrates' disciple, dismissed the human senses as providing opinion but no real knowledge. The Qur'ān, however, sees our natural senses as a special gift from God,[30] and maintains that we are all accountable to God for how we use them during our time on earth.[31] It also highlights its use of analogies such as those listed above, and is explicit in pointing out that nothing in God's creation is too small and insignificant to be pressed into service in the Qur'ān if an analogy can make a point clearer. For instance, it says that "God is not ashamed to use an analogy – some tiny gnat

---

22 Q. 2:17-8.
23 Q. 2:19-29.
24 Q. 16:92.
25 Q. 39:29.
26 Q. 2:261.
27 Q. 14:23-6; Gwynne, 2009, 118.
28 Iqbal, 1989, 3-7.
29 Q. 2:164; 24:43-4; 30:48; 35:9; 45:51; 5:16; 25:6; 37:6; 41:12; 50:6; 67:5; 85:121; 36:40; 16:68-69.
30 Q. 16:78; 23:78; 32:9; 67:23.
31 Q. 17:36.

or something larger."³² It also warns that only God can coin analogies to describe Himself, saying, "Do not coin "amthal" (analogies) for God: God knows and you do not."³³

Through these messages, God's intention for the Qur'ān is that it should be the foundation for an egalitarian and ethical social order. It was this that Goethe had in mind when he said, "You see this teaching never fails; with all our systems, we cannot go, and generally speaking no man can go, farther than that."³⁴ Indeed, anyone who reads the Qur'ān cannot escape the conclusion that one of its central aims is the creation of a social order that is based on ethics and justice. Thus, the individual is seen in the context of the broader society in which he or she lives, with the understanding that there is, quite literally, no such thing as the "societiless individual".³⁵ The concept of justice as revealed by the Qur'ān quite simply makes no sense unless one assumes a social context, and even when the Qur'ān speaks of being "self-destructive", it is clear that it refers to "the self-destructiveness of a way of life, of a society, of a type of civilisation."³⁶ Quite simply, whatever we do, and whomever we interact with, God is always there. He is there as a third party in every single relationship between two people, whatever the nature of that relationship. The Qur'ān says:

> Do you not see that God knows everything in the heavens and the earth? There is no secret cliquing of three but that God is their fourth, nor of five but that He is their sixth, nor of less than these or more but that He is with them wherever they be.³⁷

While this message is true everywhere, and in every historical context, it is interesting to consider it in the context of the time at which the revelation

---

32   Q. 2:26.
33   Q. 16:74.
34   Iqbal, 1989, 7.
35   Rahman, 1989, 37.
36   Rahman, 1989, 37.
37   Q. 58:7.

was received, when small groups of Muhammad's opponents were meeting to discuss how he and his followers could be thwarted. God is reminding them, as He is us, that he knows and sees all, because He is always present.

The first elements of the Qur'ān that were written down were committed to paper in the sacred city of Mecca, during the special month of Ramadan. The Qur'ān itself is a sacred document, whose power is difficult to comprehend by the human mind. In the Qur'ān, it clearly states that, "Were we to cause this Qur'ān to descend upon a mountain, you would see it humbled, torn asunder in awe of God.[38] This power, strong enough to destroy mountains, is really a source of peace and healing. The Prophet said that the Qur'ān is right guidance from error and a light against blindness, a support against stumbling, a source of illumination against sorrow and a protection against perdition, as well as the best way leading from this world to the next. Turning away from the Qur'ān is like turning oneself in the direction of hell. The Qur'ān shapes and governs all aspects of the life of the Muslim community – individual and collective, religious and social, political and financial, legal and moral.[39]

Throughout the Qur'ān there are references both to itself and to other holy books and scriptures, inviting us to draw comparison between them. In various instances, the Qur'ān situates itself within the context of an already extant *corpus* of documentation of God's word as revealed to various prophets. For example, it states that, "We believe in God and what has been revealed to us and what was revealed to Abraham and Ishmael, and Isaac, and Jacob, and the tribes, in what Moses and Jesus were given and in what the prophets were given from their lord."[40] In this way, while the Qur'ān is an entirely new vehicle in which God makes known His plan for mankind, it is also the final volume in a series of works that have already been made known through diverse prophets over the course of history.

---

38 Q. 59:21.
39 Ayoub, 1984. 8.
40 Q. 2:136.

It was not always easy for Muhammad to deal with the strains of being a prophet in the context of a society that often rejected him and his teaching. The Qur'ān stepped in to reassure him that, like other prophets before him, he was not to blame when people listened to his revelations, but refused to hear their message.[41] Throughout the Qur'ān, God reminded Muhammad of the sufferings of earlier prophets, some of whom, while ordinary human beings,[42] had even been killed by their own people for speaking out.[43] Other prophets had also suffered actual persecution, such as the threat of expulsion, and false accusations.[44] In earlier times, for example, the pharaoh had accused the prophet Moses of being a sorcerer.[45] Muhammad, likewise, was accused of knowing more than he should. It was suggested that he was "too well versed "in certain earlier books. That he had "studied well",[46] was a "well-taught mad man";[47] all accusations that had also been levelled at Jesus.[48]

The Qur'ān makes it clear that Muhammad was above all a man. In fact, it goes out of its way to clarify that *none* of the prophets, regardless of what claims might be made about them, were other than fully human. In other words, there was nothing supernatural about them at all. The Qur'ān compares Jesus to his forefather Adam in terms of his being the fruit of God's creation, rather than a supernatural entity, as some have claimed.[49] It also points out that just as some people had mistakenly considered prophets to be other than human, they had often confused God with man-made idols, which they had foolishly worshipped: "Those whom they invoke

---

41 Q. 6:34.
42 Q. 14:10; 17:94; 36:15; 64:6.
43 Q. 2:61-91.
44 Q. 14:13.
45 Q. 26:27.
46 Q. 6:105.
47 Q. 44:14.
48 Q. 5:110; 61:6.
49 Q. 3:59.

besides God create nothing and are themselves created – dead things, not living, nor do they know when they will be raised up."[50]

The Qur'ān discusses how some of the people who encountered Muhammad's message used the very evident fact of his humanity as a way to try to discredit him, suggesting that an ordinary man should not and could not be taken seriously. They sneered at Muhammad for engaging in everyday activities such as shopping in the marketplace for his daily necessities,[51] and for having a wife and children, just like everyone else.[52]

The Qur'ān pointed out some of the trials and tribulations of the prophets who had gone before, and how their detractors had used personal qualities of theirs to ridicule them and their message. Moses was said to have a speech defect,[53] and both Moses and Aaron belonged to an oppressed minority,[54] while Noah had a great following from among the lower classes,[55] and Lot observed very different rulings around sexual morality than other people in his day.[56] Gwynne identifies the stories of the prophets as related in the Qur'ān as analogies that should be read as stories that back up and validate Muhammad's mission as the voicepiece of God on earth.[57]

While it must have been very challenging for the people of Mecca to accept that the people and things they had long venerated were not special at all, the fact of Muhammad and the other prophets' humanity truly makes their sacrifice particularly notable. As otherwise ordinary human beings, the fact that they accepted God's decision for them to become conduits for His message speaks to great courage and forbearance, especially because they had to face so much hostility.

---

50 Q. 16:20-1.
51 Q. 25:7.
52 Q. 13:38.
53 Q. 43:52.
54 Q. 23:47.
55 Q. 11:27.
56 Q. 7:80-1.
57 Gwynne, 2009, 115.

WHAT IS THE QUR'ĀN?

By reminding him that others had suffered just as he did, Muhammad was reminded that he was not, and never would be, alone. He was, like the other prophets who had gone before him, someone who saw the difference between the world of men as it was, and how it should be, and felt a sense of impatience and urgency about returning humanity to God's plan for them.[58]

All of the prophets who are recognised by Islam are considered people who, while fully human, are also special and free from any serious deviations from God's law. Muhammad, as Islam's prophet, is considered a model for humanity, whose exemplary behaviour on earth illustrates the important role that God called him to.[59]

Despite being God's divine word, and thus in a very real sense timeless in its significance and importance, the Qur'ān also serves as a historical document of the time. Or, rather, as the central message of any Surah is equally important and valid at any point in history, the incidental text provides a certain amount of historical context that reveals something of how Muhammad lived and the various struggles that he and his followers endured. However, most of what is known about Muhammad's life comes not directly from the Qur'ān, but from a huge biographical literature that developed over the years following his death, which is known as "sira".[60] While this information is both valuable and important, it does not share the divine quality of the Qur'ān which, as we have seen, is both inimitable and relevant at all times and in all ways.

The Qur'ān relates how the pagans of Mecca demanded that Muhammad change the message it embodied to something that they found more palatable. They said, "Bring us a discourse other than this (Quran), or alter this one." In response, Muhammad said, "It is not conceivable that I should alter it of my own volition, I only follow what is revealed to me.

---

58 Rahman, 1979, 32.
59 Rahman, 1979, 32.
60 Donner, 2006, 23.

Behold, I would dread, were I (thus) rebel against my Sustainer, the suffering (which would befall me) on that awesome Day (of judgement)."[61]

Muhammad never doubted that he had been chosen as prophet for reasons that he would never understand, and that the revelations he received came from the mercy of God, and had nothing to do with any natural talents he might have. In the Qur'ān it states:

> Do they say that he (Muhammad) has forged (the Qur'ān) as a lie upon God"? If God wills, He shall seal up your heart, again. "If We willed, We would surely remove the Revelation We have given you; then you will find no one who can help you with it despite us.[62]

The Meccans who refused to hear Muhammad's message are denounced in the Qur'ān as possessing no understanding; they are deaf and dumb and blind and their hearts are sealed: "Verily, the vilest of all creatures in the sight of God are those deaf, those dumb ones who do not use their reason",[63] and, "The parable of those who are bent on denying the truth is as that of him who cries unto what hears nothing but a cry and call. Deaf are they, and dumb, and blind: for they do not use their reason".[64] Again, the Qur'ān says: "they want to extinguish God's light with their mouths, but God will not allow (this to pass), for He has willed to spread his light in all its fullness, however hateful this may be to all who deny the truth."

The Qur'ān threatens those who are so wilfully deaf that, if they do not mend their ways, they will suffer. It says:

> And most certainly have we destined for hell many of the invisible beings and men who have hearts, with which they fail to grasp the

---

61 Q. 10:15.
62 Q. 17:86.
63 Q. 8:22.
64 Q. 2:171.

truth, and eyes with which they fail to see, and ears with which they fail to hear. They are like cattle-nay, they are even less conscious of the right way, it is they who are truly heedless.[65]

They are compared to those who refused to listen to earlier prophets, and mend their ways, and who were accordingly punished by God.

The Qur'ān comforts Muhammad, for whom the role of prophet was often a very difficult one. There must have been times when he wondered why God had chosen him for such an arduous task. The Qur'ān reassures him, "We did not bestow the Qur'ān on thee from on high to make thee unhappy,"[66] and that the discipline demanded by the Qur'ān was not intended to make his life harder but, rather, to make it *better* by giving him a much deeper understanding of right and wrong.[67] It states that God knows very well how hard Muhammad's task is, saying, "It may well be that thou wilt torment thyself to death with grief over them if they are not willing to believe in this message".[68]

Indeed, Muhammad did suffer awfully when he worried about the pagan Meccans and the fate that awaited them if they continued not to heed his message. It was frustrating for him to know that, by refusing to listen, they were likely to anger God and endanger their immortal souls. The Qur'ān speaks just as clearly to anyone who is distressed when those around him will not listen to a message that he knows to be true.[69]

Muhammad is told that there is only so much he can do for those who obstinately refuse to hear God's message to them. Much as he might have liked to force the Meccans to listen to him, he could not. His task was only to preach, and he could not make anyone listen through will power: "God

---

65 Q. 7:179.
66 Q. 20:2.
67 Asad, 2003, 470.
68 Q. 18:6.
69 Asad, 2003, 438.

it is Who can make those hear whom He wills—you cannot cause the dead to hear in their graves."[70]

Those who refused to believe Muhammad's message, and to change their ways, would be doomed, either during Muhammad's own lifetime or after his death:

> And whether We show thee (in this world) something of what We hold in store for those (deniers of the truth), or whether We cause thee to die (before that retribution takes place), it is unto Us that they must return, and God is witness to all that they do.[71]

It can be very hard to see pious Muslims have difficult lives, while those who break God's law seem to prosper and have a good time without having done anything to deserve this fortune. However, the Qur'ān makes it clear that our time on earth is but a brief moment compared to the immensity of the infinite afterlife, and that it is here that man's destiny is ultimately unfurled: "only on the Day of Resurrection will you be requited in full (for whatever you have done)."[72]

The Qur'ān is very clear in stating that it was not composed by any human being, and that it both confirms and provides a definitive account of God's eternal truths, which had been revealed before to various prophets throughout history, but had been altered and made less than clear through inaccurate interpretations, omissions and the loss of the original text,[73] whether because of deliberate or accidental corruption of the original message.[74]

The Qur'ān is equally clear on the issue of its definitiveness. While other scriptures are also the word of God, the Qur'ān alone is to be considered pre-eminent, and the "final word" on what God wants for humanity; the

---

70 Q.35:22; 11:12; 88:21-22; 3:20; 5:9-99; 50:45.
71 Q.10:46, in the same vein Q.13:40, 40:77; 43:41-42.
72 Q. 3:185.
73 Asad, 2003, 297.
74 Dammen McAuliffe, 2006, 4.

Qur'ān is the determinant factor in deciding what is genuine and what is false in the earlier scriptures.[75] With the messages revealed to Muhammad, and written down in the Qur'ān, God has given his "full and final guidance for humankind."[76]

As if to pre-empt any queries or questions about its content, the Qur'ān is what Dammen McAuliffe describes as an "argumentative text".[77] It often poses itself questions and answers them, and it indulges in polemical arguments, provides evidence to justify arguments it is making, and produces conclusions after a series of reasoned discussions, comparisons and contrasts.

It appears that, in foreseeing the many arguments and attempted refutations that would be made against it, through Muhammad God is already providing the answers that he, and all Muslims, will need to launch a strong counter-argument against would-be detractors.

The Qur'ān also argues for its definitive nature not just at the time of the revelations but in the future, stating that no future prophet would ever be able to produce a comparable document, or even a single Surah that could be compared to those of the Qur'ān; quite simply, no human being would ever be capable of carrying out such a feat.[78] It also uses a range of techniques to discuss God's all-powerful and transcendent nature. Certain verses describe God as transcendent and incomparable in a positive, stand-alone way, but many others do so with implicit comparisons to other entities, with the clever use of rhetorical questions,[79] such as, "Whose word is truer than God's?";[80] "Who is more faithful to his Covenant than God?"[81]

---

75 Ridda, 1999, 410.
76 Dammen McAuliffe, 2006, 4.
77 Dammen McAuliffe, 2006, 4.
78 Dammen McAuliffe, 2006, 4.
79 Gwynne, 2009, 119.
80 Q. 4:11.
81 Q. 9:111.

and "Who is better than God at judging a people whose future is certain?"[82] It also uses lavish terms of praise to highlight God's transcendence.[83]

The Qur'ān uses arguments around the issues of similarity and reciprocity, particularly when it discusses arguments of relevance to legal matters. For example, it makes it clear that when two people take similar paths in life they will come to a similar end. Christians and Jews who believe as the Muslims do, for instance, are on the right path,[84] while those who do not believe seek to reduce others to their level, thereby creating similarity between them.[85] In all the rulings of relevance to legal disputes, the Qur'ān makes extensive use of this law of similarity; for every action there is an equal reaction. The thief who repents will receive mercy,[86] and those who make space for God in their lives on earth will find that He makes space for them in the afterlife.[87]

The Qur'ān also discusses, with particular reference to legal matters, actions that are not the same or similar, but that are legally equivalent, such as accepting an indemnity rather than insisting on a murderer's execution.[88] Equally, those who behave in a similar way to those who do not follow God will suffer similar consequences.

Although God and humankind are clearly not equivalent in any way, they are both parties to a Covenant and, as such, they are bound in a relationship of mutual obligation.[89] Ultimately, however, the only similar thing to an act of God is another act of God, because nothing that any human can achieve can truly be compared to it. The Qur'ān makes it clear in numerous instances that if God has done something in the past, He can easily do something comparable or equally momentous in the future. For

---

82 Q. 5:50.
83 Gwynne, 2009, 119.
84 Q. 2:137.
85 Q. 4:89.
86 Q. 5:39.
87 Q. 58:11.
88 Gwynne, 2009, 112.
89 Gwynne, 2009, 112.

example, "Is not the One Who created the heavens and the earth capable of creating something like them?" and "Say: 'Who will bring us back to life?' Say 'He who created you the first time?'"[90]

God's choice of Muhammad as prophet is revealing. This is a man who, despite living in a culture in which poetry, oratory and eloquence were prized, had never composed even a single line. He had reached the age of forty without learning to read, and was known to be singularly truthful. Yet, somehow, he had produced a series of revelations that led to a document with extraordinary inner logic and psychological insights.[91] The Qur'ān deals with suggestions that Muhammad might have composed the Qur'ān for his own political ends by saying that: "Those who are bent on denying the truth say (unto one another): 'Do not listen to this Qur'ān, but rather talk frivolously about it, so that you might gain the upper hand.'"[92] The implication is that those who were exposed to the Qur'ān instinctively understood its force, but wished to reject its message of social justice and faith in God, which threatened their lives of privilege and self-complacency.[93]

The Qur'ān points out the similarities between Muhammad and the prophets who came before him, and castigates those who failed to observe these similarities, saying:

> O, People of the Book, our apostle has come to you, clarifying (matters) for you after a break in (the sequence of) Apostles, so you will not say, "No bearer of good news came to you, no warner." Now a bearer of good news, a warner, *has* come to you. And God has power over all things.[94]

---

90 Q. 36:81; 17:51.
91 Asad, 2003, 291.
92 Q. 41:26.
93 Asad, 2003, 734.
94 Q. 5:19.

Some of those who sought to discredit the Qur'ān, the pagan chiefs of Mecca, demanded the Muhammad produce an angel or turn the local mountains into gold. They demanded that he also cease to defame the deities they worshipped, and said that, instead, he should respect and glorify them. If he did all these things, they promised that they would make him their leader and recognise him as their prophet. The Qur'ān makes it very clear that Muhammad immediately rejected this offer. The pagans insisted that they simply worshipped as their ancestors had before them, saying, "Behold, we found our forefathers agreed on what to believe and verily it is but in their footsteps that we follow."[95] According to their own testimony, therefore, they had not arrived at their religious views through reason, but by doing what had always been done by their forefathers, without ever thinking about it.

In a society that was organised around tribal lines, the Qur'ān provides a revolutionary message: that *anyone* who believes in and follows God's Covenant with man, regardless of who he is and where he comes from, is a true Muslim and should be supported. All the followers of the Qur'ān are asked never to turn away anyone who believes in God, even when not all of his beliefs are consistent with the Qur'ān's teachings. Instead, they should be helped to reach a true understanding of the Qur'ān's message.

One of Islam's great sorrows has been that too many Muslims over the generations have turned from the refreshing, revolutionary message of the Qur'ān, and instead have tended to accept views that Rahman describes as "almost out-and-out predeterministic",[96] which he ascribes in part to the contribution of certain medieval formulations of Islam.

Returning to the original text, and understanding the social context in which it was received and written, reveals the extraordinary clarity and beauty of God's plan for humanity as revealed to Muhammad.

---

95 Q. 43:23.
96 Rahman, 1979, 241.

CHAPTER 4

REVELATIONS OF THE QUR'ĀN

THE CONCEPT OF "revelation", understood in a broad sense to mean communication from God, either directly or via an intermediary, with someone chosen by Him to act as His prophet and messenger to the world, is central to the three historically related faiths of Islam, Christianity and Judaism. It is absolutely fundamental to understanding the nature of Muhammad's experience of communication with God, and the manner and content of His communications with Muslims throughout his lifetime and subsequently.

All three above-mentioned faiths share a belief in the one true God, and the belief that God can communicate with humankind by providing the revelations received by prophets. This monotheistic tradition is not just a variant among a range of beliefs, but a significant departure, culturally as well as theologically, from animistic and other nature-based belief systems such as prevailed in Arabia in Muhammad's time.

Historically, the emergence of monotheistic theology was associated with a rejection of the idea that the world is filled with spirits, demons, and so forth, with spirituality rooted in nature, and introduces the idea of a supreme being, who exists in a realm located beyond nature,[1] ineffable, and difficult to understand in His enormity. Only through revelation, in which God's will for humanity is transmitted through a human agent, a prophet, can this be understood.

---

1   Saeed, 2006, 22.

In Islam, the Qur'ān is the most important way in which God discloses information about what He wants from humanity, and He does so with the revelations that were received by His prophet, Muhammad.[2]

Revelation has two essential characteristics: It comes directly from God to particular humans chosen by Him, and it is communicated in a supernatural way, by means of dreams, visions, ecstatic experiences, and sacred documents or words.[3] Moreover, the purpose of these revelations is not simply to reveal the presence of God, but to teach humanity by revealing what God wishes them to do, and how they might be punished or rewarded, depending upon their actions.

When Muhammad received his first revelation in the cave of Hira, to which he had long been going when he felt the need to meditate and pray away from the hustle and bustle of Mecca, he initially felt a presence and then saw an angel in the form of a man. The angel told him to "read" or recite. When Muhammad replied that he could not recite, the angel then held Muhammad so tightly that he thought he was dying. Three times, the angel repeated the command that Muhammad should recite. Finally the angel Gabriel (for it was he) began to recite what would become the first five verses of chapter 96 of the Qur'ān, saying:

> Read in the name of your sustainer, who has created, created man out of a germ-cell. Read-for your sustainer is the most Bountiful One who has taught (man) the use of the pen - taught man what he did not know.

These were the first words of the Qur'ān revealed to Muhammad.

In Muhammad's earliest accounts of what was initially the very frightening experience of receiving revelations from God, it is clear that this experience took place in a state of vision or quasi-dream. The Prophet is

---

2 Saeed, 2006, 22.
3 Saeed, 2006, 22.

reported to have stated after narrating the experience, "Then I woke up".[4] The angel Gabriel is mentioned by the Qur'ān specifically as the bringer of revelation to Muhammad, a process that "ends at the prophet's heart".[5]

Abdel Haleem has given a detailed account of the prophet's first revelation as follows:

> For the first experience of revelation Muhammad was alone in the cave, but after that the circumstances in which he received revelation were witnessed by others and recorded. When he experienced the "state of revelation", those around him were able to observe his visible, audible, and sensory reactions. His face would become flushed and he would fall silent and appear as if his thoughts were far away, his body would become limp as if he were asleep, a humming sound would be heard about him, and sweat would appear on his face, even on winter days. This state would last for a brief period and as it passed the Prophet would immediately recite new verses of the Qur'ān. The revelation could descend on him as he was walking, sitting, riding, or giving a sermon.[6]

Gabriel is mentioned twice in the Qur'ān as the source of the revelations received by Muhammad, a fact that has become an important tenet of Islamic belief.[7] In cases where it appears that Muhammad is receiving revelations from an identified spirit, this is assumed to be Gabriel.[8]

The Qur'ān tells us that God's prophets or human messengers are receiving some special or extraordinary power that emanates from the ultimate source of all being and fills their hearts with something that is light, whereby they see and know things as others cannot. At the same time, this

---

4   Rahman, 1979, 13.
5   Rubin, 2006, 237; Q. 2:97.
6   Qattān, 1983, 38-40.
7   Rippen, 2006, 24.
8   Gilliot, 2006, 42.

power determines them upon a course of action that changes the destiny of entire cultures.⁹

Muhammad was entrusted with the mission of bringing God's message to humanity in the form of the Qur'ān: "calling the entire world to righteousness and justice, to morality and decency, and to a life of prayer and fasting, and surrender to the will of God."[10] Clearly, Muhammad had been given an immensely important task; one that could change the future of humanity.

The Qur'ān is wonderfully clear in its instructions to humanity. For example, in just five words, the first verse of Surah 96 offers us a command, "read"; information about the authority behind the command; and a definition of Who the author of the command was. The second verse elucidates the author's authority, verse three repeats the initial command, and verses three through five reaffirm the author's identity as the giver of the Covenant between God and humankind; a Covenant that has many benefits, including existence itself, and the blessing of knowledge after the ignorance in which humans laboured for so long. The remainder of humanity's obligations in fulfilment of the Covenant are not yet revealed, apart from the command "read", but in these few words we find an extraordinary richness of what Gwynne summarises as "divine command, authorization, identification, and Covenant, a combination of logic and sacred history".[11]

It would be a mistake to assume from Muhammad's ability to receive revelations and communicate them to the people that he should be seen as somehow more than human or supernatural. Indeed, the Qur'ān itself makes it clear that Muhammad, although a prophet, was an ordinary, flesh-and-blood man.[12] The Qur'ān also makes it clear that God alone, and no human intermediary, can create miracles.[13] As Asad notes, the very term

---

9 Rahman, 1989. 98.
10 Saeed, 2006, 23.
11 Gwynne, 2009, 71.
12 Saeed, 2006, 23.
13 Q. 6:109.

"miracle", as it is generally understood, "comprises of an unusual message from God, indicating sometimes a symbolic manner - a spiritual truth which would otherwise have remained hidden from man's intellect."[14] In fact, the Qur'ān elucidates that one of God's infinity of miracles was, and remains, the Qur'ān, which is a document embodying a message that is entirely clear, and utterly comprehensive, designed to be valid to guide humans at all times, and in all places. It is meant to appeal not just to the emotions, but also to the intellect, and to be relevant to everyone, regardless of their background and situation. As such, it must never change.[15]

Moreover when – as they did on numerous occasions – Muhammad's critics asked him why God did not send an angel to earth to prove that the Qur'ān was truly His word, the Qur'ān clarified in many verses that if God *had* granted this request and sent an angel to earth, it would have meant the end of times and the beginning of Judgement Day, which in turn would have meant that humans would not have had the opportunity to repent of their foolish ways and instead seek guidance and help from God. In any case, even if an angel *had* been sent to earth it would, of necessity, have taken the form of a human being, as no human is capable of seeing the real shape of an angel. In other words, the presence of an angel would not have clarified things at all, but would simply have contributed to even greater confusion.[16]

In fact, God's only miracle was, and still is, the Qur'ān itself. To this day it remains a message that is clear, lucid and easy to understand, while also providing comprehensive ethical guidelines that are as relevant in the modern age as they were when they were first received by Muhammad. The Qur'ān speaks not just to the emotions, but also to the intellect, and it is relevant to everyone, whatever their sex, ethnic and social background,

---

14 Asad, 2003, 188-9, note 94.
15 Asad, 2003, 188-9.
16 Q: 6:8-9.

and historical context.[17] Unchanging in its perfection, it is a beacon of hope for humanity.

In fact, there are areas in the text where the time and place in which Muhammad lived, and even his personal domestic situation, are referenced.[18] Over the next twenty-three years, during which Muhammad received revelations, these were recorded, written down and edited by his followers, sometimes a number of years after the revelation was received.[19] Early writers recorded the verses of the Qur'ān using whatever materials were available to them, such as leaves and branches, stones, leather, animal bones, and so forth,[20] and the evidence indicates that all, or most, of the Qur'ān as it is known today was written down at some stage during Muhammad's lifetime.[21]

As stated above, Muhammad himself was illiterate, like the majority of people in Arabia at this time, but Mecca had long been involved in trade and other relations with literate cultures, and literacy was becoming more common.[22] Evidence of the influence of both Jewish and Christian scholarship (which is not surprising, given what we know about the historical and cultural links between these three monotheistic faiths, all of which emerged in the east) can be seen in the fact that some of the words used in the Qur'ān are not Arabic in origin.[23]

The Quranic term for Revelation is "wahy," which is roughly approximate to the English word "inspiration". In the Qur'ān, God says that:

> It does not belong to any human that God should speak to him (directly) except by Revelation (i.e., infusion of the spirit) or from behind a veil (i.e., by a voice whose source is invisible) or that He

---

17   Asad, 2003, 188-9.
18   Gilliot, 2006, 41.
19   Gilliot, 2006, 42.
20   Saeed, 2006, 23.
21   Gilliot, 2006, 42.
22   Gilliot, 2006, 42.
23   Gilliot, 2006, 43.

should send a (spiritual) Messenger who reveals (to the Prophet) by God's permission what He wills - and He is exalted and Wise. And even so have We revealed unto you (i.e., infused in your mind) the Spirit of our Command – you did not know before what the Book is nor what Faith is, but We have made it a light whereby We guide whomsoever We will of our servants, and you, indeed, guide (people) to the straight path.[24]

The first part of this passage is especially important. It tells us that, rather than speaking directly to a human being, in the person of Muhammad, God infuses a spirit in the prophet's mind. This makes him both see and state the truth, saying, "This is my path- I call people (to God) on the basis of a clear perception."[25] In this way, although Muhammad was an ordinary man, he was also gifted with extraordinary powers of perception that made him exceptionally able to be still and listen to the word of God.

When Muhammad spoke about the revelations he received – initially to a sceptical audience, but over time to a growing group of followers – he was not giving his own opinion but the information that had been given to him directly by God,[26] in the form of a mental "sound" rather than a physical one, and the formation of words in the brain, rather than spoken aloud. The Qur'ān makes it clear that he "heard" words in his mind, when it says that the prophet actually mentally "heard" words and cautions him not to rush to speak before he has received a revelation: "Do not hasten your tongue with it (the revelation) in order to anticipate it. It is our task to collect it and recite it. So when we recited it, follow its recital, and then it is also Our task to explain it".[27] It is clear that Muhammad heard these words in his mind. The spirit and the voice were internal to him and, while the

---

24 Q. 42:51-2.
25 Q. 12:108.
26 Q. 53:3-4.
27 Q. 75:16-9; see also Q. 20:114.

revelation came directly from God, it was also impacted by Muhammad's own personality in a very significant way.

Popular Islamic belief sometimes maintains that the revelations came from a source entirely outside Muhammad, but this is clearly incorrect.[28] Muhammad, who had been chosen by God to be His voicepiece in the world of men and women, provided the channel through which God's word could be heard.

What does the Qur'ān itself say? On the one hand, it stresses that the revelations received by Muhammad were from an outside source, that they were objectively real, and that they were verbal in nature. On the other, it also rejects the notion that they were entirely external to the prophet himself. The Qur'ān states: "The Trusted Spirit has brought it down upon your heart that you may be a warner" and also says, "Say: He who is an enemy of Gabriel (let him be), for it is he who has brought it down upon your heart."[29] Thus, while it would be incorrect to describe Muhammad as the author of the Qur'ān (because the "author" can only be God),[30] its revelations are filtered through him. While there are verses in the Qur'ān in which God's voice is given in the first person,[31] most frequently revelations are not given directly to Muhammad, but come via an intermediary in the person of Gabriel, as mentioned above.[32] Throughout the history of Islamic scholarship, this very nuanced understanding has often been quite difficult to understand. Rahman states of Islamic scholarship in the Middle Ages that:

> The orthodoxy (indeed, all medieval thought) lacked the necessary intellectual tools to combine in its formulation of the dogma the otherness and verbal character of the revelation on the one hand, and its intimate connection with the work and religious personality

---

28 Rahman, 1989, 99-100.
29 Q. 2:97.
30 Saeed, 2006, 22.
31 For example, Q. 2:41; 44:3; 76:23; 97:1.
32 Rubin, 2006, 237.

of the Prophet on the other, i.e. it lacked the intellectual capacity to say both that the Qur'ān is entirely the Word of God and, in an ordinary sense, also entirely the word of Muhammad.[33]

In the Qur'ān, various verbs are used to communicate the notion of prophetic revelation. That which is used most frequently comes from the root n-z-l, or "nazzala" and "anzala". These suggest an act of "bringing down", evocative of the idea of the revelations being sent "down" to Muhammad from God in Heaven, which was conceived of as a higher realm.[34] Another often-used term to describe revelation is "tanzil".[35] The term "wahy matluww", which indicates a revelation which is recited, or a revelation that is spoken in words, is used with specific reference to the prophets, but the Qur'ān speaks also of revelation in terms of its connection with the earth,[36] the heavens,[37] the honeybee,[38] angels,[39] the mother of Moses,[40] and the disciples of Jesus,[41] as well as discussing the various modes of revelation.[42]

The Qur'ān records the revelations received by Muhammad over the course of a period of twenty-three lunar years; in other words, from his middle years to his old age.[43] With the passage of time, Muhammad's experience of receiving revelations changed somewhat. Whereas in the early years, he often experienced revelations when he was in a semi-dream like state, from which he "awoke", later on he seems to have also experienced some physical manifestations of religious ecstasy; physical symptoms that

---

33 Rahman, 1979, 31.
34 Rubin, 2006, 237.
35 Q. 20:4; 26:192; 32:2.
36 Q. 99:5.
37 Q. 41:12.
38 Q. 16: 68-9.
39 Q. 8:12.
40 Q. 28:7.
41 Q. 5:111.
42 Q. 42:51.
43 Saeed, 2006, 22.

only occurred in the context of revelation.⁴⁴ As stated above, the texts reflect the revelations from God, but they also reflect some of the things that were happening in Muhammad's own life when they were being recorded, as well as broader shifts and trends relating to the spread of Islam, and to the things that were happening around Muhammad and his followers at this time. For instance, there are clear differences in style between the manner in which revelations were recorded early in the key period of twenty-three years, when Muhammad and his followers were in Mecca, where they had to deal with persecution, and when they were in Medina, when they had a degree of support, and Islam had started to become much more widespread.⁴⁵

Whereas in the earlier days of Islam, Muhammad had had to commit all the revelations he received to memory before they were written down, later on, in Medina, he was in a position to employ literate men who were tasked with writing his revelations down so that they could be shared by the Muslim faithful and all of mankind.⁴⁶ Obviously, there are bound to be stylistic differences between the written Qur'ānic revelations received during such diverse periods of the Prophet's life.

While Muhammad is clarified by the Qur'ān to have been, in many ways, a relatively ordinary man, the Holy Book also stresses that, in having been selected to bring God's message to the world, he was also special. In various verses⁴⁷ the text refers to the spirit of God descending and bringing revelation down to mankind, using the term "amr", which is used to indicate a command of God. This revelation is considered the essential element of a sort of "primordial book"⁴⁸ (to put it into terms that ordinary mortals can understand) from which the spirit that enters the hearts of prophets (such as Muhammad) ultimately comes. The Qur'ān is clear in stating that while God's prophets are human beings, they have also been gifted with

---

44 Rahman, 1979, 13.
45 Gilliot, 2006, 43.
46 Gilliot, 2006, 43.
47 Q. 16:2; 17:85; 40:15; 42:52; 97:4.
48 Rahman, 1989, 98.

some sort of special power that comes from God, and that enables them to see and understand things in a way that other people simply cannot.[49] This in turn puts them in a position of great power, and great responsibility, as it is within their capabilities to change the destinies not just of individual men and women, but of entire cultures, and indeed of any person or group of people that is willing to listen to their message. As such, they offer hope to humanity; that there is always a chance to turn away from blind and foolish behaviour and to adopt, instead, a way of living that is closer to God's plan for humanity.[50]

A great deal has been said about the supposed sacredness of the Arabic language that is the first medium through which Muhammad received, and spoke of, the revelations in the cave; Arabic has been describe as a "lingua sacra."[51] However, regardless of what one might think of the special nature of the Arabic language, the revelations of the prophet Muhammad are central to Islam in *any* language.

Clearly, the revelations received by Muhammad were of immense importance to all Muslims, then as now, but it is not always recognised that the massive cultural shifts that occurred in response led to several streams of thought that would have a profound impact on the development of Western culture, as well as Arabian and Middle Eastern cultures. The desacralisation of nature, and the replacement of an assortment of minor deities and nature spirits with an understanding of a one true God with a grand plan for humanity led, over time, to a more defined understanding of nature and science. Over the years that followed Muhammad's revelations, Islamic philosophy and science interacted and blended with other influences to create Western civilisation.[52]

From when he first received revelations, to the end of his life, Muhammad never doubted that the messages he received were indeed the

---

49 Rahman, 1989, 98.
50 Rahman, 1989, 99.
51 Gilliot, 2006, 43.
52 Saeed, 2006, 22.

word of God, even when they directly contradicted some of the supposedly historical material preserved in Judaic and Christian tradition.[53] In his communications with Muhammad, God's voice was unwavering, distinct, and clear. As such, to Muhammad, and to all Muslims to this day, the Qur'ān is the Word of God and thus provides a unique template for life according to His wishes.

---

53 Rahman, 1979, 31.

CHAPTER 5

STAGES OF REVELATION

As we have seen, the Qur'ān emerged gradually over a period of many years, starting from when Muhammad was about forty and received his first revelation in the cave of Hira. This fact was quickly seized upon by some of the disbelievers, who wondered why he had not been given all the messages from God in one fell swoop, rather than little by little. The Qur'ān itself reports that:

> They who are bent on denying the truth are wont to ask, "Why has not the Qur'ān been bestowed on him from on high in one single revelation?" (It has been revealed) in this manner so that We might strengthen thy heart-for We have so arranged its component parts that they form one consistent whole.[1]

The disbelievers suggested that the gradual nature of the revelations implied that the Qur'ān had been composed by Muhammad as he went through life in order to suit the changing needs emerging from his changing circumstances.[2] They queried whether the Qur'ān had anything to do with God at all. In response to these doubters, the Qur'ān provides three distinct reasons behind the gradual nature of revelation:

- "To strengthen thy heart". Given the tribal culture, dispersed population and polytheistic religious practices that prevailed at that

---
1 Q. 25:32.
2 Asad, 2003, 435.

time, the task of converting the people of Arabia and, through them, the entire world, would call for immense patience and persistence, and these qualities would be fostered in Muhammad and his followers by ensuring that he received the revelations gradually, giving them time to adapt and learn the skills to deal with each situation as it arose.
- "Slow, well arranged stages". Although the process of receiving revelations was a gradual one, taking place over the course of twenty-three years, the ultimate result was perfect, an impeccably arranged set of instructions, as an examination of the Surahs soon shows.
- "Questions put and answers given."[3] The Qur'ān itself makes it clear that another reason why it was revealed in stages was so that, by degrees, it could be read out to mankind, giving them time to incorporate its teachings into their lives. It is, the Qur'ān affirms: "A discourse which We have gradually unfolded, so that thou might read it out to mankind by stages, seeing that We have bestowed it from on high step by step, as (one) revelation".

Although the Qur'ān was revealed to Muhammad over a period of twenty-three years, together it forms an integral, perfect whole. As such, it can only be fully understood when it is read from start to finish, in its entirety. Each passage, and each Surah, is enlightened by a knowledge of all of the others.[4] This extraordinary level of complexity is in turn cited by the Qur'ān as further proof of the divine origins of the document. Moreover, if the Qur'ān had been revealed to Muhammad as a whole, already finished and complete, it would have been impossible for the people of the time to take its complex, far-reaching message on board. The task of confirming that it is a practical guide to living, as well as a spiritual guide, would have been lost on a population without the ability to truly understand its meaning, and the implications for their lives. Instead, as it was revealed in stages

---

3   Yusuf, 1934, 1041, note 3088.
4   Asad, 2003, 436; Q. 20:114.

to a community that was enabled to grow spiritually and intellectually, as the Qur'ān grew in length and complexity, the nascent society of Muslims was able to evolve alongside Muhammad's revelations.[5]

In short, the benefits that have accrued from the Qur'ān being revealed in stages can be summarised thus:

- Muhammad, who had been tasked with an enormous responsibility, was comforted by the episodic nature of revelation, and was given the opportunity to allow his faith to strengthen in this process.[6]
- Since time immemorial, society had been plagued by vice and immorality. These had become ingrained aspects of how people lived, and it would not have been possible for them to completely rewrite their way of life overnight. In recognition of this, the Qur'ān was revealed gradually in such a way that, little by little, people could start to live in a different way before accepting and establishing a way of life governed by the regulations and laws set down by God.[7]
- During the course of the gradual revelation of the Qur'ān, those who heard it expressed occasional doubts. One by one, their doubts, as well as the problems that were affecting them, were addressed. For example, when the people asked when the Day of Judgement would take place, saying, "When will it come to pass?"[8] the Qur'ān replied, saying, "Say, knowledge thereof rests with my sustainer alone, none but He will reveal it in its time".[9] When they asked about what would happen to the mountains, saying, "What will happen to the mountains when this world comes to an end?" the

---

5 Qaṭṭān, 1983, 110-1.
6 Al-Zurqani, 2012, 57-8; Qaṭṭān, 1983, 107-8.
7 Al-Zurqani, 2012, 59-60.
8 Q. 79:42.
9 Q. 7:187.

Qur'ān informed them that, "Say, my sustainer will scatter them far and wide."[10]
- If the Qur'ān had been revealed all at once, Muhammad and his followers would have had to adapt to and implement all the laws it contains overnight. This would have been a practical impossibility, especially considering the hostility they faced from those who doubted the veracity of the revelations. However, because it was revealed over time, it was possible to gradually create a community free of immoral behaviour.[11]
- As previously stated, Muhammad was an illiterate man. The gradual revelation of the Qur'ān to one such as him made it possible for him to memorise the instructions he received and pass them on free of omissions and mistakes, to people who could record them in writing.[12]
- Because the Qur'ān was revealed incrementally over time, the followers of Muhammad were enabled to study everything it raised, memorise its instructions, and change their way of living to be consistent with God's teaching. The compilation of the Qur'ān could also take place alongside these incremental changes. God Himself, the instigator and revealer of the Qur'ān, was also responsible for its compilation. The Qur'ān states: "It is for Us to collect it and to recite it. But when We have recited it, follow thou its recital (as promulgated)."[13]
- A great deal of the Qur'ān's content consists of factual responses to the questions posed to Muhammad by his followers. Understandably, many of these questions relate to the changes that were occurring in their lives. As each new change came on the

---

10 Q. 20:105.
11 Al-Zurqani, 2012. 61-2.
12 Al-Zurqani, 2012. 59.
13 Q. 75:17-8.

scene, they were enabled to ask Muhammad for clarification and counsel.
- Gradually, the number of Muslims grew and, as it did, they were able to look beyond the confines of their immediate environment. They started to understand their mission in the world as they lived in it, and their place in the afterlife. All of these realisations led to further questions, to which the Qur'ān responded as part of an ongoing process of revelation.
- The Qur'ān forms a bridge between past, present and future. It refers to events that took place long before Muhammad's birth, as well as speaking of events that have not yet taken place (in this world, as well as the afterlife). It also addresses events that were taking place during the period of revelation, with specific reference to the many difficulties and challenges faced by the Muslim community during Muhammad's years of revelations. If the Qur'ān had revealed this depth of complexity overnight, it would have appeared nonsensical to an unprepared public, and would have contributed to the criticisms of Muhammad from those who claimed that he was a madman, and not inspired by God at all.[14]
- Another benefit of the gradual nature of the revelation of the Qur'ān is the fact that it allowed Muhammad's followers to ask questions about how best they could serve God, and how they should conduct their everyday lives. The Qur'ān states: "And they cannot bring thee a question, but we have brought thee the truth and the best explanation."[15]
- Finally, on a pragmatic note, at the time of the revelations, many centuries before the invention of printing, there simply were not enough scribes and materials to write everything down in a short period of time.

---

14 Al-Zurqani, 2012. 59.
15 Q. 25:33.

Despite the fact that it was revealed over many years, to a man who was neither literate nor versed in literature, the Qur'ān is utterly free of inner contradiction. This alone (although there is also ample proof from other areas) is convincing evidence that it was not composed by Muhammad, as many of his contemporaries accused, and as non-believers in later times have also suggested every time they seek to discredit the teachings of Islam. The ultimate origins of the Qur'ān can only be from a power external to, and far greater than, any human being. The Qur'ān itself states:

> God bestows from on high the best of all teachings in the shape of a Divine writ fully consistent within itself, repeating each statement in manifold forms (a Divine writ) whereat shiver the skins of all who of their sustainer stand in awe (but) in the end their skins and their hearts do soften at the remembrance of God.[16]

A very special quality of the Qur'ān is that it is a Holy Book that serves to provide humankind with all the guidance it needs; advice that is applicable now and in the future, as it was in Muhammad's time. Unlike the Torah, which came before, it goes far beyond providing a simple series of legal requirements. The Qur'ān reaches deep, providing the means by which any individual or any society can grapple with the eternal problem of decadence by means of transforming thoughts and beliefs, rather than by tackling the mere symptoms of said decadence. By starting with thought and belief, transformation in terms of morality and values can be assured.

---

16 Q. 39:23.

CHAPTER 6

MUHAMMAD IN MEDINA

MUHAMMAD FACED SUCH a degree of persecution and harassment in Mecca that, eventually, he was forced to move to Medina with a small number of followers. That this took place at a time when Medina was in the throes of a terrible feud between a number of local clans shows how desperate the situation in Mecca had become. Muhammad had often been asked to intervene in cases of conflict before, but he knew that this would have been a very risky thing to do in Medina, where he was unknown. Rather than getting involved in the local squabbles, he initially asked pilgrims in Medina to provide him and his followers with protection.

A few months after arriving in Medina, Muhammad drew up a pact that explained how Muslims should deal with the inhabitants of Medina who continued with their polytheistic ways and refused to listen to the message of the Qur'ān. The pact also outlined ways in which Muslims and local Jewish tribes should treat one another in a spirit of respect and mutual help. This pact formed the first original ruling that determined how Muslims' loyalty should be, above all, to other Muslims and true believers, regardless of any obligations they might have to their family and clan. In other words, the faith community transcended family in terms of commanding reverence and respect. This faith community, known as the ummah (as it still is to this day), was bound together by the oath that there was only One God, that his prophet was Muhammad, and that Muhammad's words should be obeyed, as he was God's messenger on earth. In this context, Muhammad was responsible for his people's welfare, and even their survival.¹

At first, life was very hard for Muhammad and his followers. Having arrived in Medina with practically nothing, they survived for a time on little more than dates and water. Muhammad was an experienced man of business, but local business was dominated by a number of Jewish tribes at the time, and they operated a closed shop. It was hard, almost impossible, for newcomers to get a toehold in local commerce.

When he and his followers had been in Medina for seven months, Muhammad took the decision to attack caravans coming from Syria. He did this despite the fact that he and his followers had been effectively free of persecution by members of the Quraysh tribe since their departure. One reason was the fact that one of Mecca's major sources of wealth was the caravan trade; if Muhammad's expedition was successful, Medina might replace Mecca as the most important centre for commerce in the area. Moreover, Muhammad had received an order from God to take this action.² Given his rather tenuous position in Mecca, he was both brave and daring to do so. Two of the major Arab tribes in the area continued to view Muhammad and his Muslim followers as suspect, while the local Jewish tribes, despite sharing a faith in the one true God, saw him as a direct threat to their integrity, and viewed his teachings as blasphemous.

Despite these difficulties, Muhammad gradually managed to attain the position of religious leader in Medina, and also became effectively its political and practical leader. Two of the local tribes, the Aws and the Khazraj, had converted from their pagan, idolatrous ways to following Muhammad's teachings. They were dubbed "ansar", which means "helpers", because of the support they extended to Muhammad and his followers at this difficult time. Each ansar was required to adopt one of Muhammad's followers as his "brother", to feed him and give him shelter.³ Information about these

---

1   Gabriel, 2004, 70-4.
2   Q.22:39-40.
3   Ishaq, 1967, 232.

groups can be found in *Life of the Prophet* by Ibn Ishāq. Although both the Aws and the Khazraj were supportive, they did not manage to rid themselves completely of the tradition of enmity between the two groups.

The Jewish clans of the area, who had long been so integral to local commerce, included three large groups known as the Qaynuqa', the Nadir and the Qurayza, and there were also various smaller groups that had formed alliances with diverse Aws and Khazraj clans.

As they became established in this religiously and ethnically diverse town, Muhammad and his followers came to be known as the "Muhājirūn", or those who had made the Hijra. Once established, Muhammad and his followers forged an agreement with all the people in Medina that would see all the groups coming together to form a single community with the goal of protecting themselves and the area, while recognising Muhammad as leader.

Although this agreement was formally made, some people (mostly from the Aws and Khazraj groups) pretended to support Muhammad, but privately acted against him and his teachings. Despite many efforts to rein in this situation, it would continue throughout Muhammad's time in Medina. These people are recorded by history as "munāfiqūn", which means "Hypocrites".

The local Jews also continued to oppose Muhammad's position as leader. When he first encountered this group, Muhammad had hoped that they would accept him as their political leader, and that they would also come to accept that he was a prophet, just like Abraham, Moses, and Joseph, whose teachings they followed. Although history relates many instances in which the Jews opposed Muhammad, it is not entirely clear whether this opposition was primarily political, or primarily in relation to his religious claims.

With his leadership confirmed, Muhammad turned his attention back to his ongoing struggle against the Quraysh people who had made life impossible for him and his followers in Mecca. One reason for this was his belief in the Ka'ba shrine in Mecca, which had first been established by the prophet Abraham, and which was important to Christians and Jews as well. For Muhammad, the fact that monotheistic worship had been established in Mecca all those years ago was crucial, and he felt strongly that monotheistic worship should be restored there, with a focus on the holy site of the Ka'ba. Muhammad instructed his followers that, from now on, they should turn themselves in the direction of the Ka'ba in Mecca to pray, rather than towards Jerusalem, as they had done to date.

As part of his struggle to take control of Mecca, Muhammad went to great effort to convert members of the various nomadic groups who lived in western Arabia. Their support could make all the difference in determining which town, Mecca or Medina, would come out on top.[4]

By now, an effective situation of war prevailed between the Muslims of Medina and the people of Mecca. Muhammad and his followers found out that a large trade caravan from Mecca, which had travelled to Syria a few months before under the leadership of a man called Abu Sufyan, was on its way back, and would pass Medina in a few weeks' time. Muhammad informed his followers of his plan to attack the caravan when it approached their adopted home of Medina. Unfortunately, news of the plan came to the attention of Abu Sufyan before he left Syria. Knowing what was supposed to happen, Sufyan sent scouts ahead to survey the area for any evidence of Muhammad and his followers. The scouts learned from some nomadic Bedouins that Muhammad had left Medina and was in the area outside the town, waiting for the caravan to pass.[5] As Sufyan was still several weeks away, he had time to plan a counter-attack and he sent a messenger to Mecca requesting help and pointing out that the caravan, with about a thousand camels laden with previous goods, was guarded by only forty armed men. When they got Sufyan's message, the Quraysh put together an army under the leadership of a man called Abu Jahl, who

---

4 Donner, 2006, 27.
5 Ishaq, 1967, 239.

had sworn opposition to Muhammad and his people. The army set out to rescue the caravan.[6]

This train of events forces the question of how and why Muhammad made his plans known so far in advance. It would have been easy for him to raid the caravan; there was no need for him to tell everyone many weeks in advance about his plans, and had he not done so, it would not have occurred to Sufyan to request backup from Mecca. A careful reading forces one to conclude that his real plan had been not to attack the caravan, but to force an encounter with the army of the Quraysh. Although they had clashed with them before, Muhammad and his followers had never been involved in a decisive battle with them and, instead, lived with the constant threat that the Quraysh might attack. It seems likely that Muhammad wanted to end this stressful situation and, hopefully, definitively defeat the Quraysh and thus provide a safer future for his people,[7] while also securing the future of Islam in Arabia.

With Sufyan's caravan safely making its way to Mecca via an alternative route, a Quraysh army of about a thousand soldiers in chain mail armour, with seven hundred camels and more than a thousand horses, assembled in the southern part of the Badar Valley, about a hundred miles from Medina. Unaware that Sufyan had taken another route, they expected to encounter him there.

Meanwhile, Muhammad and a ragged army of followers numbering a little over three hundred, with few arms and just seventy camels, had left Medina and set up camp in the northern part of the Badar Valley.

One of the military chiefs accompanying Muhammad saw that a mistake had been made. He turned to Muhammad and asked him, "Is this the place where God has ordered you to encamp?" Muhammad replied that the position of his troops was *his* idea, rather than God's, and that he had not received a revelation on this matter.[8]

---

6 Ishaq, 1967, 293.
7 Asad, 2003, 236.
8 Ishaq, 1967, 284,

By now, Sufyan's caravan had reached the general area, and was passing by just a few miles away from the army of Muslims. In fact, Sufyan passed directly by a spot where the Muslim camel trainers had let the animals rest. He deduced from the fact that the camel dung contained date stones that the animals were from Medina.[9] He quickly moved his caravan further south to safety, and sent a messenger ahead to inform the Meccan army that he was now safe, and there was no need for them to continue north towards Medina. Sufyan and his caravan continued to travel safely through the coastal lowlands.[10] This is recorded in the Qur'ān, which states:

> … (remember that day) when you were at the near end of the valley (of Badr), and they were at its farthest end, while the caravan was below you. And if you had known that a battle was to take place, you would indeed have refused to accept the challenge: but (the battle was brought about none the less), so that God might accomplish a thing (which He willed) to be done, (and) that he who would perish might perish in clear evidence of the truth, and that he who would remain alive might live in clear evidence of the truth. And, behold, God is indeed all-hearing, all-knowing.[11]

Unaware of Muhammad's greater plan, his followers had believed that they were on a mission to attack Sufyan's poorly guarded caravan. Instead, on the 17th day of Ramadan, they realised that they were about to come face-to-face with a huge Quraysh army, with more than three times as many warriors as they had. Unsure how to react, they held a council of war. Some felt that the enemy was simply too big and strong for them and that they would be better off going back to Medina, but most, led by Abu Bakr and Umar, opted for an immediate advance. With great charisma, they

---

9   Ishaq, 1967, 295.
10 Gabriel, 2007, 91.
11 Q. 8:42.

persuaded the rest of the army to follow them. So it was that Muhammad and his followers attacked the might of the Quraysh.

According to the custom of the day, the battle began with a number of single combats, and then general fighting broke out. Despite being vastly outnumbered, somehow Muhammad and his followers prevailed. The Meccan forces were utterly defeated and a number of their most important leaders and chieftains, including Abu Jahl, died that day.[12]

The Qur'ān describes the Battle of Badar as: "the day when the true was distinguished from the false".[13] This historic day represented the first overt hostility between the pagan Quraysh people and the emerging community of Muslims in Medina. The startling outcome of the battle brought home to the Quraysh that Muhammad and his message were no fleeting thing, but the beginning of a new political power, and of a new era that represented a complete break from everything Arabia had seen before. This was the moment when the people of Mecca, who had been anxious about Muhammad and his message from the start, began to see the decay of Arabian paganism and a massive shift in the way of life and the mores of the area.

The Battle of Badar also represents the moment when a critical mass of Muhammad's followers started to understand the vast political implications of his message and his mission. Until now, only a few of his closest companions can have understood all the ramifications. For most of them, their forced move to Medina had simply meant that they were seeking a release from the terrible persecutions that they had endured in Mecca. Now, however, it had become obvious that Muhammad and his message represented the start of a new way of living. For them, the sacrifices they had made in the early days of Islam were now becoming transformed into direct action.[14]

---

12 Watt, 1956, 7.
13 Q. 8.41.
14 Asad, 2003, 237.

Humiliated by their defeat at Badar, and deeply anxious about what Muhammad and his message meant for them,[15] the people of Mecca realised that if they wanted life to continue as they knew it, they would have to defeat the Muslims. Abu Sufyan, who was an experienced leader, was tasked with creating a massive army that would defeat Muhammad decisively.

A year after their catastrophic defeat at Badar, the pagans of Mecca, with the help of a number of tribes that were also hostile to the Muslims, formed an army of ten thousand men, which marched on Medina under the leadership of Sufyan.[16] The Battle of Uhud, which followed, represented a very difficult time for the Muslims. When Muhammad heard that the army was on its way, he convened a council of war to discuss their approach. Because the Meccans had a vast cavalry and the Muslims did not, he was of the opinion that the best way to retaliate would be to fight from behind Medina's fortifications and, if necessary, in the streets and lanes of the town. Despite this counsel, most of the Muslim leaders disagreed. They felt that they should go out and meet the army on open ground. Conceding to the majority, Muhammad reluctantly agreed, and he and his followers made their way to a plain below the mountain of Uhud, just outside Medina.[17]

Muhammad's army was even more outnumbered than before. They started out with fewer than a thousand soldiers, and on the way to the mountain of Uhud about three hundred defected from the army under the leadership of Abd Allah ibn Ubay, who pretended to believe that the Muslims did not really intend to fight. Ubay was in strong disagreement with the decision to fight on open ground rather than within the confines of urban Medina.[18]

---

15 Ali, 1991.
16 Ishaq, 1967, 372.
17 Asad, 2003, 85-6, note 90.
18 Gabriel, 2007, 114.

The Qur'ān records how, shortly before the battle, two other groups from among the Muslims were tempted to defect as well: "When two groups from among you were about to lose heart, although God was near unto them and it is in God that the believers must place their trust."[19] At the last moment, they decided to follow Muhammad after all. The Qur'ān records what Muhammad said to them: "When thou didst say unto the believers: 'Is it not enough for you (to know) that your Sustainer will aid you with three thousand angels sent down.'"[20] By referring to God helping the true believers with thousands of angels, he is referring metaphorically to how God's spiritual forces could strengthen the hearts of the faithful.[21]

Now with fewer than seven hundred men, Muhammad ordered most of his soldiers to stand with their backs to the mountain and positioned his fifty archers on a nearby hill so that they could fight against the enemy cavalry. He ordered the archers to stick to their posts, regardless of what happened in the heat of battle.[22]

The vast army of Meccans advanced on the Muslims, and the latter quickly gained a decisive advantage and almost won. In that moment the archers, believing that they had won, decided to ignore Muhammad's instructions because they were afraid of losing their portion of the spoils of war. They abandoned their posts and rushed down to the Quraysh camp, hoping to be able to seize whatever riches were available.

Now that an opportunity had opened up, most of the Meccan cavalry, led by Khalid ibn al-Walid, moved around in a vast arc and attacked the Muslims from behind. Without the archers to cover them, and with hostile forces on both sides, the Muslim army was forced to retreat, and many of its soldiers perished. Muhammad himself was seriously injured. When they saw him fall amid all the disorder, people started to shout, "The Apostle of God has been killed!" Muslim soldiers began to run away, and some even

---

19 Q. 3:122.
20 Q. 3:124.
21 Rida, 1999, 78-87.
22 Hamidullah, 1939.

planned to plead for mercy from the enemy. But a few of Muhammad's loyal followers, including Umar ibn al-Khattab and Talhah, shouted, "What good are your lives without him, O believers? Let us die as he has died!" With the strength that comes from knowing that one has nothing to lose, they threw themselves into battle, and the ordinary Muslim soldiers, who had meanwhile learned that Muhammad was actually alive, but wounded, followed their example.

The day was saved, but because the Muslim soldiers were so exhausted the battle ended in a draw rather than a resounding victory. The Meccans retreated. The next day, Muhammad and about seventy of his followers started to follow them, but when they reached the area known as Hamra' al-Asad, about eight miles south of Medina, they could see that the Meccans had no intention of engaging in battle. The miniscule force that Muhammad had brought with him retreated in turn to Medina, and that was the end of the Battle of Uhud.[23]

The Muslims had survived to fight another day, but yet more hostilities were on the horizon, in the form of a battle that would become known as the War of the Trench. This war took place when the Jewish Nadir tribe, which had been expelled from Medina and the greater Yathrib area after breaking a treaty they had made with the Muslims, instead forged an alliance with several of the most powerful Arabian tribes in the area, including the Quraysh. Together, the Jewish Nadir and the pagan Arabs planned to thwart Muhammad and his followers for once and for all. They could all see that Islam was a threat to their way of life and this commonality united them, despite their differences.

A vast army of more than 12,000 men, including the Quraysh, the Nadir, various tribes from the coastal area, and the Najd tribe with its allies, came together in Medina to defeat the Muslims.[24] By now, five years had passed since Muhammad and his followers had moved from Mecca. Among them were the Jewish Qurayza tribe, a local group that had been

---

23 Asad, 2003. 86, note 90.
24 Asad, 2003, 640, note 13.

in alliance with the Muslims, pledged to come to their aid in case of necessity. Now, five years after the arrival of Muhammad and his followers in Medina, they switched sides and attacked their former allies, betraying them.

Muhammad heard some men discussing the construction of a particular type of ditch or trench that the Muslim army could use, possibly an idea that came from a man called Salman al-Farsi, a Muslim convert from Christianity. Al-Farsi was originally from Persia, and had become a Christian as a child, but when his teacher died he journeyed to Arabia, having heard that there was a new prophet. His caravan had been ambushed and he had been sold into slavery to a Medinan Jew. However, Muhammad had helped him to raise the funds he needed to become free, after which al-Farsi had become a Muslim.[25]

Trenches had previously been unknown in Arabian warfare, but Muhammad ordered that a trench be constructed. Al-Farsi's trench had been completed before the gathered forces arrived in Medina, and it was of great help to the Muslim army, which had plenty of food and water for their troops, while the coalition of forces lined up to fight them was limited to what they had been able to carry, and the ground provided nothing for the animals to forage.[26]

A siege of several weeks ensued. Thanks to the construction of the trench, which was manned by a small, relatively weak and not at all well-armed Muslim army, the Muslims were able to repel the attackers, who suffered many losses. The uneasy alliance between the various elements of the confederation quickly gave way to internal strife, fuelled by the fact that none of the disparate groups had ever trusted one another anyway.

Morale among the confederation reached an all-time low. The weather had become bitterly cold and very windy. Even for the most hardened soldiers among them, this was very much the final straw.[27] As a final at-

---

25 Hamidullah, 1939.
26 Gabriel, 2007, 137.
27 Asad, 2003, 641, note 13.

tempt to rout the Muslims, the Ghatafan group tried to take the trench by assaulting it from the eastern part of the plain, while the Quraysh and its allies attacked from the lower, western end (each thus attacking from the direction from which they had originally come). The Qur'ān states with reference to this event, "When they came upon you from above you and from below you, and when (your) eyes became dim and (your) hearts came up to (your) throats, and (when) you thought all (manner of) thoughts about God".[28] The Qur'ān is referring to whether God would save the Muslims or allow their enemies to win. In the event, the confederates were unsuccessful, and the army dispersed.

Various members of the Qurayza tribe were captured or died on the battlefield. Most, surprised by how effective the Muslim defence had been, and realising that their betrayal had put them in a very vulnerable situation, retreated to their fortified territories, where the Muslim army placed them under siege. About twenty-five days later they surrendered, relinquished their possessions, and were sent into exile.

Six years after Muhammad and his followers had come to live in Medina he decided that they would make another journey, this time one of return to Mecca. This would be known as a "lesser pilgrimage" or "pious visit"; the "umrah". Despite the fact that the Muslims had been more or less constantly at war with the Quraysh and its allies for six years, Muhammad did not anticipate any hostile action, because he planned their arrival for the month of Dhu'l Qa'dah. According to Arabian custom, Dhu'l Qa'dah was one of four sacred months during which all warfare was forbidden, particularly in the environs of the holy city of Mecca.

Muhammad invited some Bedouin tribes who had formed an alliance with the Muslims to travel with them to Mecca, but most abstained. Thus, Muhammad left for Mecca in the company of between 1400 and 1500 men, all in traditional pilgrims' dress and, apart from their swords, which

---

28 Q. 33:10.

they wore unsheathed, unarmed to indicate that they had no bellicose intensions and simply intended to visit the temple.[29]

Despite Muhammad's declaration of his peaceful intentions, the people of Mecca decided to defy Arab tradition and prevent them from entering with the use of weapons. About two hundred horsemen, led by Khalid ibn al-Walid,[30] went to meet Muhammad and his followers while, back in Mecca, thousands of armed soldiers adopted positions of defence. As Muhammad had never intended to go to battle, he and his followers took a westward route from their position in Bir Usfan, about a day away from Mecca, and made camp for several days on the plain of Al-Hudaybiyyah. During this stay, they opened negotiations with the leaders of Mecca, with a view to securing a lasting peace.[31] Some preliminary negotiations were held with representatives from both groups in attendance, and then Muhammad sent his follower Uthman ibn Affan, who was also a member of a very powerful Meccan clan, as his emissary.

Uthman made his way to Mecca, and shortly afterwards the Muslims heard that he had been killed. Expecting the Meccans to attack, Muhammad gathered his followers under an acacia tree. There, his followers pledged allegiance and promised that they would fight for Islam to the death.[32] History has recorded this pledge as "By'at ar-Ridwan", or "the pledge of God's goodly acceptance". In the event, however, Uthman was perfectly unharmed. Instead of fighting, by working together, the two sides created a treaty, which would be remembered by history as the Truce of Hudaybiyyah, agreeing that there should be no more war between Mecca and Medina for a period of ten years; that Muhammad and his followers would not visit Mecca as pilgrims that year, but could do so the following year, if they agreed to stay for just three days during Umrah, during which period the Quraysh would leave the city; that any individual or tribe could

---

29 Ishaq, 1967, 500.
30 Shortly after the events described here, al-Walid actually embraced Islam and he eventually became one of the greatest Muslim generals of all time.
31 Ali, 1991, 1572.
32 Q. 48:18.

join any side; that if any child or other person with a guardian converted to Islam without his guardian's permission, he would be returned; that if any Muslim, whether a child or an adult, wanted to join the Quraysh, he or she would be allowed to do so.

While one might assume that the final clause of the agreement was intended to be to the Muslims' disadvantage, clearly Muhammad agreed with it because of his already-stated view, expressed in the Qur'ān, that "there shall be no coercion in matters of faith".[33]

Some of the Muslims were unhappy with the truce and felt that Muhammad had conceded too much. He had agreed, for example, not to raid the Meccans' caravans. However, the wisdom of his decision soon became clear. He was able to consolidate his position while Mecca became ever more isolated, both politically and militarily. In retrospect, one can clearly see that the Truce of Hudaybiyyah was of immense strategic importance for Islam, and one of Muhammad's greatest achievements in his mission to destroy the enemies of Islam and convert all virtuous Arabs to the new religion. Shortly after the truce, Meccan leader Abu Sufyan agreed for his daughter, Umm Habibah, to wed Muhammad.

The new peace that prevailed made it much easier for Muhammad's message to reach the pagans of Mecca. Those who visited his camp at Hudaybiyyah had been struck by the spirit of community among the Muslims, and they began to feel much less hostile towards the faith Muhammad preached than before they had seen Islam for themselves. Some converted, and this movement snowballed until Muhammad was surrounded by thousands of new Muslims. (In fact, although the remaining Quraysh pagans actually broke the truce two years after it was made, so many Meccans had converted to Islam that Muhammad and his followers were eventually able to occupy the city with practically no resistance at all, marking the beginning of the dominance of Islam over Arabia.)[34]

---

33 Q. 2:256.
34 Asad, 2003, 857.

Meanwhile, however, Muhammad was having to contend with other hostile forces. The truce with the Meccans was a huge breakthrough, but there were also other groups that opposed Muhammad and Islam. After the truce, Muhammad and his followers returned to Medina, but they stayed there for less than a month, during which time he put together an army of about 1400 soldiers and 200 members of the cavalry, so as to attack a Jewish settlement at Khaybar.[35] Khaybar, about eighty miles to the north of Medina, was an oasis area inhabited by farmers, and home to several Jewish clans whose ancestors had introduced farming to the area, and now operated a vast date farming business. In the surrounding areas there were a number of Arab tribes, the most important of which was the Ghatafans.[36] The Nadir tribe, which Muhammad had forced to leave Medina, had taken refuge in Khaybar, where they had persuaded the Ghatafans to join with Mecca against Muhammad and the Muslims. Knowing this, Muhammad had no doubt that it would be impossible to reach a truce with the peoples of Khaybar and that it would be far more efficacious to remove the threat they represented by force. Thus, he and his army left Medina and started to travel towards Khaybar.[37]

Although the Jews of Khaybar outnumbered the Muslim army by about four to one, they were quite quickly defeated. Rather than presenting a united front, their troops fought in isolated groups with no unified leadership. Moreover, they quickly ran out of the food, water, and forage for their animals that they needed to maintain a sustained battle. Finally, it seems that Muhammad's army was simply better; better at fighting, and more motivated. History records that while ninety-three Jews died in battle, only fifteen Muslims did.[38]

The outcome of the Battle of Khaybar was that Muhammad and the Muslims had succeeded in capturing the city that opposed them almost as

---

35 Ishaq, 1967, 522; Rodinson, 2002, 253.
36 Hamidullah, 1939.
37 Gabriel, 2007, 153.
38 Gabriel, 2007, 56, 157.

much as Mecca had done. Muhammad was gracious in victory. Although he could have had the Jews killed or sold as slaves, he offered them both peace and protection in return for a share of their harvest. The inhabitants of the oasis were allowed to keep their farms, orchards and gardens, so long as they paid a tax of fifty percent to the Muslims each year. Many copies of the Torah had been seized during the fighting, and Muhammad returned all these to the Jews.[39] Of the war booty, most was given to those soldiers who had been with Muhammad at Hudaybiyyah, with a double share given to the approximately two hundred members of the cavalry.[40]

After agreeing terms in Khaybar, Muhammad and his followers returned to Medina and, a year after the Truce of Hudaybiyyah, they made their pilgrimage to Mecca, knowing that this would be a test of the sincerity of the Quraysh. He need not have worried; as promised, the people of Mecca camped on the hills of the town for the requisite three days, keeping watch while Muhammad and his followers completed their pilgrimage. In this way, the Quraysh were compelled to recognise Muhammad as their equal, and to recognise the authority and reputation he had acquired.[41]

Following the truce, Muhammad had gone to great effort to forge alliances with the Bedouin people, something that was aided by his growing reputation for power. In fact, many clan chiefs sought his support against their rivals while others, who had previously been in alliance with the Meccans, tried to remain neutral as they anticipated that, despite the truce, violence would break out again between the Muslims and the Meccans. However, within two years of the truce, Muhammad had grown so powerful that the Meccans could not hope to defeat him.[42]

In November 629, the Beni Bakr, a Bedouin group that was still in alliance with the Quraysh, ambushed the Khuza'a tribe, a group that had been loyal to Muhammad since shortly after the truce, while they rested at

---

39   Hamidullah, 1939, 113.
40   Ishaq, 1967, 522.
41   Gabriel, 2007, 159.
42   Gabriel, 2007, 166.

a well in the environs of Mecca. Apparently, the Beni Bakr had acted at the instigation of the Quraysh, using weapons supplied by them.[43] They were brutal in their assault as they attacked the Khuza'a homes and slaughtered about twenty men.

Realising that the incident might lead to problems for them, the leaders of Mecca sent Abu Sufyan to Medina to meet Muhammad and reaffirm the agreement that had been reached in the truce. Sufyan travelled to Medina, but Muhammad refused to see him. It must have been obvious to Sufyan that this implied that Muhammad's intention was to conquer Mecca, either peacefully or through force, and convert its people to Islam.[44]

Indeed, Muhammad was working tirelessly towards attacking Mecca. He started by sealing the doors to Medina so that nobody could leave or enter the city. In this way, he could be sure that nobody would bring news to the Meccans. A Medinan called Hatib bin Abu Balta attempted to smuggle out a written warning hidden in a woman's hair, but Muhammad was warned of this by God. He sent guards after the woman, and they retrieved the letter.[45]

Together with a relatively small army of about three thousand, Muhammad left Medina. Along the way, their Bedouin allies joined them, and by the time they had reached the outskirts of Mecca, his army numbered about ten thousand. They camped at Marr al-Zahran, two days away from Mecca.

The people of Mecca panicked, sure that Muhammad planned to attack them. They sent Abu Sufyan again, hoping that he would be able to negotiate with Muhammad. Sufyan was met by Abbas, Muhammad's uncle, who brought him to Muhammad, but Muhammad told him to leave, and asked Abbas to bring him back the following morning.[46]

---

43 Watt, 1956, 62.
44 Gabriel, 2007, 167.
45 Ishaq, 1967, 545.
46 Ishaq, 1967, 546.

The following morning, Abu Sufyan returned. Muhammad told him that his wish was for there to be an amnesty and that if the Meccans surrendered their city to them, there was no need for anyone to be killed. The citizens who remained in their homes rather than taking up arms would all be safe, as would anyone who sought safety in the courtyard of the Ka'ba or in Abu Sufyan's own house.[47]

Abu Sufyan returned to Mecca and ensured that everyone had heard the news, while Muhammad divided his army into four groups, each of which he instructed to enter Mecca from a different direction.

The occupation of Mecca by Muhammad has been recorded in Muslim history as the "fat'h" or conquest. Shortly after taking Mecca, Muhammad sent emissaries to the surrounding Bedouin tribes, with the goal of forging an alliance with them. One such was the great tribe of Hawazin, to the northeast, which was allied with the people of Ta'if, a town to the southeast. Muhammad's emissaries soon realised that the chief of the Hawazin tribe had started to prepare his men for war. This would be a very strategic battle as, if the Hawazin were defeated, Muhammad would be in control of the important caravan routes in the area.[48]

The Valley of Hunayn is to be found on the way between Mecca and Ta'if, and this is where Muhammad's army, of about twelve thousand, faced that of the Hawazin and the Ta'if, with only about four thousand men. Perhaps because of their recent victories, which may have led to carelessness, and despite their greater numbers, the Muslim army did not perform well. Near the Oasis of Hunayn, they were ambushed and suffered great losses at the hands of the Bedouin archers, after which they began to retreat in disarray. However, Muhammad and some of his earlier followers, including the muhajirun, from Mecca, and the Ansār, from Medina, managed to turn this ignominy into victory.[49] The soldiers of Hawazin were killed or captured, or scattered to escape the Muslim army, and the

---

47 Ishaq, 1967, 548.
48 Gabriel, 2007, 179-80.
49 Asad, 2003, 260, note 33.

women, children, animals and property became the spoils of war. As the last few men made their way out of the area, Muhammad sent his cavalry after them so that they could not try to rescue their families. After the Battle of Hunayn, Muhammad and his army marched on Ta'if. Having seen what had happened, many of the other clans in the area decided that they would have a better future within Islam, and many of them converted.

Now that Muhammad could count on so much support from the Bedouins, there had been a significant shift in the balance of power. Ta'if was now cut off from both Meccan commerce and the caravan routes that brought goods to and from Iraq. After a year, the leaders of Ta'if travelled to Medina and told Muhammad that they agreed to all his terms.

The victory at Hunayn, and subsequent seizing of power in Ta'if, was an important turning point in Muhammad's long term battle to make all of Arabia Islamic.[50] The Qur'ān refers to this battle, saying:

> Indeed, God has succoured you on many battlefields,(when you were few) and (He did so, too) on the Day of Hunayn, when you took pride in your great numbers and they proved of no avail whatever to you –for the earth, despite all its vastness, became (too) narrow for you and you turned back, retreating. Whereupon God bestowed from on high His (gift of) inner peace upon His Apostle and upon the believers, and bestowed (upon you) from on high forces which you could not see, and chastised those who were bent on denying the truth: for such is the recompense of all who deny the truth.[51]

In this verse, we can clearly see that Muhammad and the Muslim army were aided by God in their mission: "forces you did not see". True support can only come from God, and even large numbers, kinship ties and

---

50 Gabriel, 2007, 186.
51 Q. 9:25-6.

worldly wealth matter not at all if they are "dearer to you than God and His Apostle and the struggle in His cause".[52]

After taking Ta'if, Muhammad stayed in Medina for six months. At this point, he received information that the Byzantines, who were increasingly anxious about how quickly Islam was spreading in Arabia, had begun to assemble a huge army near the borders of the Arabian Peninsula, from where they planned to march to Medina and rout the Muslims. They had been incited to do this by Muhammad's enemy, Abu 'Amir. Abu 'Amir (which means "the monk") who was an important member of the Khazraj tribe, had converted to Christianity as a young man, and was well known in both Arabia and among the Syrian Christians. From the start of Muhammad's mission, he had gone into alliance with the Quraysh of Mecca, and he had supported them during the Battle of Uhud. After the battle, he had gone to Syria and applied himself to persuading the Emperor of Byzantium, Heraclitus, to invade Medina and destroy the Muslim community.[53] Within Medina, he had some secret followers, and he had remained in contact with them. He told these followers that Heraclitus had agreed to send an army to defeat Medina, and that preparations were underway.

Now that he knew what was afoot, Muhammad put together the biggest army he could, and they set out towards the border. When they reached Tabuk, about half way between Medina and Damascus, Muhammad realised that the Byzantines were either not yet ready to invade Arabia or did not plan to do so for now, and he returned with his followers to Medina. The Islamic principles by which he lived stated that war should only be waged in self-defence.[54]

The history of Muhammad in Medina reveals he was not just a prophet and a man of God, but a very able general. Well advanced in middle age, within the space of ten years he fought eight large battles, led eighteen

---

52 Asad, 2003, 260, note 34.
53 Asad, 2003, 265, note 59.
54 Asad, 2003, 281, note 142.

raids, and planned thirty eight operations that were under others' commands, albeit acting to his orders and strategic instruction. In the process he was wounded twice, endured defeats, and had two near misses. Muhammad was also a sophisticated "military theorist, organizational reformer, strategic thinker, operational level combat commander, political and military leader, heroic soldier, revolutionary, and inventor of the theory of insurgency and history's first successful practitioner."[55] He was usually able to count on information from an extensive intelligence network which kept him informed of his enemy's location and plans.

Whereas most generals intend simply to defeat a foreign enemy, Muhammad's goal was a much greater one; the replacement of the Arabian social order with a new way of life. In the course of pursuing his goal he used a vast array of means to mount a highly successful overthrow of the dominant powers. With each victory, he introduced new social programs and an ideology that brought together religion and politics. With charisma, he attracted growing numbers of followers and expanded his military might.

Islam challenged traditional Arab beliefs, values and social institutions by showing them to be against God's law, oppressive, and ripe for change. Amid the violence that is inevitable in social change on this scale, Muhammad created a community of true believers to replace a society that had once been formed of ever-squabbling clans and tribes.

---

55 Gabriel, 2007, 18-22.

CHAPTER 7

UNAMBIGUOUS VERSES AND AMBIGUOUS VERSES

WHAT IS THE best way to read the Qur'ān? Can *anyone*, from any background, read it, understand it, and put its wisdom into practice, or can this only be aspired to by experts and holy men? What do the structure and the style of the Qur'ān reveal about God's intentions for how we should read, interpret and understand it?

The Qur'ān is the written word of God and therefore, while the text clearly uses a vocabulary that was familiar to Muhammad and the other people of his day, it is a stand-alone document that should be explored and understood as a discrete entity, with its own internal referencing system, and its God-given authority.

The Qur'ān has often been described as an interactive text because, unlike the sacred scriptures that had come before it, the Qur'ān often addresses the reader or listener directly, challenges them, and demands that they act upon, rather than simply passively receive, the words it contains.

The Qur'ān also comes with its own reading guide, insofar as it contains passages of self-reflection which, with a thoughtful exploration, provide a key to how we should interpret and understand it.[1] As Dammen McAuliffe says:

> The Qur'ān... makes reference to itself, characterizes itself in various ways, and defines (at least in a preliminary way) what might be

---
1 Dammen McAuliffe, 2000, 56.

termed the exegetical relationship between God, the Prophet and the faithful.[2]

While the Qur'ān features complete internal consistency, and remarkable comprehensiveness, being a guide to how good Muslims should conduct themselves in every aspect of their daily lives, it is useful to understand the difference between those verses that are unambiguous, and require no interpretation (known as muhkam), and those that are ambiguous, and can only be understood (and thus applied to life) when they are seen as allegories, and properly examined and explored (known as mutashābih). The distinction between these two categories is the central point of this chapter.

Early in the Qur'ān, it states:

> He it is who has bestowed upon thee from on high this divine writ, containing messages that are clear in and by themselves- and these are the essence of the divine writ – as well as others that are allegorical. Now those whose hearts are given to swerving from the truth go after that part of the divine writ which has been expressed in allegory, seeking out (what is bound to create) confusion, and seeking (to arrive at) its final meaning (in arbitrary manner); but none save God knows its final meaning. Hence, those who are deeply rooted in knowledge say: 'We believe in it; the whole (of the divine writ) is from our Sustainer – albeit none takes this to heart save those who are endowed with insight'.[3]

This verse, Q. 3:7, is generally recognised as a key instruction to readers of the Qur'ān, in terms of how they should understand and interpret the Holy Scriptures,[4] and it has received particular attention and scholarly exploration, both in the earlier period of Islamic scholarship and in recent

---

2 Dammen McAuliffe, 2000, 56.
3 Q. 3:7.
4 Dammen McAuliffe, 2000, 56-7.

years. According to Asad, this passage is a key to understanding the Qur'ān in its entirety.

Unambiguous verses are clear in and by themselves; they are instructions or statements from God that are perfectly clear, easy to understand, and non-ambiguous. These include messages that can only be interpreted in one way, although there may be a range of ideas as to the full implications of the statement or instruction. The Qur'ān describes these messages as "essence of the divine writ", and as messages upon which actions can be based.[5] This refers to the fact that they contain the fundamental principles of Islam, and in particular its teachings in the area of ethics and society. In other words, the Qur'ān instructs us that we should live in a particular way, or abstain from a particular range of behaviours, and we can exercise free will to decide whether or not to do as God directs us via the pages of the Qur'ān.

Because these passages are quite straightforward and easy to understand, they can be followed by just about anyone. They tell us "Do this," or "Don't do this" and are useful guides to a virtuous life. Among these unambiguous messages we find a wealth of information about God's intentions for us in terms of what is permitted (halal) and what is forbidden (haram).[6] Thus, for example, Muslims know that they may behave in a certain way and not in others. As everyone knows, it is haram for Muslims to eat pork, whereas it is halal for them to eat other certain foods that have been prepared in a certain way.

By looking a little more deeply, we can also see that these factual statements also provide us with the context within which the more complex allegorical passages can be understood,[7] because they comprise the fundamental principles underlying its message and, in particular, its ethical and social teachings. It is only on the basis of these clearly enunciated

---

5 Asad, 2003, 58.
6 Asad, 2003, 58.
7 Asad, 2003, 66, note 5.

principles that the allegorical passages or ambiguous verses can be correctly interpreted.

While some scholars have contrasted these straightforward messages with the Qur'ān's allegorical content, it would be a mistake to assume that all the content that is unambiguous are allegories. Instead, there are many messages that are open to more than one interpretation but that are not allegorical, while others, although allegorical in style, are simple and unambiguous in interpretation.

While the two types of message are different in a very significant way, they are similar in another respect; they are both perfect:

- The unambiguous verses, or muhkam, are protected by their simplicity from any contamination, and thus perfectly encapsulate a message from God, even in the limited format provided by human language.
- The ambiguous verses, or mutashābih, are perfect insofar as they embody goodness, truth and freedom from contradiction and imperfection,[8] despite being so complex that they require study in order to understand them, and are not easily understood by everybody.

In the mutashābih, the meaning is implied through the use of metaphor and not directly stated. The issue of how to understand these messages has long been a matter of intense debate by Islamic scholars, many of whom have, over the years, attempted to devise a way of categorising them. For example, the scholar ibn Kathir, working in the 1100s, tends to focus on their apparent ambiguity, saying that these are "verses in which there is doubt about the meaning for some people or many of them."[9] Yet others, such as Jarir al-Tabari, have proposed that this aspect of the Qur'ān contains information that is simply unknowable by human beings. It is

---

8 Dammen McAuliffe, 2000, 64.
9 Asad, 2003, 59.

just too difficult for them to understand, and only God knows what certain passages of the Qur'ān truly mean.[10] Other scholars have maintained that, while they are undoubtedly complex, these allegorical elements of the Qur'ān are not necessarily completely beyond the capacity of humankind to understand. They might not "stand alone" the way the muhkam do, and their meaning may be very complex and difficult to interpret without supporting information, but with patience and intellectual curiosity, they can ultimately be decoded.[11]

In the Qur'ānic verse cited above, Q. 3:7, it states that "none save God knows its final meaning". How can this be interpreted? Most of the early Islamic scholars maintained that this refers to interpreting allegorical passages that discuss metaphysical subjects. These include such topics as the attributes of God, the resurrection of the dead and the Day of Judgement, what we are to understand as the meaning of time and eternity, and the nature of heaven and hell and beings described in the Qur'ān as angels. In other words, these are all aspects of the Qur'ān that deal with the things that are simply beyond the capacity of ordinary human beings to understand because they have never, and cannot, witness them for themselves. Because they simply have no everyday criteria by which to judge such matters, the only way in which God can communicate information about them to humankind is by using allegorical language.

While this view has some merit, it also overlooks the many elements of the Qur'ān that are allegorical in both intent and expression, but that do not deal with metaphysical matters at all. As Asad sees it, there is no way to properly understand the passage cited above without considering the question of what an allegory really is.

In its truest sense, an allegory is a way of using figurative speech to describe something that is so complex that ordinary language cannot express it properly. Because of this complexity, the only way to understand the subject matter is to use language imaginatively, so as to evoke a mental image,

---

10 Asad, 2003, 59.
11 Asad, 2003, 59.

rather than to make a series of detailed statements of fact. Asad believes that this is the meaning of the apparently ambiguous phrase, "none save God knows its final meaning".[12] Thus, Asad's hypothesis is that even those elements of the Qur'ān that are immensely challenging and appear to defy all efforts to understand them have been written for us, for our instruction and edification, and that we can and should make efforts to know what God means.

In tandem with this relatively straightforward concept of the metaphysical, we find information about the nature of the human mind. This complex entity, which comprises conscious thought, dreams, intuition, memory and imagination, works and interprets in light of what it has already experienced, either in part or completely. The human mind is utterly unable to visualise or begin to understand something that is completely outside experiences it has already had. For this reason, even when we *think* that we have come up with a completely novel idea or image, careful consideration invariably reveals that it is not as new as we thought; it is made up of elements of our previous experience.

According to Asad, the statement in verse Q. 3:7 occurs just once in the whole Qur'ān. This verse represents a key to understanding the Qur'ān and the message it contains, making its entire content accessible to those who really think deeply. Its importance, which has been much pondered in recent decades, was not lost on earlier Islamic scholars. One of them, Muqatil, who was writing in the eighth century (and thus just about one hundred years after Muhammad first received the revelations that would become the Qur'ān), placed the work squarely in the context of earlier revelations, such as those received by Abraham and Jesus, and stresses that the messages it contains are relevant for all believers.[13]

This is potentially a tricky issue. On the one hand, the Qur'ān itself is both complete and perfect, and nobody needs to use any other scripture in order to know the will of God. On the other hand, the Qur'ān itself places

---

12 Asad, 2003, 67.
13 Dammen McAuliffe, 2000, 60-1.

its text within the context of the genre of holy books, and also makes references to the prophets who went before Muhammad. However, rather than referring to these earlier books as sources of information, or as a means to bestow authority on it, the Qur'ān turns the tables and, instead, provides a means to better understand the scriptures that have gone before.[14] The Qur'ān bestows authority on them, rather than vice versa. Whereas the earlier texts were written by genuine prophets and offer some information about God and the earlier covenants He had made with humanity, the Qur'ān is the last, and definitive, guide to God's intentions for mankind.

Another scholar, Qutayba, who was writing in the ninth century, devoted a great deal of thought to verse Q. 3:7, and asked the important question why God, in all his wisdom, had sent his message down in both simple and complex, allegorical language. What was the meaning of this? Qutayba concluded that the reason for the inclusion of complex allegories was to ensure that the ignorant and the educated would not be in the same position. Why should those who have made no effort to expand their minds and enrich their intellects be rewarded in exactly the same way as those who have spent all their lives working hard to better themselves and learn more about God? If all of the Qur'ān was perfectly transparent and easy to understand, there would be no motivation for anyone to stretch themselves intellectually and reach towards the higher understanding that God wants for humanity. In this situation, there would no longer be any intellectual competition at all, and nobody would strive to improve their mind.[15]

Yet another scholar, Abul-Faraj, who lived and worked in the thirteenth century, believed that the mutashābih fall within the Qur'ānic system of endeavour and reward. Just as the virtuous are rewarded by God when they respond to His call to live a good and pious life, readers of the Qur'ān are invited to take part in the challenge of exploring its more difficult passages, even though this may be difficult for them. In the process of using their

---

14 Dammen McAuliffe, 2000, 66.
15 Dammen McAuliffe, 2000, 61.

UNAMBIGUOUS VERSES AND AMBIGUOUS VERSES

God-given human minds to understand God's intentions for humanity better than ever before, they are given the opportunity to receive an eternal reward for all of their efforts, alongside the efforts they have expended on living a virtuous life. He makes his argument as follows:[16]

> People of every field of endeavour set forth abstruse concepts and subtle issues in the area of expertise so that by means of them they can make things difficult for their students and can train them to extract the right answer. This is because when students can handle the abstruse, they will be more capable of dealing with the obvious… it may be that God's sending of the mutashābih acts analogously.[17]

Another thirteenth century scholar, Fakhr al-Din al-Razi, broadly agreed, stating that the bigger effort involved in interpreting the verses results in a greater reward, that they provide an opportunity for theological growth and the use of reason, and that they call for the development of specific skills in the area of interpreting sacred manuscripts and the niceties of language.[18]

Another aspect of the complexity of the mutashābih is that they are not accessible to everyone. Only some people will have the time and the intellectual capacity to investigate and understand these complex messages, while others – perhaps less blessed with intellectual gifts, or without the time or availability to devote to Qur'ānic scholarship – must depend on the insights of others to access the wisdom embedded in these sophisticated elements of the Holy Book.

Understanding the mutashābih is rarely, if ever, a one-off event. Those who read them must read again, and again, and again, and endeavour to place them within the broader context of the Qur'ān, while those who

---

16 Dammen McAuliffe, 2000, 64.
17 Dammen McAuliffe, 2000, 64.
18 Dammen McAuliffe, 2000, 65.

listen must similarly listen again, and again, and again, to even start to benefit from the wisdom they contain. This process, of studying, listening, and opening oneself to the realisation that true understanding demands effort, and is a gift from God, provided to us through the medium of the Qur'ān. It offers each and every one the opportunity to develop themselves, intellectually and spiritually. With each such effort, the intellect is expanded (regardless of the individual's innate giftedness or otherwise) and the individual's capacity to understand not just the verse in question but also the next one he or she explores, and indeed all of the Qur'ān, grows. The communal effort involved in exploring the mutashābih together also represents an opportunity for faith communities to grow in togetherness as well as in a deeper understanding of God and His intentions for humanity.

In this way, Qur'ānic scholarship, worship, and mutual understanding can be an occasion for transformational change; those who use the Qur'ān in such a way to understand God will find themselves becoming ever more receptive to Him and His message, and will be better able to hear His reminders of His wishes to them.[19]

Accepting that the human mind relies completely on experience, we are forced to ask how "heavy" issues such as the metaphysical aspect of religion, which refers to an area that is entirely beyond human experience, or at least that part of experience that takes place during our lives on earth, be communicated to us in a way that we can understand. How are we to comprehend matters that lie completely behind our experience, and that have nothing to do with anything we have ever seen or heard of?[20]

Let's look at some examples:

The Qur'ān teaches that those who believe in God, are pious, and live virtuous lives will be rewarded in heaven. No living human being has ever experienced heaven, so how are we to understand what it will be like? Comparing it to even the most blissful of familiar experiences will be pointless. Clearly, ordinary human language is simply unable to

---

19 Dammen McAuliffe, 2000, 73.
20 Asad, 2003, 989, appendix 1.

UNAMBIGUOUS VERSES AND AMBIGUOUS VERSES

communicate this information to us. Instead, the Qur'ān makes abundant use of rich allegorical language to help us to understand what it will be like in heaven, or at least to experience some of the richness of emotion. It uses this language to evoke images of beautiful gardens lush with running water, shade from the sun, beautiful spouses and countless other delights. The Qur'ān refers to heaven thus:

> Whenever they are granted fruits therefrom as their appointed sustenance, they will say, "It is this /that in days of yore was granted to us as our sustenance' – for they will be given something that recalls that past.[21]

In these lavish, beautiful descriptions of the afterlife, the Qur'ān does not suggest that we will literally be placed beside a stream of water, or whatever, but simply to evoke the wonder and joy experienced by people who are submerged in the splendour of God's creation.

In describing the uniqueness of the concept of heaven in the afterlife, the Qur'ān says, "No souls knows what joy is kept hidden in store for them as a reward for what they have done."[22] When asked to expound on the Qur'ān's description of heaven, the Prophet was reported to have offered the following explanation as to what God has promised to His righteous servants: "I have readied my righteous servants what no eye has ever seen, and no ear has heard, and no heart of man has ever conceived".[23] To help us come to terms with the baffling concept of heaven, the Qur'ān describes it as "a heaven as vast as the heavens and the earth".[24] Similarly, as no living human being has ever experienced the agonies and horrors of hell, the Qur'ān resorts to complex, deep allegorical language to convey the experience to us.

---

21 Q. 2:25.
22 Q. 32:17.
23 Al-Asqalani, 1929, 418.
24 Q. 3:133.

Another area where the Qur'ān uses allegory is in discussing God and His activities. Clearly, God is not something that any ordinary human mind can ever hope to completely understand, and human language is simply unable to discuss Him in all His vast complexity. Allegorical language offers us the closest thing to glimpsing the face of God that we will experience in this lifetime.

Of course, the Qur'ān also refers to God in terms of identifiable human emotions, such as anger or love, but these restrictive terms are there because of the limits of language; no more and no less.

The Qur'ān draws our attention to its extensive use of allegory when it states that those areas of reality that are beyond all human understanding can really only be discussed in this way. One implication is that the reader of the Qur'ān should ask, on reading any verse, whether it can be read as an allegory and, if so, what the potential implications are.[25] Again, this is particularly relevant to any passages that deal with material of which no living human has any direct experience. For instance, when the Qur'ān refers to God as being in the heavens, or seated upon his throne, it is important to understand that these remarks cannot be taken literally; God is not sitting on a chair! Similarly, when the Qur'ān mentions God as being "all-seeing" and "all-hearing" we must understand that this does not mean the senses of sight and hearing as they are experienced by ordinary men and women. Human language is a very restrictive medium of communication and, therefore, phrases like this are simply attempts to convey something that is unknowable in language that can be understood. Since no human being can ever see or directly experience God because "no human vision can encompass Him",[26] we must learn what we can about Him from the Qur'ān and also look attentively at the world around us for, in the perfection of nature, the changing seasons, and the movement of the animals, we can observe His hand at work ceaselessly, all around us. Throughout all of this, we also need to remain conscious that in our brief time on earth, our

---

25 Boullata, 2000, 990.
26 Q. 6:103.

behaviour, including but not limited to our religious observance, will be weighed on the Day of Judgement, when God will decide what becomes of our immortal soul.

With the extensive, clever use of allegory, the Qur'ān invites us to contemplate the vastness of the difference between our experience as ordinary human beings during our short time on earth, and our lives as they will be after our death. While, with our limited experience, we can never hope to understand, by beginning to appreciate the scale of all that is unknowable, at least we can start to appreciate the magnitude and splendour of God and all His creation.

CHAPTER 8

QUR'ĀNIC OATHS

THE TRADITION OF swearing oaths was widespread throughout Arabia during the pagan era. The procedure often involved visiting the Ka'ba, reciting the oath, and pouring the blood of a sacrificial offering onto the site. Oaths were made in the open, and invariably witnessed by third parties who could testify to what they had heard.[1] Anyone who took an oath was bound not to renege on his word, as this was seen as an immense disgrace and a threat to his honour and dignity.[2] Witnesses who saw and heard someone making an oath knew immediately that this was something that they should take very seriously indeed.[3] All of this is evidenced in the poetry that was left behind from this era.

However, it is also clear from the historical documents of the period that oath-swearing in Arabian culture of the time had become a rather degenerate practice, and the ideas of nobility and honour that were originally attached to oath-swearing had gone by the wayside. People commonly took the name of God lightly, and they also used their oaths as an excuse not to do the right thing.[4] In fact, oath-swearing had become so ubiquitous that any sense of solemnity associated with the act had become effectively meaningless by the time of the Muhammad. For example, oaths were used before unjust acts were carried out, as well as in the course of the wholescale oppression of women (as was common in Arabia at that time).

---

1 Farāhī, 2008, 35.
2 Farāhī, 2008, 39.
3 Farāhī, 2008, 13.
4 Asad, 2003, appendix 7, 2004.

QUR'ĀNIC OATHS

In his book, translated into English, *The Study of Qur'ānic Oaths*[5], Hamid al-Din Farahi explores how the tradition of oath swearing evolved after the revelation of the Qur'an. With the arrival of Islam, the tradition of oath-swearing did not disappear, but it was reformed. The Qur'ān itself features many instances of oaths, particularly in the earlier Surahs.

Gwynne[6] discusses the prominence of oaths in the Qur'ān, stating that they are elements of the Covenant between God and humankind as revealed to Muhammad. On the first hand, God commands people to keep their oaths, which were already part of the original Covenant laid down in earlier scriptures and, as we have seen, an integral aspect of Arabian culture at the time. On the second, there are yet more oaths in this new document. Gwynne asks us to consider whether these two sets of oaths can be distinguished from one another.

In fact, the Surahs that refer to oaths and those that discuss the relationship between God and man, reminding man of his Covenant with God, have much in common, and three Surahs in particular contain both oaths and reminders. The earliest is Surah 77, al-Mursalat, with both oaths and reminders in the first seven verses. The second is Surah 51, al-Dhariyat, with a series of oaths in verses 11-14. The third is Surah 52, al-Tur, which starts with the swearing of oaths. The Qur'ān also covers the issue of false oaths, or oaths that were given thoughtlessly, which were a big problem in seventh century Arabia. Although, as discussed in more detail below, people were not to be punished for oaths that were not made seriously,[7] the person who consistently makes oaths with no discrimination is referred to as "despicable"[8] and God warns those who swear oaths so as to take part in evil acts that He will call them to account.[9]

---

5   2008.
6   Gwynne, 2009, 103-4.
7   Q. 2:225; 5:89.
8   Q. 68:10.
9   Q. 2:224-25; 16:94.

In his exploration of the Qur'ān, drawing on Qur'ānic sources, Arabic literature, and also classical Greek and Biblical Hebrew, Farāhī[10] has traced the origin of oaths, explored the conventions behind them, and established that not every oath necessarily involves glorifying the object of it. In this case, we can understand how oaths were sometimes made by invoking apparently insignificant objects of God's creation, including plant matter such as figs and olives.[11]

Within the Qur'ān, oaths – which often occur in clusters within the text[12] – differ from Biblical oaths insofar as they do not invoke authority figures external to the text.[13] They can invite the reader to look at various aspects of God's creation, and to think deeply about the planning, divine decree, and justice that even the humblest of these display.[14] Oaths are used as a clever device that introduce a topic, and invite the reader to apply his or her own power of reason to it. For instance, the Qur'an uses oaths as a device to symbolise the giving of life through the use of winds, clouds and rain.[15] While readers might automatically reject certain contentions if they were presented with them in an abrupt, blunt way, by starting with an oath framed with an unlikely reference point, they are less likely to default to immediately negating or rejecting the argument. Moreover, as the Qur'ān explicitly teaches us that we should not venerate anyone other than God, the true believer runs no risk of confusion when he hears oaths being sworn by invoking other things. Frequently, the same argument appears in the Qur'ān in different formats, in the context of oath-swearing in some instances, and without oaths in others. In each case, it is the word of God and should be taken equally seriously, regardless of the specific context.[16]

---

10 2008; 2013.
11 Farāhī, 2008, 7.
12 Neuwirth, 2006, 110.
13 Neuwirth, 2006, 104.
14 Q. 89:1-5.
15 Q. 51:3-5.
16 Farāhī, 2008, 64.

QUR'ĀNIC OATHS

The Qur'ān which is, as established above, an "argumentative text", often uses oaths to affirm the claims it makes. For example, God is described as swearing by both Himself and many of His creations, such as the sun, moon, stars, winds, fruits, towns, and so forth. He swears that sinners will be punished,[17] that He has sent apostles to serve His people,[18] that His covenant is the truth[19], and that those who choose to disbelieve His message can easily be replaced with better people.[20]

The instances when God is shown as swearing oaths by what seem to be unimportant things was baffling in an Arabian context, in which oaths were supposed to be sworn only by things that are "great" and "glorious".[21] To people who were used to this convention it was strange, even unseemly, for God to invoke the small and apparently insignificant aspects of creation in the context of oaths when discussing weighty matters. According to tradition, one should only make oaths by invoking something of huge importance. What, then, could it mean for God to invoke things that seem to be of little importance? In many cases, it may be a question of perspective.[22] A tiny creature like an insect, or a piece of fruit like a fig or an olive, might seem at first glance to be very unimportant, but perhaps we overlook their significance. After all, even the smallest creature is part of God's creation and has its purpose in the grand scheme of things.

However, the cases when God swears by Himself, which is seen in seventeen instances,[23] are perhaps the most puzzling of all the Qur'ānic oaths. One might ask why this oath swearing is necessary at all, as everything in the Qur'ān is the word of God and therefore true believers are bound to accept it all, while those who do not believe are unlikely to suddenly start believing, just because the text features an oath.

---

17 Q. 15:92.
18 Q. 16:63.
19 Q. 51:22-3.
20 Q. 70:41-2.
21 Farāhī, 2008, 7.
22 Farāhī, 2008, 19.
23 Gwynne, 2006, 84.

Gwynne points out that oaths are an integral aspect of the Covenant between God and His people.[24] Together with evidence from history and from the scriptures that were provided to us by the prophets who went before Muhammad, they provide reassurance in a human context that God will keep His word, as there is no power greater than Him. While those who fail to honour the Covenant will be punished, those who are faithful to it need not doubt that they will receive their reward in heaven when the time comes.

Asad notes that these passages are often very difficult for even the most accomplished translator to render accurately, as they typically feature multiple layers of meaning, coupled with a lack of verbal precision that gives them spiritual power, but represents a linguistic challenge.[25] From the earliest days of Islamic scholarship, these questions have fascinated commentators, who have often struggled with explaining the sacred text while also dealing with the multiple questions that arise from the meaning and nature of the oath.

In everyday language, people often take oaths by invoking something holy to make those around them notice and register the truth of what they are saying.[26] So what does it mean when God swears by Himself and His creation? The person who believes in God will believe in him even without an oath, whereas the person who does not believe is not going to be further persuaded by an oath.

The eleventh century Islamic scholar Al-Qushayri stated that "judgement proceeds either by witness or by oath, and that both are in the Qur'ān." If, for example, someone asks how God can swear by the things he has created when people are not allowed to do so, there are three possible responses: the expression "Lord of" has been left out; or it was customary in Arabian culture at the time; or all oaths should involve swearing

---

24 Gwynne, 2006, 84.
25 Asad, 2003, 2006.
26 Farāhī, 2013, 1.

according to something greater than oneself, but all of God's oaths point to the Creator Himself.[27]

There are other areas where it appears that the oaths may be used simply to provide emphasis, and also to bring the readers' attention to the glorious nature of something or other. Oaths of this sort are generally restricted to matters of enormous theological importance, as when things are made the focus of oaths given in evidence of sworn statements, like when the Qur'ān urges the faithful to remember when God entered a Covenant with them regarding the prophets:

> (God stated) "Whatever I give you of the Book and Wisdom and then there comes to you a Messenger, in confirmation of that which is with you, you shall believe in him and help him." And He asked: "Do you agree, and do you accept the responsibility which I lay upon you in this matter?" They said: "We agree." He said: "Then bear witness and I am with you among the witnesses. Now whoever turns away after this, then surely, those are the transgressors."[28]

An oath in the Qur'ānic context is considered to be an invocation of the name of God, or of something else held sacred to the person making the oath, in order to testify to the great importance and truth of their affirmation. The Qur'ān is completely unequivocal in condemning the inappropriate invocation of God in oaths, as well as oath-taking in the area of committing to doing something that is contrary to the laws of God.[29] The Qur'ān states:

> Take not your oaths to practice deception between yourselves, with the result that someone's foot may slip after it was firmly planted, and ye may have to taste the evil consequences of having hindered

---

27 al-Zarkashi, 1988, iii, 121-3.
28 Q. 3:81-2.
29 Asad, 2003, appendix 7, 2004.

men from the Path of Allah, and a Mighty wrath descend upon you.[30]

While humans can invoke God when they make oaths to one another, they should never invoke God Himself when making an oath to God. The Qur'ān makes it clear that this is a forbidden action, and that only evil people, knowing this to be wrong, would do such a thing. It says:

> They swear their strongest oaths by God that God will not resurrect those who die. On the contrary! It is a promise incumbent on Him, but most of the people do not know.[31]

The historico-cultural context in which Muhammad received his revelations, and in which the Qur'ān was written down, provides some examples of oath-taking that was not carried out in accordance with the will of God. For example, the Hypocrites (see Chapter Six, above) swore false oaths in which they invoked the name of God to promise to stand in alliance with Muhammad and his followers, all the while they were planning to deceive them.[32]

Shari'ah law, as set down in the sacred book, does not entail a series of strict and detailed laws as to how we should conduct our lives in the social and cultural areas, but it considers the needs of men and women in this area, and our natural weaknesses as flawed human beings, including in matters of oath-swearing. This is exemplified in the Qur'ān, where it says:

> God wants to lighten your burdens, for man has been created weak. By means of his guidance. Therefore, it was not appropriate to promulgate absolute prohibition to swear an oath, an unavoidable

---

30 Q. 16:94.
31 Q. 16:38.
32 Q. 24:53.

proceeding in the conducting of important religious and social issues.[33]

God's system of laws bears in mind that people often foolishly make oaths casually in the context of conversation, and does not hold them accountable for such throw-away comments. The relevant verse states:

> God will not take you to task for oaths which you may have uttered without thought, but will take you to task for what your hearts have conceived (in earnest): for God is much forgiving, forbearing.[34]

This verse is further backed up by a series of traditions in Islamic thought and scholarship that Muhammad said that if someone makes an oath stating that he will do or refrain from doing something, and later realises that it would be better, in the sense of righteousness, to do something else, it is preferable for him to break his oath and make any necessary atonement than to take a more foolish path. Older scriptures also inform this tradition, and the Qur'ān refers to numerous cases that are also referenced in the revelations received by the earlier prophets.[35] The Torah states that oaths should only be taken in the name of God, saying, "You shall fear the Lord your God and serve Him, and shall take oaths in His Name".[36] Also in the Torah, it relates that the famously long-suffering prophet, Job, atoned his oath.[37] During his long and apparently pointless suffering, Job's wife asked him why, in the face of all that he was having to endure, he still remained faithful, saying: "Dost thou still retain thine integrity? Curse God, and die." Commenting later on this story, the Qur'ān relates that Job swore an oath stating that if God ever gave him back his health, he would punish his wife for this blasphemous remark by giving her a hundred lashes. Later,

---

33 Q. 4:28.
34 Q. 2:225.
35 Asad, 2003, 2005.
36 Deuteronomy, 6:13.
37 The Book of Job, ii, 9.

restored to health, he was terribly sorry for what he had said, and the oath he had made when he was angry, because he knew that his wife's comments had come from a place of love and pity for her long-suffering husband. God sent Job a revelation stating that, instead of beating his wife, he could fulfil his oath symbolically by hitting her with "a bunch of grass containing a hundred blades or more".[38] In the Gospel, Jesus refers to oaths, stating, "Let your Yes be Yes and your No be No."[39]

In the Qur'ān, it states that when someone breaks an oath, they should atone for this by, for instance, feeding ten poor people with food of the same quantity and calibre as they would provide for their own families, by providing them with clothing, or by releasing them from slavery.[40] When this is not possible, an alternative would be to fast for three days. In other parts of the Qur'an, it is made clear that those who break their oaths do so for their own loss, and those who keep their oath do so for their own gain.[41]

To illustrate the fact that even very virtuous people sometimes found themselves in the position of having to atone for oaths they had not been able to follow through, we can point to the fact that even Muhammad himself had to do so, as the Qur'ān records. On one occasion, during his time in Medina, Muhammad swore an oath stating that he would abstain from conjugal relations with any of his wives, apparently because of an episode of jealousy among a number of them. When he broke the oath, he was obliged to atone for it. Needless to say, this story is not necessarily biographical in the strictest sense of the word, but it does provide the Qur'ān with the opportunity to highlight two important points: Firstly, although he was both a prophet and a leader, Muhammad was also a human man with the frailties and emotions associated with the state, and therefore could make mistakes; and, secondly, it is not appropriate to

---

38 Q. 38:44.
39 Matthew 5:37.
40 Q. 5:89.
41 Q. 48:10.

consider forbidden anything that the Qur'ān has declared lawful, such as intercourse between spouses.[42]

One of the important subjects of oaths made by God Himself is that of the Last Judgement. God swears to reward the righteous, and ensures that those who have not followed His law are duly punished.[43] These oaths, says Gwynne:

> ... are solemn, unshakeable undertakings by God that the relations between God and man, virtue and reward, sin and punishment, are the truth upon which all reasoning – indeed, all action – must be based.[44]

One possibility for the inclusion of oaths is to speak strongly to those for whom the message of God's Covenant is a new one. Whereas many people only need a "reminder" of God's message (and there are many such reminders within the pages of the Qur'ān) placing God's message in the context of an oath brings home its vast import and significance to people who might not otherwise realise how meaningful it is to their lives.[45]

In terms of the practical application of oath-making in everyday life, the Qur'ān has ample advice for its adherents. For example, if someone makes a claim against someone else, and this is denied, the former is required to provide evidence. When he can't, a final option is to ask the defending party to swear an oath so as to reject the claim. If he does so, the claim is considered null and void, and neither party is considered guilty. If they refuse to swear an oath, or do not do so for some reason, the claimant is considered guilty. During Muhammad's lifetime, he is said to have asked a claimant if he had any evidence for what they were suggesting. The claimant admitted that he had no evidence, and Muhammad told him,

---

42 Asad, 2003, 875.
43 Gwynne, 2009, 21.
44 Gwynne, 2009, 22.
45 Gwynne, 2009, 22.

"You may ask for his (the defendant's) oath". The claimant answered, "He readily swears and does not care", and Muhammad told him that he had, "naught but these: your two witnesses or the defendant's oath."[46]

Disputes have long been settled by means of making oaths that invoke God's name. He who makes the oath is thus affirming his faith in God and the truth of what he is saying. In an ideal world, this would be sufficient. In reality, however, those involved in the judiciary know that oaths are a weak form of proof, and only have a role when there is no tangible evidence. For example, if someone claims to own a particular property, they are required to swear an oath that they have not sold it, given it away, or otherwise divested themselves of ownership. If they refuse to swear such an oath, it is assumed that this is a tacit acceptance of a claim against them. If they were telling the truth, they would have no reason to shy away from an oath. Muhammad is reported as saying that, "the burden of proof is on him who affirms, the oath on him who denies".[47]

The Qur'ān's instructions on oath-making also extend to various aspects of domestic and civil law. Prior to Islam, men could divorce their wives by simply swearing an oath that stated, "thou art (as unlawful) to me as my mother's back". This form of divorce put women in a dreadful situation. From this point on, they did not belong to their husbands, but nor could they remarry. The Qur'ān rendered this practice unlawful,[48] and instigated a system of fines for men who took such oaths. Today, such an oath is not recognised as a divorce, but if a man were to swear one, he would be considered to be in a state of sin, and would have to atone by carrying out a penance, which might take the form of freeing others from bondage (which could include poverty and debt) or fasting for two consecutive months as if it were Ramadan. He would be obliged to complete his penance before resuming conjugal relations with his wife.

---

46 Mahmassani, 1961, 190.
47 Mahmassani, 1961, 192-5.
48 Q. 58:2-4.

The process of oath-taking known as "li'ān" refers to cases when someone of either gender suspects their spouse of being unfaithful but does not have recourse to the four witnesses required by law to confirm their suspicions. In this case, they have the option of swearing an oath to God that what they say is the truth, whereas their spouse is lying.[49] By making such an oath, they make themselves vulnerable to incurring God's wrath should they be lying. In the process, both members of the couple are put on an equal footing. When oath-taking of this sort occurs, divorce becomes inevitable, as it is clear that there is no longer love and trust in the marriage, and nobody of good faith would seek to remain in a relationship after their spouse has made such a serious charge against them.

Finally, the Qur'ān also provides clear instructions as to how and when oaths should be used by ordinary human beings in their everyday context. Above all, it is important to understand that oaths are serious, and should never be made lightly.[50] The person who makes oaths without considering the situation is making a grave mistake that threatens his honour. If a religious oath in particular is sworn, no being other than God should be invoked; doing so is akin to worshipping false idols, and it is blasphemous and wrong. Conversely, God should never be casually invoked when one is making an oath on a matter of little significance.

The Qur'ān, as a complete guide to life in all matters practical as well as spiritual, has provided us with clear instructions on this issue, as on so many others. While our cultural context has changed greatly since seventh century Arabia, the advice still stands.

---

49 Q. 24:6-9.
50 Farāhī, 2008, 84.

CHAPTER 9

MYSTERIOUS LETTERS

OF THE MANY interesting linguistic and stylistic features of the Qur'ān, none is more so than the presence of hard-to-explain letters at the beginning of some of the Surahs, often referred to as "abbreviated letters",[1] that at first glance appear to add nothing of any substance to the text. The Arabic language contains twenty-nine letters, and twenty-nine of the Surahs are prefaced with the so-called abbreviated letters. Not all of the letters in the Arabic language, but rather just fourteen, are featured.[2] However, all of the vocal sounds present in Arabic are included.[3] Almost all of the mysterious letters feature in the Surahs that were received in the early period of Islam, when Muhammad was still in Mecca, with just two in the Surahs that were received in Medina. It is important to note that while these letters do present a challenge to understanding, they are not entirely without precedent. There are many examples in Arabic of abbreviated letters having been used to imply quite ordinary things. The letter n, for example, which in Arabic is pronounced "nūn", can be used mean "fish",[4] while q (pronounced "qāf") means "mountains," l (pronounced "lam") means "parents" and s (pronounced "sād") means "copper".[5]

On some occasions, the abbreviated letters appear singularly in the Qur'ān and can be read on their own. Examples are a, l, and m, (pronounced: "alif," "lam," "mim"). Other examples show the letters in

---

1 Ali, 1991, 134.
2 Ali, 1991, 134.
3 Ali, 1991, 135.
4 As seen, for example, in Q 21:87.
5 al-Dīn ar-Razi, n.d., 25.

combination to form a word, including "alm", which means "not" and is pronounced "alam". This appears in phrases including "alm nashrah", which means "have we not"[6] and "alm tara", which means, "art thou not aware".[7]

These letters, which invariably appear at the beginning of about a quarter of the Surahs,[8] and which are written in a way that suggests that they should be read as separate enunciations, have often puzzled scholars, and appear at face value to contradict the general clarity of the Qur'ān, which was written in such a way that it would have presented no difficulty in comprehension to the inhabitants of Mecca and Medina at the time of Muhammad.[9] (The relevant Surahs date to Muhammad's time in Mecca, but not to the earliest period of that time. The very earliest Surahs tend to be prefaced with the oaths that were the subject of the preceding chapter.[10]) The confusion is compounded by the fact that nowhere does Muhammad refer to them, while none of his followers seem to have asked for an explanation of their meaning, leaving us to consider their relevance and meaning with very little background information to rely upon.

Some Western scholars have suggested that these confusing letters are simply the initials of the various scribes who recorded the revelations received by Muhammad, but the fact that the prophet's followers accepted them as an integral part of the Surahs and duly recited them indicates that they might actually be much more than that.

Some of Muhammad's followers, and some of the early Muslim scholars of the succeeding generations, believed that these mysterious letters were actually abbreviations of words or concepts pertaining to God. Believing this, they made various efforts to decode them, but the possible

---

6   Q. 94:1.
7   Q. 105:1.
8   Asad, 2003, 992.
9   Shahîd, 2000, 127.
10 Shahîd, 2000, 136.

interpretations are so many and so varied that these attempts can only be taken with a grain of salt.[11]

Some scholars have suggested that the letters represent those occasions when Muhammad simply did not hear or receive a particular revelation with complete clarity because he started to receive a revelation at a moment when he was not completely prepared for it, and reflected this in preserving what he thought he had heard, even though it defied understanding, so as to remain as close as possible to the integrity of the text as it was originally received.[12] This view is bolstered somewhat by a number of verses in the Qur'ān that clearly instruct Muhammad to preserve revelations precisely as he received them,[13] including, "Do not make haste in the recitation of the Qur'ān",[14] and "Do not move your tongue with it so that you may make haste in reciting it."[15] It is a position that is also somewhat supported by the traditional view, provided by the Hadith, that the process of receiving revelations was often very testing for Muhammad, who experienced symptoms including, "perspiration, fear, trembling, and the sound of bells in his ears".[16] Others attempted to decode the mysterious letters by assigning numerical values to the letters of the Arabic alphabet, and trying to decipher the resulting combinations of numbers, but the obscure results of these efforts owe more to imagination than reality and cannot be considered serious scholarship.

Another explanation, and one that may be more rooted in reason, is that the mysterious letters are intended to signify the wondrous nature of the revelations that gave rise to the Qur'ān. The relevant argument points out that all the words in Arabic consist of a combination of from one to five letters. This, too, is the format in which the mysterious letters, known as muqatta'āt, appear. In each case, they preface a Surah that refers to the

---

11 Asad, 2003, 992.
12 Shahîd, 2000, 126.
13 Shahîd, 2000, 125-6.
14 Q. 20:114.
15 Q. 75:16.
16 Shahîd, 2000, 127.

nature of revelations, either directly or obliquely. Thus, some scholars have argued that the inclusion of the letters that defy interpretation is meant to "illustrate the wondrous, inimitable nature of Qur'ānic revelation which, though originating in a realm beyond the reach of human perception, can be and is conveyed to man by means of the very sounds (represented by letters) of human speech."[17] At first glance, this explanation may seem plausible, but it is not without problems because, while all the Surahs prefaced with a mysterious letter refer in one way or another to revelations, there are also many Surahs about revelation that are not prefaced in this way at all. Moreover, there is absolutely no proof of this explanation, which is based on nothing more than simple conjecture.[18] Ultimately, as Shahîd states, the presence of these letters has above all tended to reduce Islamic scholars to a state of helplessness,[19] as no explanation is entirely satisfactory, and every possibility appears only to open up yet more questions.

Certain scholars have identified one Surah in particular as possibly containing the key to understanding the purpose of and intention behind the mysterious letters. This Surah is known as the "al-Muzzammil". Verses six and seven in this context are considered particularly relevant. This is one of the earliest Surahs, and dates to when Muhammad was still in Mecca, before the loss of his wife Khadija.[20] According to tradition, after receiving this particular revelation, the prophet returned home, whereupon his wife placed a mantel around him; this fact is referenced in the name of the Surah, above, which means "the one covered with a mantel." This Surah is noteworthy for a number of reasons, including the fact that this is where the term "Qur'ān" is used for the first time, although here it appears to refer to one particular aspect of revelation, and not the whole book. Moreover, while most of the verses of the Qur'ān are addressed to the entire community of believers, this one addresses Muhammad specifically.[21]

---

17 Asad, 2003, 992.
18 Asad, 2003, 993.
19 Shahîd, 2000, 125.
20 Shahîd, 2000, 127.
21 Shahîd, 2000, 130.

Verse six in the "al-Muzzammil" has often been thought to refer to the practice of praying at night, but can also be interpreted as the "descent" of revelation from God in His heavens to Muhammad during the night; that is, the revelation of the various Surahs to Muhammad at night.[22] Why at night? The idea is expressed that Muhammad is better able to receive revelations at night, perhaps because he is free of distraction, and in the best position to understand what has been expressed, to commit it to memory and to communicate this information.[23] We can conclude from this Surah that it was standard for Muhammad to receive revelations during the night, and therefore that the bulk of the Qur'ān contains material received by the prophet during the hours of darkness.[24] Does this, then, provide us with the key to why twenty nine Surahs have been picked out to be prefaced with certain mysterious letters? If they are different in some tangible way, it is possible that these are the relatively few Surahs that were received during the daytime.[25] Given the many stresses Muhammad was under at the time, it is likely that he might have been distracted or otherwise disturbed during the receipt of revelations in the hours of daylight.[26] Another source of the prophet's dismay could have been the rejection of his message by the vast majority of the people of Mecca. As stated above, most of the Surahs under discussion here come from a time when Muhammad and his few followers suffered ridicule and discrimination from the Meccans, who ardently rejected his message, and certainly from a time when he would have suffered immense stress. An additional source of stress may have been the Persian invasion of the Near East, which also occurred during this time, and which may have been a factor in a number of Muhammad's followers making their way to Abyssinia and finding asylum there, as mentioned above. The fall of the Byzantine Empire to the Persians, incorporating the fall of Jerusalem, represented the ascendancy of the Zoroastrian faith over

---

22 Shahîd, 2000, 130.
23 Shahîd, 2000, 133.
24 Shahîd, 2000, 134.
25 Shahîd, 2000, 134.
26 Shahîd, 2000, 134.

a monotheistic tradition that was much closer to what Muhammad was preaching at the time, and would certainly have been experienced by him as a setback to his goal of converting the peoples of Arabia to Islam.[27]

The Qur'ān, as we have discussed in various contexts, is both eternally valid and incomparable to any scripture that came before it.[28] It appears that, while we do not understand precisely what they mean, the mysterious letters at the beginning of certain Surahs are an aspect of this important quality of incomparability. Despite all the scholarship that has been devoted to analysing and examining the mysterious letters, where they came from and what they mean are still two issues that elude scholars and laymen alike. While there is much here for the scholar and the interested layman to consider, perhaps ultimately we have to accept that only God knows for sure the exact meaning of the mysterious letters that precede so many of His Surahs. As the Qur'ān is a book with many and rich layers of meaning, it may be that the full significance of these letters has simply not yet been shared with us, and that with the passage of time it may become apparent.[29] Furthermore, scholarship and exploration of the Qur'ān is a useful and worthy pursuit in any case, providing us all with the opportunity to come to know the sacred book more profoundly.

To me, it appears that if we inspect the Qur'ān and the available Qur'ānic exegesis closely, we may yet uncover the answers that we have been searching for. Considering that the Qur'ān was revealed in the Arabian Peninsula, as it is known today, and that both Muhammad and the people to whom he was sent to preach were Arabs, it is unsurprising that the Qur'ān states on many occasions, very clearly, that it was revealed in Arabic so that the people could understand the many messages it contains.[30] The following verse states its position very clearly:

---

27 Shahîd, 2000, 134.
28 Shahîd, 2000, 125.
29 Ali, 1991, 134.
30 Q: 12:2; 16:103; 39:28.

> Now if We had willed this (divine writ) to be a discourse in a non-Arabic tongue, they (who now reject it) would surely have said, "Why is it that its messages have not been spelled out clearly? Why - (a message in) a non-Arabic tongue, and (its bearer) an Arab?[31]

Given its frequent declarations that it was sent in Arabic in order to be understood by those who heard it, and that the use of similar letters is an integral element of the Arabic language, I propose that it is more than likely that Muhammad's contemporaries actually *did* know the nature and meaning, and maybe even the full significance, of these letters, but that with the passage of time, this information has been lost to us. Consider that we know, from the huge amount of scholarship that has been carried out in the fields of Qur'ānic exegesis and Hadith studies, that whenever someone wished to discuss something of relevance to the Muslim community with Muhammad, he would address those issues and request that his pronouncements on them be dispersed to the wider community. In this manner, Muhammad was asked about a huge range of matters, including family law, inheritance, and charity giving, acts of worship, judgement day, gambling, usury, and so forth. We also know that, on certain occasions, the Qur'an would enlighten the Prophet (and by extension, the entire Muslim community) on equally wide-ranging matters. On these occasions, as the following verses attest, the Qur'ān would make a proclamation, and then ask the question concerning the nature of that proclamation before providing an answer:

> (Hence,) I shall cause him to endure hell-fire (in the life to come). And what could make thee conceive what hell-fire is? It does not allow to live, and neither leaves (to die), making (all truth) visible to mortal man.[32]

---

31 Q. 41:44.
32 Q. 74:26-9.

MYSTERIOUS LETTERS

And:

> Nay, verily, the record of the truly virtuous is (set down) in a mode most lofty! And what could make thee conceive what that mode most lofty will be? A record (indelibly) inscribed, witnessed by all who have (ever) been drawn close unto God.[33]

The dialect of Arabic used in the Qur'ān is the same as that spoken by Muhammad and his contemporaries, which would have minimised any risk of the true meaning of the Qur'ān being lost to the local community at the time. Only with the passage of time (1400 years have passed since the Qur'ān was revealed) and the many linguistic developments and changes that have quite naturally occurred in the language, have we arrived at a point whereby today's Muslims require specialist teachings of the Qur'ān to understand its message. While the spoken language has changed (as all languages do), the Arabic preserved in the Qur'ān has remained intact since its first revelation, consistent with God's promise that the Qur'ān would remain forever unaltered. In the process, gaps of intelligibility have emerged between modern spoken Arabic and the Arabic in the Qur'ān, leading in turn to the widening gap in our knowledge of the significance of these letters; hence their designation as "mysterious".

---

33 Q. 83:18-20

CHAPTER 10

ARGUMENTATION

UNLIKE THE EARLIER sacred books of revelation, the Qur'ān does not present its messages merely as self-evident content to be presented to the reader or listener, who should then passively accept them as the word of God, and organise their life around them. Instead, it frames them in the context of argument and counter-argument, engaging the person who reads or listens to it in a dynamic and often exciting way, utilising arguments that can be long or short, complex or simple, formal or informal.[1]

Since the time of Muhammad, Muslims have used the Qur'ān in support of their views in the areas of life, law, and theology. However, historically relatively little attention has been given by Islamic scholars to the very important matter of *how* the Qur'ān presents its edicts as conclusions that follow from arguments that are made in an orderly and reasoned way; of the style and format in which it makes its many points.

Since the early days of Islam, the content of the many arguments contained in the Qur'ān have attracted a great deal of attention from scholars, who have applied various techniques to teasing out the discussions in its pages, and applying logic to a detailed analysis of their full implications for humanity. While some comparisons have been made to the Classical philosophers, such as Aristotle, they are not always perfectly valid. The fact that there are some broad similarities in terms of the complexity of the argument no more implies that Muhammad was influenced by Aristotle than that Aristotle was receiving divine inspiration from God.[2]

---

1 Gwynne, 2009, 194.
2 Gwynne, 2009, x.

ARGUMENTATION

Regardless of the topics at hand – how people should consider their lives and where they are heading, God's powers of creation, or why God does certain things – the Qur'ān is such an essential element of most Muslims' lives that many can assert its primary appeal to the human intellect (which is certainly fundamental).[3] The Qur'ān engages so much in both reasoning and argument in this appeal to the intellect that it is impossible to consider these elements separately. The very process of argumentation can be identified as formative to how scholars of the Qur'ān think, experience, and understand the world. Perhaps this is why the study of Qur'ānic argumentation has not received the attention that it warrants,[4] with the notable exceptions of *Logic, Rhetoric, and Legal Reasoning in the Qur'ān* by Rosalind Gwynne, which is cited extensively in this text, and of Kate Zebiri's 2006 text, *Argumentation*. In recent years, however, the topic of argumentation in the Qur'ān has begun to attract more attention in both the English- and the Arabic-speaking worlds,[5] and we can expect to see considerable growth of scholarship in this area.

It is important to mention at the outset that the Arabic word "jadal", frequently used in the Qur'ān and generally translated as "argument" (which is the term we use here), has a meaning that goes somewhat beyond the generally accepted English implications of the word to incorporate aspects of the term "debate".[6] Thus, the Qur'ān encourages the perceptive to listen, consider, and act upon its teachings in a reasoned way.[7] While today the Qur'ān is often read privately, at the time of revelation Arabia (and indeed most of the world) had a largely oral culture, so most new Muslims and potential converts would have encountered its teachings in an oral context. The argument-and-counter-argument structure lends itself particularly well to oral teaching,[8] especially in the context of the clear

---

3 Gwynne, 2009, 1.
4 Gwynne, 2009, 203.
5 Zebiri, 2006, 268.
6 Gwynne, 2009, xv.
7 Gwynne, 2009, ix.
8 Zebiri, 2006, 266.

language that dominates the Qur'ān,[9] and that must be intended to make its message accessible to as many people as possible.

To a degree, the manner in which the Qur'ān was written reflects the difficult times in which Muhammad received his message. Seventh century Arabia was a challenging environment at the best of times, and for a prophet with a new message that contradicted many of the local mores and traditions, it was difficult indeed. As we have already seen, his challenges to the status quo in Mecca and Medina were not warmly received by most of the inhabitants, particularly in Mecca (and, later, from the "hypocrites" in Medina, who merely pretended to be Muslims when it suited them). From the very outset, the Qur'ān as revealed to Muhammad pre-empted the queries, doubts and outright aggression of so many of the Arabians of the day by presenting arguments given and answered, and by dealing with their own many criticisms and attempts to undermine.[10] In the process, a range of styles was used, including rhetoric and persuasion, and with a general emphasis on a specific, practical approach rather than an abstract one. The Qur'ān's arguments appeal to both the intellect and the emotions, as one might expect from a document of tremendous theological and sociological importance.[11]

This, you will remember, was a time when the tiny, nascent Muslim community was literally struggling to survive in a very hostile cultural environment. The tone and degree of argumentation of the Qur'ān had changed somewhat by the time Muhammad and his followers had successfully established themselves in Medina and had become a physical, as well as a theological, force to be reckoned with.[12] However, it would be a mistake to see the Qur'ān as simply bound specifically to a particular place and time. In fact, the Holy Book also goes far beyond the scope of this immediate cultural context to explore the arguments of various proph-

---

9 Zebiri, 2006, 268.
10 Zebiri, 2006, 266.
11 Zebiri, 2006, 279.
12 Zebiri, 2006, 268.

ets with their people, providing arguments and counter-arguments each time. A recurring theme of binary opposition is found in many contexts throughout the book, in which heaven is compared to hell, good to evil, truth to lies, and so forth,[13] often with the vivid use of metaphor and rich, colourful language, including "rebukes, criticisms, threats and warnings, declarations of woe, curses, satire, irony, rhetorical questions, challenges, etc."[14] In a particularly evocative passage, for instance, the Qur'ān argues that all of creation indicates not just the existence and power of God, but also His merciful qualities:

> In the creation of the heavens and the earth; in the alteration of night and day; in the ships that sail on the ocean for the benefit of humankind; in the water which God sends down from the sky to revivify the earth when it is barren, scattering creatures of all kinds over it; in the change of the winds, and the clouds that run their appointed courses between the sky and the earth; here indeed are signs for a people who understand.[15]

In this engagement, the Qur'ān acknowledges the unparalleled intellectual properties of human beings, who have been created by God as thinking, rational creatures who are able (and need) to use the gift of intelligence to see and understand the reasons behind His demands that they modify their behaviour in certain ways and to respond on an intellectual level, not just because they are fearful of what will become of them if they do not comply. The Qur'ān does not simply say "do this" or "do that" but presents the reasons why certain things should be done in a certain way, or why particular behaviours or actions are best avoided. Moreover, it acknowledges that all human beings have free will. Quite simply, they can choose how they conduct their lives, and how to react to any given situation. The

---

13 Zebiri, 2006, 267.
14 Zebiri, 2006, 269.
15 Q. 2:164.

Qur'ān does not seek to hamper this exercise of free will, but to guide the individual who is open to its message towards drawing conclusions that will help him or her to wisely select the best course of action.[16] Indicative of the underlying assumption that human beings are both rational and intelligent is the fact that the Qur'ān goes to immense lengths to use persuasive language to appeal to its listenership, to encourage them to engage with it, and that it rarely issues commands without explaining the logic behind them, while also urging people to think, reflect, and learn. As God is omnipotent and omniscient, there is no imperative on Him to provide this reason, but He does anyway, presumably in recognition of the higher intellectual capacity of humanity, alone of all creation in this respect.[17] Some scholars have gone so far as to suggest that there may be a "reciprocal relationship between faith on the one hand and understanding or intelligence on the other."[18] God, of course, knows exactly what is in every person's mind at any given time. This is referenced in the Qur'ān on various occasions, including the verses that state, "Do they not know that God knows what they conceal and what they reveal?"[19] and "Fear God, for God knows what is in your hearts."[20] God also does not hesitate to remind His people that He simply exists on a higher plane: "O humankind! It is you who need God: God is free of all need, worthy of praise".[21] Furthermore, although excessive argumentation is portrayed in a negative way in various instances (see below), there is a degree of acceptance that human beings are simply inclined to disagree and argue, and that this is a function of what it means to be human, as created by God in the first instance. For example, the Qur'ān states, "If your Lord had so willed, He could have made humankind one people; but they do not cease to disagree."[22]

---

16 Gwynne, 2009, ix.
17 Zebiri, 2006, 267.
18 Zebiri, 2006, 267.
19 Q. 2:77.
20 Q. 5:7.
21 Q. 35:15 and many similar.
22 Q 11:118; 10:19; 16:93.

ARGUMENTATION

The argumentative quality of the Qur'anic text is fundamental, and in fact scholars have been able to decipher no fewer than thirty distinct types of argumentation, including the explicit and implicit, and a wide variety of demonstrations and examples. Arguments can be encapsulated in a single verse, or can be spread out over a range of verses.[23] Different types of argument can be used, in varying styles, depending on who is being addressed. For instance, through the Qur'ān God can direct a message, framed in an argument, to an individual rather than a collective, or vice versa: He can address Muhammad himself directly, address specific groups of detractors, or provide instructions for all of humanity. He tends to assume the acceptance of a higher being, even among the pagans to whom Muhammad and his followers preached, and from whom they received such rough treatment.[24] In the sacred text, God reminds the reader of the multiple signs of His glorious creation, but also of the inherently limited nature of the human mind and the difficulties we may have in perceiving it in all its splendour.

While argumentation is a very important aspect of the Qur'ān, in general Islamic scholars tend not to cite it as a proof of the document's inimitability and divine origin (which is discussed in some detail in Chapter Seventeen), because of the capacity of the human mind to apply reason, and the human tendency to engage in argument and discussion.[25] The Qur'ān references this important human quality in numerous instances such as, for example:

> Call to the way of your Lord by means of wisdom and beautiful preaching; and argue with them according to what is best. Because your Lord knows best who has strayed from His path.[26]

---

23 Gwynne, 2009, x.
24 Zebiri, 2006, 270.
25 Gwynne, 2009, xi.
26 Q. 16:125.

The arguments in the Qur'ān can be read as the voice of God Himself, addressing His people directly, or they can occur in the context of stories, histories and parables intended to make a particular point or set of points. For example, Surah 21 discusses the life of the prophet Abraham, and in particular an episode in which he engaged with some idolaters and asked them, "What are these statues to which you are so devoted?"[27] The situation places Abraham in a very difficult context, as his own father was an idolater. He is shown demonstrating that the idols his father worshipped are incapable of either speech or action,[28] and arguing that even if many people sincerely believed for a long time that it was appropriate to worship idols, this was wrong.[29] In response, the pagans rather weakly argue that even though their idols don't listen to them, or do anything for them, they continue their form of worship simply because it is what they have always done and what their ancestors always did before them.[30] Having asserted that it is not appropriate to worship idols, Abraham is shown arguing that God truly exists, supporting this argument with the proof provided in the form of God's creation of the heaven and the earth and following up with a demonstration of the idols' uselessness when he breaks all but the largest of them and demands that the idolaters ask their idols to speak. When they can't, they are forced to accept this fact.[31] It should be noted that Abraham also engaged with a king of the time, as the Qur'an recounts.[32] Abraham reminded the haughty king that only God grants life and deals death. Arrogantly, the king replied that he too granted life and dealt death. Abraham reminded him that God also causes the sun to rise from the east, and challenged the king to cause the sun to rise from the west if he really considered himself powerful. At that point, the king was dumbfounded and had no reply. With a similar message, the Qur'ān narrates

---

27 Q. 21.52.
28 Q 21:51-67.
29 Q. 21:54.
30 Q. 45:24-25.
31 Q. 21:63-5.
32 Q. 2:258.

the story of the Prophet Shu'ayb, who was sent to the people of Madyan. Shu'ayb implored that the people should believe in God, reject their sinful ways, embrace righteousness, and deal in justice and fairness. Even though he pointed out the fate of people who had rejected God's message before them, they would not relent and ultimately went to their downfall.[33]

Although in the early parts of the Qur'an it mentions the pagans and their deities, nevertheless, the central tenet of Islam - reinforced throughout the Qur'an - has always been that there is only one God and the Qur'an vehemently rejects all forms of idol worship and regards it as false. Whereas, in the early parts of the Qur'ān, it appears to go along with the notion that they are actual deities that might have some powers, with the passage of time they are represented more and more as inert beings. This incremental approach is mirrored in the Qur'ānic approach to legislation which, as we will discuss in more detail in chapter thirteen, introduces new concepts gradually to facilitate their adoption amongst the people.[34] While it might have been too much to expect the pagans, who were so attached to their idolatrous practice for a variety of reasons, to reject their idols all at once, by incrementally introducing the idea that they might not be the all-powerful beings they were supposed to be, it would be easier for the people to accept that they had been wrong all along. In a similar fashion, the ruling that Muslims should not imbibe alcohol was introduced incrementally, over time. The uniqueness of God is also underlined in the argument that if there were more than one they would each have undone the other's creation. For order to exist on earth, there is a need for a single, unifying deity: "If there were in them (earth and heaven) other gods besides God, there would be ruin in both."[35]

Another Surah, Surah 26, deals with the life of another prophet, Moses, and once again places the issue of argumentation in a biographical context. Moses is represented as arguing with his foster father, the Pharaoh

---

33 Q. 11:84-95.
34 Zebiri, 2006, 271-2.
35 Q. 21:22; 12:39.

of Egypt, with the latter issuing threats in response to Moses' prophecies.[36] While Moses has to admit that he has done wrong in the past, he counters the Pharaoh's insistence that he should be grateful for his upbringing with the argument that whatever good he did in raising Moses, he did far worse when he enslaved the people of Israel. Moses goes on to insist that there is but one true God, much to the Pharaoh's horror. While much of the story of the interaction between Moses and his foster father is familiar from the older scriptures, the Qur'ān places considerable emphasis on the content and quality of Moses' arguments against the Pharaoh's deeds and his lack of belief in the one true God.

One of the issues that the pagans found most difficult to comprehend and accept was the doctrine of resurrection, and of the final Judgement, as revealed to Muhammad, and many verses in the Qur'ān portray arguments on this topic. To assuage their doubts, the Qur'ān responds that, as God was capable of creating the world and all it contains, He is surely also capable of guaranteeing resurrection into an afterlife for His faithful followers. The Qur'ān argues:

> O people. If you are in doubt concerning the resurrection consider that We created you out of dust, then out of a drop of fluid, then out of a clot, then out of a piece of flesh, partly formed and partly unformed.[37]

Although the pagans were very clear in rejecting Muhammad's teaching on this issue, they were utterly unable to advance any arguments against it, instead demanding that he prove what he was saying. The Qur'ān responds in a range of ways: with simple assertions, with dismissals, and by imploring them to consider the wonders of nature all around them, in which they will soon see many signs of God's greatness.[38] On other occasions it

---

36 Q. 26:18-52.
37 Q. 22:5.
38 Zebiri, 2006, 278.

departs from persuasion and uses threats to assure those who will not listen to God's message that they will suffer the agonies of hell in the next life if they do not repent and start to listen to Him.[39]

The Qur'ān also calls upon Muslims to apply very high standards when they themselves engage in debate over theological matters, such as when they talk about God to non-believers, or to Christians and Jews. God instructs the reader:

> Do not argue with the People of the Book except according to what is best, except for those of them that have done wrong. And say, "We believe in what was revealed to us and what was revealed to you: our God and your God is one, and to him we submit ourselves."[40]

The implications of this argument are that Muslims should invariably debate with courtesy for their opponent, and in a state of preparedness to deal with any issues that arise. In terms of using this ability to preach the truth of Islam to unbelievers, the Qur'ān states: "Call them to the way of your Lord with wisdom and beautiful preaching and debate with them in the better way."[41] Historically, and largely inspired by this particular verse, Muslim scholars have placed great emphasis on the importance of using the correct etiquette in any debate, which they have tended to see as having parity with any relevant legal issues under discussion.

While the ability of men and women to perceive and understand argument and debate is a given, the sometimes problematic nature of humans' argumentative qualities is also referenced in the Qur'ān, which makes a number of negative comments about this quality,[42] particularly as it pertains to unbelievers, who are often seen as especially guilty of being unduly contentious and argumentative, "wilfully wrangling over God's revealed

---

39 Zebiri, 2006, 279.
40 Gwynne, 2009, 192.
41 Q. 16:125.
42 For example, Q. 18:54.

truths" as they had done throughout the ages with the revelations sent by God to each of his various prophets.[43] For example, in various locations, the Qur'ān states: "None dispute concerning the signs of God except those who disbelieve."[44] At the same time, it urges Muslims to use argumentation in a range of contexts. For example:

> They say, "None will enter the kingdom of Heaven except those who are Jews and Christians" That is what they wish! Say: "Give us your proof, if you are telling the truth."[45]

Muslims are also urged to use their capacity for argument and debate judiciously, and warned that its inappropriate use is not appreciated by God. For instance: "Those who argue about God after a positive response to Him – their argument is void with their Lord. There will be anger against them and a painful punishment."[46]

One of the most important aspects of Muhammad's message is that he brought it not just to people from Arabia, and not just to "People of the Book" but to everyone, all over the world. That is, his message was as applicable to pagans and idolaters as it was (and is) to anyone else. The Qur'ān argues against the pagan worship of idols in a range of settings. It states that they are ineffectual, incapable of either harming or helping anyone,[47] and that they are created by humankind rather than being themselves capable of creation.[48] In some cases, as in the following verse, they are directly (and unfavourably) compared to God Himself:

> They worship, besides God, that which can neither harm nor benefit them, and they say: "These are our intercessors with God."

---

43 Zebiri, 2006, 269.
44 Q. 40:4; 2:197; 6:25; 8:6.
45 Q. 2:111.
46 Q. 42:16.
47 Q. 22:12.
48 Q. 7:191.

ARGUMENTATION

Say: "Are you informing God of something He doesn't know to the heavens or the earth? Glory be to Him! Far is He above the partners they ascribe to Him!"[49]

The pagans who heard Muhammad's message, like the idolaters in Moses' day, were often reluctant to countenance it, and tried to argue against it. The techniques of argumentation that they employed were flimsy. On the one hand, they stated that because the people who had gone before them worshipped idols, they were going to do it too, and they said that Muhammad should carry out miracles to show them that his message was real, even though he had never suggested that he could or would do any such thing.[50] Although he presents a range of arguments in support of his message – saying, for example, that he cannot return their forefathers to life (as they demanded) because only God, who creates life in the first instance, can return it[51] – they reject them out of hand because he does not also provide them with the miracle that they have demanded. The Qur'ān shows how Muhammad turns the tables on them by demanding that they bring him some material comparable to the Qur'ānic verses that have been revealed to him:

> They may say "He has forged (the Qur'ān). Say: "Bring ten Surahs 'forged' like it and call on anyone you can (to help you) other than God, if you are sincere! Then, if (your false gods) do not respond to you, know that it has only been sent down with God's knowledge and that there is no deity but He."[52]

The pagans also prove themselves dishonest when they suggest that in citing Jesus as one of the prophets of God, Muhammad is trying to say that

---

49 Q. 10:18.
50 Q. 45:24-5.
51 Q. 45:26.
52 Q. 11:13-4.

Jesus was a god, when in fact he suggests no such thing. The Qur'ān references this episode, saying: "They say: 'Are our gods better, or is he?' They refer to him only (to start) an argument with you, for they are truly an argumentative lot."[53] They are also shown as making a nonsense of their flimsy arguments when they represent God as having daughters in the form of al-Lāt, al-'Uzzā and Manāt, three goddesses whom the pagans worshipped at the time and considered to be the daughters of Allah, whom they recognised as a higher being among the pantheon of deities they worshipped.[54] In the intensely patriarchal Arabian society of the day, daughters were not prized, and men tended to respond with disappointment and regret when a daughter was born to them.[55] By representing God as having offspring of the sort that they themselves often rejected, they made no sense: "For you the male and for Him the female? What an unfair division!"[56] Moreover, one of the qualities shown as discerning females from males is the ability to argue clearly, with men depicted as those who "speak with clarity".[57] This can be seen as a clear case of the Qur'ān utilising the cultural norms of the day to argue with the pagans in their own language.

While Muhammad brought his message to both pagans and "People of the Book", or Jews and Christians, his arguments to the latter were quite different. As fellow monotheists, Jews and Christians did not have to be persuaded to follow the one true God, as they already did this. However, as they already believed themselves saved, and had certain doctrines that were inconsistent with Islam, many were very reluctant to accept that Muhammad's message represented a new Covenant with the God they already held so dear. Muhammad pointed to the fact that they bowed down before a cross, which could be seen as idolatry, and that they believed that God had a son, Jesus, who drank wine, which is forbidden to Muslims. The teaching that Jesus was God's son in particular was held by Muslims

---

53 Q. 43:58.
54 Zebiri, 2006. 271.
55 Q. 43:17.
56 Q. 53:21-2.
57 Gwynne, 2009, 199.

to contradict the Qur'ān's message of God's unique nature, and when the Qur'ān argues against Christian teaching, this is the topic on which it tends to focus. For instance, it states that God cannot have a son when he has no spouse, and Muhammad is told to state that he would certainly worship God's son if such a person existed, with the implication that he clearly did not.[58] The Qur'ān also repudiates the notion that, if Jesus was born of a virgin, this of necessity meant that he was divine, pointing out that God had created Adam with no human father, and yet Adam was certainly a man and not a god.[59] While the Qur'ān argues that there should be peace between all the "People of the Book", as they all share a faith in the one true God, this argument is qualified with calls for Jews and Christians not to attempt to assume more authority than they are due,[60] not to lead true believers (Muslims) astray,[61] and more.

In many contexts, the Qur'ān deals with the accusations that Muhammad was not really a prophet of God. This, again, reflects the many and varied accusations that were levelled against him by his detractors: "that, far from being a prophet, he was a poet, a sorcerer, a soothsayer, or he was mad or possessed by jinn" and that his revelations were really nothing of the sort, but just forgeries, repeated old stories, dreams or products of the imagination.[62] The Qur'ān repeatedly refutes these accusations and affirms Muhammad's status as a prophet of God, as well as issuing counter-accusations against those who did not believe him, such as, "In truth it is they who have put forward an iniquity and a falsehood."[63] When Muhammad's critics sneered at him for not being from a noble family, the Qur'ān was quick to assert that he was of good character,[64] and that the previous prophets had all had to deal with exactly the same sort of doubt

---

58 Zebiri, 2006, 273.
59 Zebiri, 2006, 273.
60 Q. 3:66.
61 Q. 3:69.
62 Zebiri, 2006, 275.
63 Q. 25:4.
64 Q. 68:4.

and accusations from their peers. Again, the Qur'ān often uses very beautiful, poetic and argumentative language to prove its point as, for example, in the following passage:

> They say: "We shall not believe in you until you make a spring gush forth for us out of the earth, or until you have a garden of date trees and vines, and cause rivers to gush forth in their midst, or you cause the sky to fall in pieces… or you bring God and the angels before us face to face, or you have a house made of gold, or you rise up into the sky, and we won't believe in your ascension until you send down to us a book that we can read."

In response, the Qur'ān tells Muhammad to say, "Glory be to my Lord! Am I anything but a man, a messenger?"[65] Elsewhere, it suggests that the Qur'ān itself is the miracle that the incredulous seem to be seeking.[66] It is noteworthy that while the Qur'ān at times addresses Muhammad directly, many arguments discuss him in the third person, particularly in the later revelations, leading to what Zebiri describes as a "sense of detachment and objectivity, enhancing Muhammad's credibility as conveyor of a transcendent message." [67]

Many of the arguments in the Qur'ān can be used by Muslims as guidance in their everyday lives. For a start, the Qur'ān recognises some of the fundamental qualities of humankind and asserts humans' need to understand and acknowledge God and all His works, and to incorporate this into their everyday lives. In the Qur'ān, God says:

> Have they themselves been created without anything (that might have caused their creation) – or were they, perchance, their own

---

65 Q. 17:90-3.
66 Zebiri, 2006, 275.
67 2006, 276.

creators? Have they created the heavens and the earth?). Nay, but they have no certainty of anything.[68]

Of course, humans played no role in the creation of the stars in the sky or the bountiful world we inhabit. However, without faith in God they cannot explain the wonderful things they see all around them; they cannot admit that behind all the wonders of the universe there is a conscious deity who is responsible for all of creation.

The Qur'ān (and to some extent the older scriptures) provides ample evidence of God's ability to create, using a wide range of arguments and debates to do so. For example, when Zachariah beseeched God to give him a son and heir, God assured him that a son would be born, and that his name would be John. Zachariah queried how this could be the case, as his wife was barren, and he himself had grown elderly and infirm. In response, God said, "This is easy for Me, even as I have created thee aforetime when thou were nothing."[69]

At the time of Muhammad, many people venerated a range of saints, whom they believed to have divine or semi-divine qualities, and asked to bring their messages before God. The Qur'ān teaches very clearly that these beliefs have no basis in theological fact, stating: "Verily, all those whom you invoke beside God are but created beings, like yourselves: invoke them, then, and let them answer your prayer, if what you claim is true."[70] The Qur'ān is clearly stating that all humans were created by God, and must do His will. This is true of all saints, living and dead. Nor is there any need for a third party to intercede with God, Who is all-knowing and all-powerful. The Qur'ān makes it clear that Muslims should never misplace their faith in saints, nor in mere objects of any sort, including figurative images, idols,

---

68 Q. 52:35-36.
69 Q. 19:8-9.
70 Q. 7:194.

or any fetishes associated with saints or any other people who have been falsely equated with God.[71]

Elsewhere, God provides instructions to the faithful on how to challenge those who query God's existence:

> Say: Have you ever considered those beings and forces to whom you ascribe a share in God's divinity, and whom you invoke beside God? Show me what it is that they have created on earth – or do they have a share in the heavens? Have We ever vouchsafed them a divine writ on which they could rely as evidence? Nay, the evildoers hold out to one another nothing but a delusion.[72]

The Holy Book often depicts mortals as inclined to be overly hasty and to argue on all sorts of topics without knowing the facts. In order for them to allow their faith to grow, they are urged to silence the temptations that emanate from Satan and his minions. Throughout the Qur'ān, all of these issues are discussed in the context of arguments and responses.[73] They include the arguments of those who seek a universe that is eternal and ruled by fate,[74] of those who question the doctrine of bodily resurrection,[75] and those who query whether God's messenger (Muhammad) is really telling the truth, or even mock him and his message.[76] Through the Qur'ān, God argues forcefully against each of these arguments, with reasoning that continuously grows more complex and wide-ranging. All of this makes of the Qur'ān a document that is challenged, and that challenges in return.

Throughout the Qur'ān, faith is shown to be a dynamic process, rather than a static quality. The document's argumentative style shows the faithful how they can deal with their own doubts and those of others, and

---

71 Asad, 2003, 234.
72 Q. 35:40.
73 Khalidi, 2008, xvii-xix.
74 Q. 45:24.
75 Q. 17:49.
76 Q. 3:184.

teaches them how to engage with God's message on both an intellectual and an emotional level. Faith is shown to be a process of growth in the certainty and knowledge of God; a process that is facilitated by God's invitation to consider and reflect upon His message.

CHAPTER 11

COMMANDING RIGHT AND FORBIDDING WRONG

THE DUTY TO "command right and forbid wrong" is at the heart of Islam and the way of life of pious Muslim people, who do their best to follow God's law. This refers not only to the individual's need to strive at all times to do God's bidding to the absolute best of their abilities, but also their duty to prevent evil or wrong acts being committed by others, again to the best of their ability. While this is a principle reflected in broadly similar ideas in many, if not most, cultures around the world, it is most clearly enunciated and codified in Muslim thought, which springs from the teachings of the Qur'ān.[1]

Throughout the Qur'ān, we hear the Voice of God commanding us to do good, and forbidding us from wrongdoing. In terms of forbidding wrong, the term "al munkar" is used to imply which is "that which the mind or the moral sense rejects". God calls on His people to act in the spirit of justice, to be generous towards their fellow human beings, to do good, to avoid engaging in shameful and unreasonable acts, and not to allow themselves to be tempted to experience envy.[2]

The sacred obligation to correct wrong when we see it being carried out around us is also referenced in numerous other instances such as, for example, when the Qur'ān calls on the wider community of Muslims to work together as one, doing their utmost to ensure adherence to God's law

---

1 Cook, 2000, 562.
2 Q. 16:90.

for humanity: "Let there be one community of you, calling to good and commanding right and forbidding wrong; those are the prosperers."[3]

Of course, the Qur'ān is not the only sacred book to discuss matters of right and wrong; these issues are also at the heart of earlier revelations. However, the people who had been gifted God's earlier revelations (which is to say, the Jews and the Christians) had failed to be consistent with the strictures of their own scriptures, and had fallen into ways that displeased God. In sending them a new series of revelations, through the medium of His prophet, Muhammad, God was able to speak directly to the community of Muslims, assuring them that if they followed His orders, they would surely be the best representation of how His law would work on earth to bring about a true community in every sense of the word; one that worked together to serve God. In this sense, He compared faithful Muslims favourably to those peoples who had previously had the opportunity to listen to and heed His message, but who had failed to do so.[4] The Qur'ān also makes it clear that, while many Christians and Jews failed to live according to the revelations they had been sent, others did their best to fulfil God's intentions for them[5] as laid out by the earlier prophets. These were the ones who endeavoured to live well, and who believed in and acted upon His message of faith and the Day of Judgement. These, the Qur'ān states, would be rewarded in the afterlife for their virtuous lives.[6]

It is also important to note that the Torah predicts the arrival of the Prophet Muhammad,[7] placing him squarely within the Abrahamic tradition. However, the Qur'ān also makes very clear the fact that those who listen to God's message as revealed to His prophet, Muhammad, have unparalleled access to information about what God wishes of them; much more so than even the most faithful and pious Christian or Jew. They are invited to do what is right, and forbidden to do what is wrong, as explained

---

3 Q. 3:104.
4 Q. 3:110; 9:71; 9:112; 22:41.
5 Asad, 2003, 84.
6 Q. 3:113; 114; 115.
7 See especially Deuteronomy xviii, 15 and 19.

in the Qur'an. The Qur'ān states that those who followed Muhammad ("the unlettered prophet") and his teachings would have the opportunity to learn about what is right and what is wrong, and to live their lives according to this information. When they do so, they will have the opportunity to live forever with God in the afterlife.[8]

It is interesting to note that the Qur'ān emphasises the fact of Muhammad's illiteracy and, by association, his relatively humble status in Mecca as an ordinary man of business. This highlights the fact that his knowledge of the various earlier prophets who are discussed in the Qur'ān cannot be ascribed to his familiarity with the Bible, as he was unable to read.[9] Instead, it was the singular result of divine intervention. The stress on Muhammad's having been "unlettered" serves to emphasise the fact that all his knowledge of the earlier prophets and of the messages transmitted by them was due to divine inspiration alone.

In line with its frequent usage of binary oppositions, the Qur'ān refers to the Hypocrites (as stated above, those who pretended to be Muslims for purposes of expediency, but who were not really pious at all) as doing the exact opposite of those who did their best to faithfully follow God and His expectations for them. Despite their surface adherence to God's law, the Hypocrites acted against doing right, and engaged in doing wrong. As they ignored God, so would He ignore them.[10]

Cook explores the issue of whether there were cultural precedents in pre-Islamic Arabia that may have influenced the emergence of the concept of forbidding wrong and commanding right. There are hints that the idea, in the broadest general sense, may have been around before Muhammad's time. One such is found in the traditional story of Hakīm ibn Umayya, who was a member of a prominent Meccan family, and who eventually converted to Islam. Apparently, Hakīm was tasked by the tribe with the role of controlling the hot-blooded young men of the Quraysh, which is

---

8   Q. 7:157.
9   Asad, 2003, 226.
10 Q. 9:67.

described as "commanding right and forbidding wrong". However, it is not entirely clear whether the phrase and concept were already in use in those days, or whether they were appended when the story was narrated later on, when Islam had already become established in the area,[11] as seems quite likely. Certainly, this reference does not imply the well-developed, theologically-based instructions that are integral to Islamic teaching.

Further, and more convincing, evidence of the notion existing in pre-Islamic Arabia is found in the hilf al-fudul alliance, a Meccan institution that was dedicated to the matter of righting wrongs in that busy commercial hub.[12] The alliance is said to have been formed when a merchant from a particular tribe delivered goods to Mecca and sold them to a member of another tribe, who failed to make payment. When the merchant protested in public that he had not received his due, the matter drew such attention that four or five Meccan clans came together in alliance, swearing that:

> If anyone is wronged in Mecca, we will all take his part against the wrongdoer until we recover what is due to him by the one who wronged him, whether he is noble or humble, one of us or not.[13]

It is said that, in this period, before he started to receive revelations, Muhammad himself was present when the alliance was formed;[14] after all, he was one of the many local businessmen for whom it would have been in their interest to establish a functioning system of justice and retribution. For a city whose economy was based on commerce, a good reputation for ethical dealings would have been essential. From this point on, the alliance was in place to intervene whenever someone was short-changed or otherwise mistreated in Mecca. Yet this concept of righting wrongs where possible does not go nearly as far as that discussed in the Qur'ān. It seems

---

11 Al-Kalbi, 1986, 407.
12 Crone, 1987, 143f.
13 ibn Habib, cited in Cook, 2000, 565.
14 Cook, 2000, 565.

to have applied to the collective, as in the case of the alliance, but not to the individual, and is purely concerned with pragmatic affairs of business and everyday interactions.

Another potential source of information about pre-Islamic views of right and wrong is the rich tradition of poetry. As discussed elsewhere, poets were extremely important, influential people in Arabian society, with its rich oratorical language, nuanced turn of phrase, and love of eloquence. These were highly respected, extremely influential, men who typically belonged to the higher social classes and had access to the echelons of power. Arabian poetry covers many topics, from the concrete to the abstract and everything in between, and indeed the concepts of "right" and "wrong" are addressed in the poetic tradition, appearing in juxtaposition in works by a wide range of poets, including Zuhayr Abi Sulma, 'Urwa ibn al-Ward and Nābigha al-Dhubyani.[15] There is a reference, in al-Dhubyani's verse, to "taking action against a wrong", which appears to predate the Islamic period, and suggests that the notion of intervening to "fix" a bad situation was already present in the local culture.[16]

We have already discussed the Qur'ān's ability to take contemporary traditions and mores to make its message more accessible to those who heard it. For example, we can point to its use of the character Luqman, who was a legendary figure embedded in ancient Arabian tradition, as the prototypical sage, disdaining worldly honour or benefit and striving for inner perfection. Even long before the advent of Islam, the character of Luqman had become a focal point of innumerable legends, stories, and parables that expressed wisdom and spiritual maturity. For this reason, we find instances in which the Qur'ān utilises this pre-extant tradition to express some of its teachings on how people should behave. Luqman is depicted as saying, for example:

---

15 Cook, 2000, 567.
16 Al Dhubyani (ed. S Faysal), 1968, 53.

> O my dear son! Be constant in prayer, and enjoin the doing of what is right and forbid the doing of what is wrong, and bear in patience whatever (ill) may befall thee: this, behold, is something to set one's heart upon![17]

However, despite the clear presence of a concept of right and wrong in pre-Islamic Arabia, and some references to broadly similar concepts in historical and poetical sources, we can assert that the terms "commanding right" and "forbidding wrong" originate in the revelations received by Muhammad, along with a series of instructions about how these two directions from God can best be carried out. As well as being present in the Qur'ān, from this point on these themes are also found in Arabian literature generally, including literature of primarily secular content.

Of course, the concepts of right and wrong are also present and discussed in the other books of revelation, and there are some parallels with the way in which these qualities were conceived of and discussed in Islam, which are worth mentioning in the interest of providing a broader context. In Leviticus, for example, we read "you shall reprove your neighbour or you will incur guilt yourself",[18] referring to the need to correct other people when they have clearly done something wrong. There are also various instances in which people are shown in both scripture and rabbinical literature[19] as taking actions to prevent others' wrongdoing, although there does not appear to be consensus on the matter of how far someone should go to influence the behaviour of another person in such circumstances:

> One rabbi declined to rebuke members of the household… on the grounds that they would not accept it from him; another held that he should rebuke them notwithstanding.[20]

---

17 Q. 31:17.
18 Leviticus 19:17.
19 For example the Babylonian Talmud.
20 Cook, 2000, 570.

That there was a duty in Judaism to engage in actions or words intended to cause someone else to desist from doing something wrong is clear, even if the details are sometimes vague and there is a general lack of consensus about the precise situations wherein such a ruling might apply. There is a description of the destruction of Jerusalem because of its inhabitants' failure to reprove each other when they did something wrong.[21] Failure to protest against another's wrong-doing can lead to becoming responsible for it, according to some Jewish sources, and even run the risk of divine punishment for not taking action.[22] Of course, taking action against others' wrongdoing does not guarantee that they will stop doing what they should not, but God knows and sees all, and will be aware when earnest attempts have at least been made to cause the offending actions to cease.[23]

According to Cook, there are no direct parallels in Christian thinking until at least the thirteenth century (and therefore long after Muhammad's revelations and the beginning of Islam, ruling out any notion that contemporary Christian thinking influenced Islamic theology in this respect). Cook cites Thomas Aquinas, the Italian friar, philosopher and theologian, as providing a good overview of Christian thought on this topic.[24] In those late medieval days, Christian duties included admonishing sinners for their own sake, even when the admonisher is a social inferior. Even a fellow sinner can admonish a wrong-doer, so long as he does so without arrogance, and in general it is considered better to carry out these admonishments in private before proceeding to a public airing of the wrongs in question.[25] If someone is going to reform and start doing things as God has instructed, what is the point of humiliating him without giving him a chance? Aquinas divides admonishments into two key types; fraternal correction, in which someone's wrongdoing is pointed out to him for his own good, and what is essentially juridical correction, which is carried out for the

---

21 Babylonian Talmud, Ketubbet, 105b, 19.
22 Neusner et al, 1982, 11;183.
23 Babylonian Talmud, Shabbat, f 55a :23.
24 Cook, 2000, 574.
25 Aquinas, 1964, 274-205.

good of society as a whole.[26] While there are some parallels with the issue of righting wrongs as discussed in the Qur'ān, it is important to remember that Aquinas was writing many, many centuries after Muhammad received his revelations. Moreover, there are also some important differences between Christian and Islamic thought on this matter. Aquinas labours over the issue of whether correcting someone is an act of justice or charity (opting for charity) and also about the matter of whether statements should be taken from witnesses before any public denunciation takes place. Neither concept is discussed in the Qur'ān at all.[27]

As the Jewish and Christian scriptures were also revealed to the various prophets by the one true God, it is unsurprising to find traces of the concepts covered in the Qur'ān in the earlier books of revelation. However, it seems undeniable that the concepts of "commanding" and forbidding" right and wrong respectively were not present in Arabian culture prior to the birth of Islam, and that these key directions from God through the medium of His prophet Muhammad represent an important innovation to the custom and practice of the pagan Arabs and the monotheistic Jews and Christians alike, and are fundamental to Islamic practice now, as they were in the early days of revelation. Moreover, Islamic doctrine teaches that the faithful should go much farther than is proposed in either the Judaic or the Christian scriptures towards righting wrongs, including wrongs committed by others. Where Christians, for example, seem to be taught that there is often little point in trying to correct wrongs being carried out by a stranger, because there is no chance of a good outcome, and nor is there an absolute obligation for someone to correct his or her social superior, Islamic teaching comes to no such conclusion; in fact, quite the reverse.[28]

Some broadly comparable ideas about the obligation to correct wrong where we see it can also be seen in a variety of non-Abrahamic religions,

---

26 Cook, 2000, 577.
27 Cook, 2000, 576.
28 Cook, 2000, 577.

including Hinduism and Buddhism,[29] but these have no direct bearing on the development of Islam, and a full discussion of this matter is beyond the scope of this chapter. In any case, comparisons even between the three Abrahamic religions reveal significant differences in this area, so we must recognise that thinking in this area is central to Islam in a way that it simply is not in the case of other major faiths.

The Qur'ān is unique among the various books of revelation in providing perfectly clear information on who is being called upon to follow God's instructions, how they should do so, and why. Quite simply, the Qur'ān states that the faithful should heed God's word because He, in all His infinite wisdom, has sent information via His prophet Muhammad on His will for humankind. In the Qur'ān, God refers to the Ummah,[30] the world-wide community of Muslims or true believers, and to "those who believe".[31] From this we can conclude that God is instructing that His word on doing right and forbidding wrong should be read as applying equally to all Muslims, everywhere. Beyond the Qur'ān, this simple ruling is backed up by a wealth of tradition.[32] Over the years, scholars have debated a range of topics around this matter, particularly that of whether God's ruling on the matter of right or wrong should be followed "only" because it is a ruling from Him, received as a revelation by His prophet Muhammad, or also because adopting an altruistic outlook also simply makes pragmatic good sense.[33]

Alongside the teachings of the Qur'ān, there are many prophetic traditions that deal with the matter of right and wrong. Here, we see that there are various ways in which to respond appropriately to wrong-doing, and that they are a hierarchy of deed, word, and thought. The term "munkar" is used both in Qur'ānic teaching, and in Islamic tradition. In tradition,

---

29 Cook, 2000, 579-81.
30 Q. 3:104.
31 Q. 3:102.
32 Cook, 2003, 12.
33 Cook, 2003, 12.

the term "ghayyara" is juxtaposed, implying the ability to "put right". This term, however, has both positive and negative implications in the Qur'ān.[34]

Having accepted why the faithful should heed God's word on the matter under discussion, we move to the matter of precisely who should follow this ruling. Should *everyone* command right and forbid wrong, or does this apply only to a chosen few? The answer is that all faithful Muslims, and only they, can and should forbid wrong and command right, as these are the people who have listened to God's message for humanity and who know, because they have accepted His revelations, what exactly is meant by "right" and "wrong". Someone who does not believe in God or listen to His orders is simply not in a position to correct others, least of all a faithful Muslim. While Muslims can and do on occasion fail to follow God's rulings, the only person who is in a position to correct them is another Muslim.[35]

Within the complexity of society, the nature of the relationships between people invariably have an impact here. In Arabian society at the time of revelation, various categories of people, including women, slaves and children, lived under the authority of adult males. In this context, there was some uncertainty among scholars as to how God's rulings on forbidding wrong and commanding right should apply. Could people in these categories correct those in a position of authority over them, or was that inappropriate? While the scholars debated this matter, the Qur'ān does provide teaching. Women can and should engage in following God's law on this matter,[36] although the Qur'ān also states that they find their fulfilment and ultimate mission in the home,[37] and clearly there were situations in which a woman would simply never be in a situation to forbid wrong; for example, a woman could not forbid a gathering of men "of doubtful character" to do wrong, as for her to be in their company would itself

---

34 Q. 13:11.
35 Cook, 2003, 13.
36 Q. 9:71.
37 Q. 33:33.

be contrary to God's law.[38] The issue of women's role in this matter has been much debated by Muslim scholars throughout history and within the context of a range of traditions.[39]

In Muhammad's own voice, we also hear the following instructions on how one should address a situation of wrong-doing in one's midst:

> Whoever sees a wrong and is able to put it right with his hand, let him do so; if he can't, then with his tongue; if he can't, then with his heart, and this is the bare minimum of faith.[40]

What does this much-studied teaching mean? "With the tongue," clearly implies a verbal interaction – perhaps a rebuke, advice that the person in question should cease to engage in a particular behaviour, or some sort of a reproof. Of course, the word "reproof" can include a wide range of tones of voice and degrees of assertiveness, from a mild comment to a fierce tirade! Over the years, different thinkers on this ruling have proposed varying interpretations, with some maintaining that the political authorities should correct "with the hand", scholars "with the tongue", and ordinary people "with the heart";[41] a rather elitist view.

One thorny issue that has been much discussed by scholars is that of whether sinners should be excluded from the ruling that they should forbid wrong in others. Someone who does not follow God's law surely does not have the moral authority to correct others – but why should they be relieved of the responsibility?[42] In fact, the sinner has a two-fold responsibility; first, to address his own behaviour and misdeeds and, secondly, to forbid the wrong-doing of others.

---

38 Cook, 2003, 16.
39 Cook, 2003, 14-15.
40 Cook, 2003, 12. Note that these words, while attributed to the Prophet, do not appear in the Qur'ān and are a matter of tradition.
41 Cook, 2003, 17.
42 Cook, 2003, 19.

Another tricky matter is that of who is responsible for forbidding wrong when there are many witnesses. Are all equally responsible, or are some people more responsible than others? If one person speaks out, but nobody else does, are all the others guilty of a dereliction of duty? Most scholars agree that there is such a thing as a collective duty, when it is the responsibility of the people to come together to right a wrong up to and including, at times, the necessity to engage in war. When the wrong has clearly been righted, even if by the action of only some members of the collective, there is no further need to take measures.[43] Of course, there are many instances in which wrongdoing is observed by just one person. In these cases, while correcting it is the onus of whomever witnesses it, it becomes a matter for the individual.

The Islamic scholar Ghazzali proposes three basic degrees in terms of how those who are doing wrong should be corrected "with the tongue": If someone is committing a wrong-doing unwittingly because they don't know what they are doing, they should be addressed gently, and not humiliated because, while they need to be corrected, it is not their fault that they have done something wrong through sheer ignorance. This might apply to someone new to Islam, or perhaps someone who has not had the advantage of a full education, and unknowingly does something they should not. If someone knows that they are doing something wrong, but they are not doing so with malice, they should be exhorted to behave otherwise in a polite fashion and given the opportunity to mend their ways. If someone knows full well that they are doing something wrong and continues to do so brazenly and in the face of gentle correction, their chastiser can feel free to use harsh language.[44] Frequently, all that is necessary is a gentle rebuke and there is no need to escalate any further. Often, there is much to be said for rebuking a wrongdoing in a private, discreet way. A traditional proverb maintains that, "Whoever admonishes his brother in private graces him;

---

43 Cook, 2003, 19.
44 Cook, 2003, 28.

whoever does so in public disgraces him."[45] It should be remembered that the correction is for the benefit of the person who is doing wrong, and not for the purpose of displaying the piety of the person who is carrying out the correction.

"With the hand" refers to taking physical action, but of course it should not be assumed that this implies violence, or that resorting to violence before all other means have been employed is ever desirable. For example, if someone is drinking wine, which is forbidden to Muslims, their glass could be taken from them, emptied or destroyed, or if someone is in a place where they are not supposed to be, they could be physically removed from it. There may be cases when violence is necessary to stop a wrongdoing from taking place, but this should be preceded by words along the lines of, "If you do not stop what you are doing, I may have to use force," so as to give the person in question the opportunity to think about their actions and take remedial steps before things escalate. In the worst of cases, and only when all other actions fail, the person who is forbidding wrong may need to enlist the help of others to carry out whatever deeds are necessary to stop the action from taking place.[46] Physical force, when used, should not be carried out in a hot-headed way, and care must be taken to prevent it spilling over into public disarray, and that it should take place within the confines of the law in the relevant area.[47] Most often, "with the hand" can refer not to violence against offending persons, but to the physical destruction of objects that might be occasions of sin, such as containers full of alcohol, musical instruments intended for entertainment at a party that will not be held according to the edicts of Islam, and so forth. Islamic scholars do not always agree on the degree to which acting with the hand should escalate. While some feel that there are situations in which putting together a group of armed men to forbid wrong is permissible, others do not. A majority, however, believe that such drastic action should only be

---

45 Cook, 2003, 29.
46 Cook, 2003, 29-30.
47 Cook, 2003, 30.

taken in extreme cases, and even then only with the express intervention of a king or other ruler.[48]

"With the heart," implies a private action, known only to the individual himself and to God; in fact, some translations of the relevant Arabic phrase state it as "*In* the heart," which further emphasises the private nature of the deed in question.[49] This applies when we witness an act that we know to be wrong, but are powerless to do anything to prevent. Islamic scholars have suggested that there is also the implication of making one's disapproval apparent; that by turning away from the person who is committing the inappropriate act and showing them how we feel about it, we may be able to influence them to act in a different way.[50] Others have suggested that there are various ways in which we can employ the heart in forbidding wrong; purely by means of thought, by openly expressing disapproval, and by engaging in ostracising and marginalising the offending individual.[51] Clearly, this category can apply to people in many categories who are not in a position to forbid wrongdoing otherwise. Women, for example, rarely have the power or opportunity to correct wrongdoing in a physical way, and there are also many instances in which to do so would be not just dangerous for them, but also problematic in a moral sense, as it would involve them putting themselves into situations that are themselves sinful or potentially sinful. Forbidding in the heart can also imply the use of subtle cues such as facial expression to indicate to wrongdoers one's disapproval of their actions.[52]

As stated above, the Qur'ān recognises that diverse categories of people should be seen differently. Competent adults, for example, should always be considered to "own" their behaviour and are thus culpable when they do wrong and must be corrected. But what of the case of incompetent adults, such as the mentally ill, or children, who do not possess sufficient maturity

---

48 Cook, 2003, 33.
49 Cook, 2003, 35.
50 Cook, 2003, 36-7.
51 Cook, 2003, 37.
52 Cook, 2003, 36.

to know that what they are doing is wrong? Understanding that such people are not always in a position to make judgements on their own does not imply that they should not be corrected. If a child or someone living with mental illness drinks alcohol or fails to observe the rules on fasting and prayer, for example, they should certainly be corrected. However, because they are not able to understand the full ramifications of their behaviour, their wrongdoing should be seen as simply that, and not a sin in the eyes of God, Who is merciful. These loving corrections do not fall under the edict of forbidding wrong.[53]

Over the years, there has been much debate over precisely what the Qur'ān means when it orders us to command right and forbid wrong. The words seem clear enough, but what exact behaviours are considered to be covered? Some scholars have maintained that to "command right" simply means that one should believe in God, His unique nature, and the message of His prophet, Muhammad, and that to "forbid wrong" applies merely to forbidding the opposite, such as polytheism. However, most experts take a wider view.[54] Moreover, while the teachings of the Qur'ān are clear and unequivocal, historically some Muslim communities have had slightly different rulings on matters such as chess-playing and some dietary restrictions. As these are not matters that are mentioned in the Qur'ān, it is best to observe local norms. However, this also raises an interesting question. While some acts are obligatory, or forbidden, others are merely desirable or disapproved of, begging the question of whether commanding right and forbidding wrong also applies to these matters. Most scholars feel that, while supporting optimum behaviour and making disapproval of lesser behaviour is ideal, this does not fall under the edict that all Muslims should command right and forbid wrong.[55]

Another complex issue is that of when a wrong is committed. Clearly, the principal purpose of the ruling that Muslims must strive at all times to

---

53 Cook, 2003, 21.
54 Cook, 2003, 22.
55 Cook, 2003, 23.

forbid wrong is to prevent wrong-doing from occurring in the first place. But what happens when someone has already done something wrong? There is, of course, no longer any obligation on anyone to forbid it, as it is too late. In many cases, the wrongdoing will be a matter that can be punished according to state law (say, for example, in the case of an assault or murder). Conversely, when a wrong has not yet been committed, but it is clear from someone's behaviour that one is being planned (let's say that a young man buys alcohol at a local shop, or boasts about planning to go out and assault someone later on), it is incumbent on any good Muslim to take steps to prevent the misdeed from occurring.[56]

As a guide to living for all Muslims, which it is among other things, the Qur'ān addresses many issues of right and wrong; of good moral living and how to follow God's law while also living in the world of men. For example, God addresses the believers by saying: "Be a community that calls for what is good, urges what is right, and forbids what is wrong: those who do this are the successful ones."[57] He urges them to ensure that they do not behave like those who have ceased to live like a community, and have adopted views at odds with the message sent to them via His prophet Muhammad, and warns that if they do, inevitably they will suffer dreadfully.[58] The latter refers to the followers of the Bible, who are divided into "Jews" and "Christians" despite the fact that their beliefs have a common source and are based on the same spiritual truths. In this, they can be seen as having departed from the fundamental religious principles that they once shared in their entirety, and they have gone different ways with respect to doctrine and ethics.

While God enjoins us to do good, the Qur'ān also warns us that Satan is ever-present, and that he urges us to follow him and to commit evil acts. Those who succumb to Satan's temptations will invariably find themselves

---

56   Cook, 2003, 24.
57   Q. 3:104.
58   Q. 3:105.

doing dreadful things. Only by listening to God can the faithful attain and grow in purity.[59]

How far are Muslims expected to go when it comes to taking actions to prevent or correct the wrongdoing of others? The answer is that they are considered to have an obligation to do all they can, up to and including putting their own lives at risk.[60] This includes the obligation to stand up to unjust rulers, using violence if there is no other recourse and, when all else fails, to the idea of a holy war.[61] Judaism and Christianity simply do not teach their adherents about what they should do if they find themselves treated unjustly by a ruler.

Those who are not true to Islam are not, of course, expected to following this teaching. As they have no faith to uphold, they are not in a position to take action to protect it. Some Islamic scholars have even gone so far as to suggest that there is no sense in someone who does not believe in God and Islam reprimanding even the execrable behaviour of a Muslim. According to this line of thought, while a Muslim is committing wrong when he commits adultery, or steals, or whatever, the non-Muslim is committing a graver wrong by failing to recognise God's message to the world.[62] It should be noted that this way of thinking is properly seen as a relic of the past. Today, in most societies Muslims and non-Muslims live peacefully side-by-side. This means that the responsibility of commanding right and forbidding wrong rests on everyone's shoulders, regardless of their background or faith.

In the past, when Muslim societies still included slaves. and adult women tended to have secluded lives under the authority of their husbands or, if they were unmarried or widowed, other adult males in their family, they were nonetheless considered to be completely obliged to correct wrongdoing whenever they encountered it, notwithstanding their relatively

---

59 Q. 24:21.
60 Crollius, 1978, 281.
61 Cook, 2000, 582.
62 Cook, 2003, 13.

unempowered position in society at the time. Among Islamic scholars, views on women's role in this area have not always been very consistent, with some feeling that women's position in the home, as wives and mothers, and the need for them to be modest, were not compatible with their taking action in the area of correcting wrongs.[63] While this view has not historically been held by all Islamic scholars, we can take a generally egalitarian view on this matter as the one that has come closest to approaching consensus. Of women's role in this area, God's message in the Qur'ān is very clear when He says: "... and the believers, the men and women, are friends of one another. They command right and forbid wrong."[64]

By and large, the rulings about forbidding wrong and commanding right are taken to apply to all adult Muslims.[65] These laws apply even within families; adult sons and daughters should chastise their parents if needs must, although the nature of the filial relationship will clearly have an impact on the form that this chastisement takes, with similar implications when, for instance, a student chastises his teacher, or a citizen his ruler.[66] Throughout much of history, it appears that most of the overt correction of wrong doing was in fact carried out by Islamic scholars themselves.

The Islamic teachings about commanding right and forbidding wrong are revolutionary in a number of respects. For one, these teachings are a great "leveller" and show no regard for social standing or hierarchy. In the eyes of God, all Muslims are equal, so when a person of relatively lower social standing, or another person who might usually be seen as inhabiting a position of weakness, sees a wrong being committed by another, he or she is just as obliged (or empowered) to do whatever they can to correct the wrong as would be someone with much more obvious access to power and authority. Exceptions to this ruling, as stated above, include children and the mentally unbalanced, who are not considered to have sufficient

---

63 Cook, 2003, 14-15.
64 Q. 9:71.
65 Cook, 2003, 16.
66 Cook, 2003, 17.

maturity to make a considered judgement on the matter of what is right and what is wrong. This is not to suggest that Muslim societies have invariably been bastions of social equality (at various times and in various places, Muslim communities have actually been intensely hierarchical), but that *before the eyes of God* all Muslims are equal and have an equal right and duty to do whatever they can to correct the wrongs and injustices that they see being carried out around them.[67]

---

67 Marlowe, 1997, 6-10.

CHAPTER 12

THE QUR'ĀNIC CONCEPT OF JUSTICE

"And when you voice an opinion, be just, even though it be [against] one near of kin".[1]

IN ALL SOCIETIES around the world, there is (understandably) intense interest in the issue of what society owes to each of its citizens. People whose experience of life is that they feel themselves to be at the bottom of the social pile often speak out about what they believe to be injustice directed towards them, while many more fortunate individuals also believe that society should be fair, and that due consideration needs to be given to those who appear to be weaker and more vulnerable. However, while that might sound all very well, it is actually very difficult to reach consensus on the matter of what fairness and justice actually are, in real and practical terms. This is where things start to become much more complicated. Is it "fair" to take from the rich to give to the poor? Is it "fair" to accept that some people work much harder than others? Philosophers, social scientists and more have all battled with the idea of justice, and even within cultures and schools of thought there is often a great deal of disagreement. Today, in our complex and interconnected world, every society has the opportunity to learn from every other about how different issues can be dealt with fairly,

---

1 Q. 6:152.

from both a social and a legal point of view. The Qur'ān, which deals at length with these issues, provides all the answers we need.

Although all cultures develop their own individual "scales of justice", each of which is derived from the local society and by the exertion of that society's legal system, it is fascinating to observe that they all have a great deal in common. In this context, when someone makes assertions about what they feel to be their due and their right, this needs to be measured against the legal system. In many societies God (or in the case of non-monotheistic societies, whatever concept of the supernatural applies there) is invoked as the divine authority from Whom all justice ultimately derives.

The great monotheistic traditions of Judaism, Christianity and Islam all subscribe strongly to the view that true justice comes from God, and only God, and is revealed to humankind via the revelations received by His prophets. As God's revelations are the ultimate Truth, they are equally applicable to everyone, and must be at the heart of any justice or legal system that is permitted to develop. This system was referred to by the great philosopher Aristotle as "natural justice", and after Aristotle the concepts of natural and divine justice were often conflated.[2]

Christian and Islamic scholars generally agree that justice derives ultimately from God, and have developed systems of justice predicated around the will of God and the ultimate destiny of humankind. Thomas Aquinas referred to this notion as the "Eternal law" and, earlier, Muslim scholars designated this Eternal Law with the name Shari'a, which refers to a system of justice derived from God and rooted in the Qur'ān.

Over the years since Muhammad received the Qur'ān as a series of revelations, Islamic scholars have debated long and hard about Shari'a; what it implies, how far and where it should extend, and how Muslims can strive towards establishing Shari'a law here on earth.[3] Whereas in some cultures religion and justice are seen as inhabiting completely different realms, even as mutually exclusive, for Muslims religion and justice are inextricably in-

---

2 Khadduri, 1983, iii-xiv.
3 Khadduri, 1984, 1-2.

terlinked and both are considered elements of God's will for humanity.[4] In Muslim communities, religion and justice come together to form the law, and the law is enforced to create a just and equitable society in which people can live together in a harmonious fashion.

Under Shari'a, the primary source of law comes from Revelation – in other words, from God's message as received by His prophet Muhammad, and recorded in the Qur'ān – and the secondary source is found in what are referred to as "derivative sources," including matters on which Islamic scholars are in consensus.[5] These elements come together to form the substance of the law, which is to say, the overarching, guiding principles that allow us to understand what the law is, and how it should be interpreted.

Substantial law includes issues of what is permissible and what is forbidden; both topics on which the Qur'ān has much to say. God's law states what we should do and what we should not do, with the underlying assumption that permitted things (known as halal) are just, and forbidden (haram) are unjust, because our merciful God would not expect us to do unjust things.[6] God's law as revealed in the Qur'ān is designed for the greater good of humanity in general, and recognises that human beings, in all their frailty and with all their manifold shortcomings, are not always able to make the best decision for themselves in terms of understanding what is best for them.[7]

While individual rights are clearly important, in Shari'a law the rights of the individual are subservient to the rights of the collective. In other words, individual rights can be protected so long as they do not infringe on the general good of society.[8] For example, Shari'a law recognises the right of the individual to own property, such as land, so long as this goes hand in hand with a series of factors intended to facilitate the better functioning

---

4 Khadduri, 1984, 135.
5 Khadduri, 1984, 136.
6 Q. 16:116.
7 Q. 2:216.
8 Khadduri, 1984, 139.

of society, such as a tax to raise funds for the poor, and various legal undertakings intended to ensure a just use of property.[9]

The Qur'ān also contains many provisions about the general rules for living well on an individual level. The Arabian society into which Muhammad had been born was often very difficult and dog-eat-dog in its approach to life, and it had many aspects that were not pleasing to God. Although some of the cornerstones of Arabian society, such as hospitality and honour, were retained, Islam introduced values including kindness, justice and mercy which, over time, came to dominate over the earlier core values.[10]

The Qur'ān provides detailed instruction on the rules governing political law, which refers to law as it is dictated and administered by a sovereign leader. Leaders, like everyone else, are frail and subjective human beings who are in need of guidance from a Higher authority. It is in the great interest of society to have a clear set of rules and principles that will help them to administer the law in accordance with the greater good of society and with God's intentions for humanity.

Muslims believe that political law should derive ultimately from God's divine law, revealed primarily in the Qur'ān and to some extent in the Prophet's traditions. Thus, matters of political justice come from God, and are discussed and administered by His servants on earth in the form of the Imams who succeeded Muhammad. All of God's people are clearly instructed to follow the ruling of His representatives on earth.[11] The Qur'ān states (among other verses): "… obey God and obey the Apostle and those in authority among you; if you quarrel about anything, refer it to God and His apostle."[12]

Following from the substance of the law is the procedure of the law. In other words, this aspect of Shari'a is all about how the law should be

---

9 Khadduri, 1984, 141.
10 Khadduri, 1984, 141.
11 Khadduri, 1984, 14.
12 Q. 4:59; Q. 42:38.

applied and imposed, and how those who break the law should be dealt with. Procedure allows for a consistent and fair application of the law, regardless of individual or collective circumstances and mitigating factors.

As the Qur'ān is a complete guide not just to establishing a good relationship with God, but to living on earth in all its aspects, a careful reading of the Qur'ān reveals all we need to know about God's intentions for us. The Qur'ān is the direct word of God, and Muslims also find a great deal of information about Muhammad's teachings in those aspects that are related in his own words, rather than God's. These teachings, which were originally referred to as the Sunnah, are now known as the "Hadith," which means the "Prophet's tradition". However, Muhammad died before the formation of a political system had been completely established. After his death, the Muslim community came together to establish a system and a successor (in leadership) by means of consensus. A Caliph was duly enthroned, creating a precedent in terms of the future source of political justice.[13]

After the very early Islamic period, the law developed under various Caliphs (considered to be political and religious successors of Muhammad), who made decisions based on what was for the general good of society. In this way precedents were gradually established, and a formal legal system gradually developed. An early legal expert, Mālik, set the precedent for using the greater good of the people as a foundation for law, and a later scholar, Najm al-Dīn al-Tawfi, even argued that when something that would serve the general good was in conflict with direct teaching from the Qur'ān, it should nonetheless be done, because the general good of humanity is the Qur'ān's ultimate goal.[14]

At this point in Muslim history, a number of schisms emerged, two of which, the Sunnī and the Shī'ī, agreed that Imams were necessary; that they should come from the same tribe as Muhammad (the Quraysh) and understand the Will of God; and that they should have certain key

---

13   Khadduri, 1984, 15.
14   Khadduri, 1984, 137-8.

qualities that made them suitable for a leadership position.[15] These guidelines were generally accepted, but the Sunnī and the Shī'ī came to disagree on the point of tribal membership; the Sunnī maintained that it was merely necessary for an Imam to come from the wider tribal group, while the Shī'ī maintained that the first Imam, Alī, had left the position to his direct descendants. Thereafter there was a tendency for doctrinal differences between the two groups to widen and, ultimately, become irreconcilable.[16] For the Sunnī, the consensus of the community in deciding who would take on the mantel of leadership was fundamental, whereas for the Shī'ī, the matter of leadership was predestined by birth. Sunnī Imams are also required to consult with scholars before making their rulings.[17]

As Islam grew in geographical scope, and with the passage of time, Islamic scholars (beginning with al-Kindi) came into contact with the work of other great philosophers, including those from the Greek schools of thought.[18] Muslim thinkers sought to introduce some of the elements of Greek philosophy in terms of making the Qur'ān's teachings easier to understand and more accessible. Prior to al-Kindi's time, Muslim scholars had generally considered it unacceptable to apply the methods of the Greek philosophers to Islamic thinking. Al-Kindi believed that there was no conflict at all between Reason and Revelation, and that philosophical thought could help the believer to better understand the awesome truth of the one God. The implications for the justice system lie in al-Kindi's view that truth could be divided into two categories; the ultimate truth of God, and the practical truth, which lies in applying the former to ordinary situations, or natural justice. The qualities of natural justice can be understood as "wisdom, justice, temperance and fortitude".[19]

Al-Kindi's thinking proposes that natural justice is an innate quality that leads us to do the right thing in diverse situations, with practical

---

15 Khadduri, 1984, 16.
16 Khadduri, 1984, 16-17.
17 Khadduri, 1984, 19.
18 Khadduri, 1984, 78-9.
19 Khadduri, 1984, 81.

justice, inspired by Reason, providing a means to apply it. While innate, justice is also a quality that we can foster in ourselves. In this way, it can become not just a fundamental quality, but a means of balancing a range of other virtues. Al-Kindi did not discuss the matter of "rational justice", which Islamic thinking sees as reaching its ideal form as a justice system based in God.[20] This matter was discussed at length by later scholars, including al-Fārābī and ibn Rushd.

Ultimately, it is from God that all matters of justice and the law derive, but the Qur'ān makes it clear that human beings have the capacity to understand the difference between what is just and what is not.[21] Ibn Rushd discusses the thorny issue of why some people do dreadful things. For what reason does God create some people with the capacity to do evil? He concludes that this is an element of Divine wisdom.[22] Most people are born with the inherent capacity to do and be good, but some also have the capacity to be evil. Without this means of contrast, how would we recognise good in the first place? This idea is supported by the Qur'ān, which states in the voice of God addressing the angels:

> They (the angels) said: Wait, wilt though set therein one who will do corruption there, and shed blood, while we proclaim Thee praise and call Thee holy?
> He (God) said: Assuredly I know that you know not.[23]

People have sometimes found it hard to accept that God, who is One and Unique, created evil. It is important to understand that He created evil for the sake of good, for without means of comparison, how would we understand good? Justice flows from humans' natural desire to see good and to experience good for themselves and in their societies. Whereas God

---

20 Khadduri, 1984, 95.
21 Q. 23:78; 90:8-10.
22 Khadduri, 1984, 95.
23 Q. 2:28.

is inherently, naturally just, human beings must see justice performed, and engage with it, for the sake of humanity itself. This occurs best within the context of human beings as the rational, engaged citizens of the state in which they live, and when that state is properly run.[24]

In Islamic teaching on matter of justice, various different words are used to describe the concept, each of which has its own nuances. The most common word is "'adl", followed by "qist," "wasat", "istiqama", and "mizan" (not necessarily in this order). The word "'adl", which comes from the verb "'adala", has a number of implications: to straighten up; to deflect from a wrong path to a right one; to be equivalent or equal to something; to balance or weigh, or to be balanced.[25] Both "'adl" and "jawr" imply the dual concepts of right and wrong in the religious and moral sense.

The concept of justice summed up in the word 'adl is described in various locations in the Qur'ān, including the following verses:

> Behold, God enjoins justice, and the doing of good, and generosity towards (one's) fellow-men, and He forbids all that is shameful and all that runs counter to reason, as well as envy, and He exhorts you, so that you might bear (all this) in mind.[26]
>
> Behold, God bids you to deliver all that you have been entrusted with unto those who are entitled thereto, and whenever you judge between people, to judge with justice. Verily most excellent is what God exhort you to do: verily, God is all-hearing, all-seeing.[27]

A fundamental principal of Qur'ānic justice is the idea of equality; that all Muslims (of both genders) are equal in the eyes of God,[28] regardless of whatever hierarchical and social divisions there are in society. In accordance

---

24 Khadduri, 1984, 96-7.
25 Manzur, 1997, 275.
26 Q. 16:90.
27 Q. 4:58.
28 Q. 49:11.

with this basic precept, all Muslims are called by God to consider this principle of equality.

In legal terms, the Qur'ān is very clear in stating that this equality needs to be borne in mind in every instance of assessing the motives, outlook, and actions of others. The term "amanat", which means "trust", is used to imply anything that we have been tasked with, be it physical or moral; Muslims have been entrusted with certain truths, given to them by God in the form of the Qur'ān, and these truths must be held as sacred, not just in our own lifetimes, but as precious heirlooms that should be passed on to all humanity, as God has intended. God orders Muslims to uphold justice at all times and to be truthful in all their dealings, even if doing so has difficult repercussions for themselves, their families and their people. Regardless of whether someone is rich or poor, God's truth matters more than anything they say. We cannot allow someone's wealth to prejudice us towards or against him and, similarly, the compassion we feel for another's poverty must not dissuade us from sticking to the truth. We must never let our own wishes cause us to ignore justice and truth. After all, God knows all that we do.[29] Similarly, in our devotion to God and the pursuit of His truth, we must never allow our personal negative feelings towards someone to cause us to swerve from the truth. By upholding justice at all times, we can be as close to God as possible.[30]

Qur'ānic teaching on justice is also relevant when it comes to helping Muslims to live their personal lives in accordance with the Will of God. For example, while Islam provides for men to marry two or several women under certain circumstances (as Muhammad himself did), it also stresses that any man who is concerned that he might not be able to treat his wives in a perfectly equitable way should marry only one, as to risk being less than fair is to risk angering God.[31] Similarly, if someone is in debt to us, we

---

29 Q. 4:135.
30 Q. 5:8.
31 Q. 4:3.

should watch over his interests in a fair and equitable manner, by allowing the debtor (who is the weaker party to the transaction by definition) to lead the way in formulating the agreement.[32]

God urges His people to "give full measure and weight, with equity" in everything they do, and also stresses that God does not give anyone more than he can deal with. He expects each and every one to stick to the path of justice, even when that has negative implications for those close to them, and to consistently bear their relationship with God in mind.[33]

Of course, God knows that human beings are imperfect. Realistically, as naturally subjective beings, none of us can be completely impartial in all our interactions with everyone else; all God asks is that we do our absolute best to be as fair and impartial as we possibly can.[34] Many verses in the Qur'ān enjoin us to this task. Addressing the prophet David, the Qur'ān states that he should "judge then, between men with justice, and do not follow vain desire, lest it lead thee astray from the path of God" and warns that anyone who deviates from the path of justice will experience a terrible punishment on the Day of Judgement.[35] All the faithful must believe in the revelations God has sent down to them, and to His teaching on justice.[36]

Throughout the Qur'ān God urges justice and tolerance. He recognises that there will be times when different groups have conflicting views, and encourages Muslims to recognise that God is the sustainer of them all.[37] When two groups of Muslims reach a stage of conflict, He urges that peace should be made between them, but that if one group continues to treat the other badly, that right-thinking people should fight against them until they return to God's command for them. At that point, despite all

---

32 Q. 2:282.
33 Q. 6:152.
34 Asad, 2003, 199, note 151.
35 Q. 38:26.
36 Q. 2:82; 5:9.
37 Q. 42:15; 2:15.

that has happened, God urges that they should be treated fairly, stressing His love for those who put equity first.[38]

The Qur'ān illustrates many of its teachings by way of parables and offers the story of two men, one dumb and unable to do anything on his own account, who represents little but a burden to his employer, and another who "commands justice and himself follows straight away."[39] The "dumb" man cannot help his master in any way, and possibly actually creates damage rather than doing any good. The other not only "commands what is good and righteous" but also ensures that everything he does is "on the path of righteousness."[40]

"Amanat" or "trust" can also apply to actual physical objects or specific responsibilities. In the broadest sense, it also applies to Muslim communities, nations and states exercising power and political authority in the world.[41] Collectively, God expects Muslims to strive to become "a nation in the middle".[42] This ruling has considerable implications for matters of international justice, which are basically a legal issue. Attaining justice around the world does not necessarily derive from all nations reaching agreement on all the important matters in life, and in fact such an agreement is probably impossible. Throughout history, we have never seen a single public order that applied to every society in the world, with the result that different societies develop their own unique systems of justice. Instead, international justice tends to be served when one or a number of nations plays a central role that oversees the relationship between various nations. Most nations that have risen to a position of prominence on the world or regional stage have attempted to establish systems of public order that, ideally, provide peace and security to humankind.

As Islam became ever more prominent in world affairs, the issue of how it could develop an important role in the establishment of lasting peace and

---

38 Q. 49:9.
39 Q. 16:76.
40 Ali, 1991, 755, note 2108.
41 Asad, 2003, 115.
42 Q. 2:143.

justice emerged. While Islam is theological, it is also a political ideology, equally applicable to all communities, that has been gifted by God with the responsibility for overseeing both the internal matters of Islamic nations, and international relations with diverse cultures and nations, always in accordance with the divine laws of God.[43] The Qur'ān states:

> O men, Behold, We have created you all out of a male and female, and have made you into nations and tribes, so that you might come to know one another. Verily, the noblest of you in the sight of God is the one who is most deeply conscious of Him.[44]

In this verse, God makes it clear that all humans are His creation and that, as such, all are equal. Nobody is born with any inherent superiority over anyone else. By our division into social groups, described here as "nations and tribes", we are supposed to be inspired to experience curiosity and a desire to learn about one another. Despite the many superficial differences between us in terms of physical appearance and culture, we are all God's servants, loved equally by Him. The Qur'ān is entirely unequivocal on the matter of prejudice on grounds of appearance, nationality or tribe; this is invariably wrong. Muhammad too, when speaking in his own words, explicitly condemns such tribalism, saying, "He is not of us who proclaims the cause of tribal partisanship; and he is not of us who fights in the cause of tribal partisanship; and he is not of us who dies in the cause of tribal partisanship." Of those who foolishly boasted of the glories, real or imagined, of the past of their tribe or nation, Muhammad commented:

> Behold, God has removed from you the arrogance of pagan ignorance with its boast of ancestral glories. Man is but a God-conscious

---

43 Shaltūt, 1992, 453.
44 Q. 49:13.

believer or an unfortunate sinner. All people are the children of Adam, and Adam was created out of dust.[45]

Throughout the Qur'ān, justice as conceived and applied is a great equaliser. In society, some people have more power and resources than others, but to God we are all the same in value and worth, and we are all equally bound to express and live justice in the best and most complete way possible.

---

45 Shaltūt, 1992, 452.

CHAPTER 13

QUR'ĀNIC LEGISLATION

THE QUR'ĀN CONTAINS many verses that deal with moral and legal matters, incorporating moral and legal precepts, and commands and prohibitions to do with lawful (halal) and unlawful (haram) actions. It promises that those who live well will be rewarded in heaven after their deaths, while sinners will be punished in hell. It discusses the lives and teachings of the prophets of old and their people, as well as parables, similes, metaphors, and admonitions. It discusses every Muslim's need to pray, fast during the requisite periods, give to the poor, engage in pilgrimage and to struggle throughout their lives to do God's work.

The Qur'ān is a complete guide to spirituality, and it also provides detailed information about how we should conduct our everyday lives, and how legislation can help to create and sustain a just society. In this respect, how does the Holy Book stand up in today's modern world, and how has it adapted to changing social circumstances throughout history? This is a complex matter. On the one hand, the Qur'ān is God's immutable law, which is eternally valid for all humanity. This means that the answers to the questions of how we should live, individually and collectively, and to how we should understand and apply the law, can be found within its pages. On the other hand, it is essential to understand that the Qur'ān was revealed to a certain individual, at a certain time and in a certain place, and that this historical, geographical and social context is reflected in the language and metaphors it uses, some of which may have shifted in meaning subsequently.

QUR'ĀNIC LEGISLATION

To understand these important questions, and to appreciate the relevance of context, it is necessary to return to the Qur'ān itself, and to explore both its social context and the testimony of Muhammad.[1] Above all, we need to note that while Qur'ānic legislation has been a matter of intense interest for jurists and reformers to this day, Muhammad himself made no hasty decisions about how Islamic public policy should be developed, but rather waited to receive the relevant legislation from God in the form of a revelation. We know from the Qur'ān and from historical sources that Muhammad was a rather retiring individual whose tendency was not to interfere with the lives of others unless there was a problem. While some of the later literature about him presents him as endlessly pronouncing decisions on both pressing and theoretical matters, this is in no way accurate or consistent with what the historic record reveals, and in fact he *never* made decisions about issues in the theoretical realm, or that were not brought specifically to his attention.[2] While Islamic scholars generally agree on the timeless, eternal validity of the Qur'ān, they can differ on the details; where the meaning of a particular verse is opaque, is this because today we do not understand every nuance of classical Arabic, or because the actual details of the meaning of the verse, albeit not its essential qualities, are something that shifts over time? Those who answer "yes" to the latter question, an approach which Saeed describes as "contextualist", can be summarised as considering the Qur'ān to contain "ideas, values and principles that can be applied through changing times and across different places."[3] This view is in line with the concept of the Qur'ān as a document primarily dedicated to empowering "the poor, the weak and vulnerable", positing Muhammad not just as God's messenger but as an important social reformer.[4] This is the view that was held by the great Islamic scholar Rahman (who is quoted and referenced extensively throughout this book), who said: "The imple-

---

1 Saeed, 2006, 220.
2 Rahman, 1984, 16.
3 Saeed, 2006, 221.
4 Saeed, 2006, 223.

mentation of the Qur'ān cannot be carried out literally in the context of today because this may result in thwarting the very purposes of the Qur'ān."[5] Although some scholars have tended to believe that considering the historic context of the Qur'ān undermines its universality, in fact by exploring the connection "between the contents and contexts of divine speech" it is made relevant for today's purposes.[6] According to Rahman, one should not assume that the opinions and interpretations of earlier scholars will work today; it may be that their findings were inherently insufficient even during their lifetimes, or that they were valid in their historical context, but are not in ours.

Muhammad was naturally a reticent person and did not intrude into people's affairs so long as they ran smoothly – the portrayal of him by later juristic literature as ceaselessly coming forth with decision upon decision on real or hypothetical questions is decidedly false. It goes without saying that he never gave decisions on purely hypothetical issues or on issues that were never brought to his notice. Initially, of course, Muhammad did not have the requisite standing in Mecca to wield much influence on legislation and social change, but he relatively quickly acquired the necessary status after he and his followers had established themselves in Medina. For this reason, while in Mecca he received revelations against usury (for example), this could not be legally banned for all Muslims until sometime after his arrival in Medina, when the community was on a stronger footing to propagate the messages that he was receiving from God. Similarly, while he received many revelations in Mecca that emphasised the great importance of acting to improve the situation of the poor, there were no specific laws to provide for this until he and his followers were firmly established in Medina.

In order to understand the Qur'ānic teaching on legislation it is essential to explore the issue of the historical background to each law. This context is known to Islamic scholars as "occasions of revelation". Sadly,

---

5 Saeed, 2006, 223.
6 Barlas, 2006, 267.

however, the information available to us from the literature about these "occasions" tends to be rather patchy and full of contradiction. Quite simply, although Muhammad's contemporaries and Islamic scholars had some understanding of how important situational context was in order to understand specific laws, this understanding did not go far enough. Rather than taking a nuanced view, they tended (wilfully or otherwise) to stress their opinion that even though a particular injunction may have come about because of a specific historic set of circumstances, it was still universally applicable. While this concept works so long as we understand it to mean the underlying *value* of the injunction rather than the literal words in which it is made, the fact is that we can only truly understand this value when we comprehend the language in its situational and historic context.[7]

Qur'ānic legislation is intended to reform the corrupt beliefs and morals of Muhammad's day, as well as completely reconfiguring society along with all the relevant customs and traditions of the time. While it is truly revolutionary in scope, it did and does make allowances for local customs when these do not flout the laws revealed in Qur'ānic legislation. These allowances date from the earliest days of Islam, when Muhammad would consider local traditions, and found that some did not run counter to the Qur'ān. Muhammad's silence on the matter of many of the Arabs' traditional customs has been taken to imply his acceptance of them.

Generally speaking, it is relatively easy to see the point of a particular verse or injunction and, by and large, the Qur'ān tell us why orders are being given, and why it makes a particular statement or comment, despite the fact that it rarely nominates specific cases. Typically, the Qur'ān's prohibitions and injunctions are issued in a series of increments.

We will turn now to an exploration of some of the key tenets of Islamic legislation.

First of all, most people are aware of Islamic legislation against usury, which is referred to in the Qur'ān as "riba". But how many are aware of the historical context? The Qur'ān does not refer to the Arab tribes of

---

7   Rahman, 1984, 17.

Muhammad's time, which were threatening to cause trouble, but it first refers to the practice of usury by denouncing it very strongly as a dreadful form of exploitation that should never be engaged in: "Whatever you may give out in usury so that it might increase through (other) people's possessions will bring (you) no increase in the sight of God".[8] The terminology used here leads us to an understanding of what the Qur'ān considers usury to be; it is clearly intended to mean adding to the money or goods lent by someone, or by a confederation of people, to another, in the context of the economic situation at the time of revelation. Later, the Qur'ān refers again to usury, saying, "O You who have attained to faith! Do not gorge yourselves on usury, doubling and redoubling it".[9]

To give the above teachings some context, we need to know that, in those days, the pagan people of Mecca had mainly acquired their considerable wealth through the practice of usury. This is what had made it possible for them to establish and supply their vast army, with which they had almost managed to defeat the small, badly-armed Muslim army at Uhud. There was clearly a temptation at the time for the early Muslims to likewise increase the funds available to them by engaging in usury. While they had ultimately prevailed at Uhud, they were in a very vulnerable situation, with few funds at their disposal, and the knowledge that they had many enemies. In order to clarify that usury was unacceptable, not just for them but for all future generations of Muslims, the Qur'ān is unequivocal on this matter.[10] As well as issuing statements that clearly forbid it, it warns of the punishment that awaits those who refuse to stop:

> O you who have attained to faith! Remain conscious of God, and give up all outstanding gains from usury if you are (truly) believers. For if you do it not, then know that you are at war with God and His apostle. But if you repent, then you shall be entitled to (the

---

8 Q. 30:39.
9 Q. 3:130.
10 Asad, 2003, 87, note 97.

return of) your principal: you will do no wrong, and neither will you be wronged. If, however, (the debtor) is in straitened circumstances, (grant him) a delay until a time of ease, and it would be for your own good, if you but knew it, to remit (the debt entirely) by way of charity.[11]

Clearly, the Qur'ān condemns usury strongly. Humankind's experiences of the ebbs and flows of the global economy throughout the centuries should clearly show us why. As a general rule, we can affirm that the Qur'ān's condemnation of this practice relates to the fact that the profits earned from loans that bear interest almost invariably involve the exploitation of the economically weak by those in a position of financial strength. The owner of the capital is entitled by contract to earn money from his loan irrespective of what or how much the borrower loses in the process. Thus, we can see that this prohibition is a strictly moral one that has everything to do with the motivations of the lender. Rather than placing all the onus on the borrower, Islamic law requires both lender and borrower to assume some of the risk, and to have the opportunity to reap the rewards of any enterprise. While this ruling is an eternal, timeless one, the exact nature of how it can be followed must, of necessity, be influenced by the social and economic environment in which both parties to the transaction operate. As our society is in a constant state of flux, every new generation needs to learn and understand for itself what the prohibition on usury means in the current context.[12]

The Qur'ān condemns apostasy, which is the renunciation of the faith. However, it is merciful, as we can see in the following words:

> There shall be no coercion in matters of faith. Distinct has now become the right way from (the way of) error; hence, he who rejects the powers of evil and believes in God has indeed taken hold of a

---

11 Q. 2:278-80.
12 Asad, 2003, 623, note 35.

support most unfailing, which shall never give way: for God is all-hearing, all-knowing.[13]

The term used in the discussion of apostasy is "din", which implies the contents of a morally binding law, and the Muslims' compliance with it. Thus, the ruling refers to religion in a very broad sense, incorporating elements of faith, of doctrine, of the practical implications of both, and of the individual person's attitude towards their God. In translation, "din" can be rendered as "religion", "faith", "religious law" or "moral law", depending on the context of the discussion.

A widespread view holds that Islam gives unbelievers the option of "conversion or the sword",[14] but nothing could be further from the truth. Forcible conversion is meaningless, and any Muslim who attempts to coerce a non-Muslim to embrace Islam against their will is committing a dreadful sin. God holds the free will of each and every person to be crucial: "Had We so willed," God says in the Qur'ān, "We could indeed have imposed Our guidance upon every being: but (We have not willed it thus)."[15] Another verse brings home the same message: "Had We so willed, We could have sent down unto them a message from the skies, so that their necks would (be forced to) bow down before it in humility."[16]

Clearly, as faith is meaningless unless it results from free choice, had God provided a visible or audible message "from above", the bluntness of the message would remove the element of free choice, and render faith empty of moral meaning. The Qur'ān says:

> As for anyone who denies God after having once attained to faith – and this, to be sure, does not apply to one who does it under duress, the while his heart remains true to his faith, but (only to) him

---

13 Q. 2:256.
14 Asad, 2003, 58.
15 Q. 32:13.
16 Q. 26:4.

who willingly opens up his heart to a denial of the truth: upon all such (falls) God's condemnation, and tremendous suffering awaits them.[17]

This verse refers to those believers who pretend to renounce their faith so as to save themselves when they are being tortured, or when they are being threatened with death. Here, and elsewhere, the Qur'ān explains that God does not give any of His people more than they can deal with.

Elsewhere in the Qur'ān, the following rhetorical question is posed: "But wouldst thou, perhaps, torment thyself to death with grief over them, if they are not willing to believe in this message."[18]

This question is posed primarily to Muhammad himself. At the time of revelation, he was very upset when his message was greeted by the pagan Meccans with great hostility and resistance. It is also posed to anyone who is distressed when those around him simply don't care about what he or she sees as the fundamental truth embedded in a moral matter.[19]

As we have seen, the Qur'ān was revealed in an environment of considerable religious diversity. In this context, when it criticises Jews and Christians, it asks them to correct specific issues within their communities, and to recognise the fact of Muhammad as prophet. It also builds on earlier revelations around apostasy that they would have been familiar with. Long before the emergence of Islam, Judaism and other Semitic religions recognised apostasy, and punished it with death. In early Jewish law, the following ruling was often implemented:

> ... he who blasphemes the name of the LORD shall be put to death; all the congregation shall stone him; the sojourner as well as the native, when he blasphemes the Name shall be put to death.[20]

---

17 Q. 16:106.
18 Q. 18:6.
19 Asad, 2003, 438.
20 Leviticus 24:16.

The Qur'ān, however, does not suggest that those who engage in apostasy in general should be punished in this life. Apostasy becomes a crime in the legal sense only when it occurs in the context of physical hostility against Muslims. Again and again, Qur'ānic verses clearly state that no one should be forced to follow a particular religion, and that the role of Muhammad and other messengers of God was to relate revelation, not to force anyone to accept it. Every human being has been created by God with the innate ability to tell the difference between right and wrong.[21]

The life of Muhammad illustrates God's rule in action. When he moved to Medina, he found there an established community of Jews. Although they were invited to become Muslims, they chose not to. In response, Muhammad swore that their religious practices and traditions would be respected while they, in return, promised to defend the new community of Muslims, if it was ever attacked. Furthermore, as Islam expanded in its early years, wherever it came into contact with Christians and Jews, and members of other faiths, all were granted the right to worship in their own way without the threat of intimidation or violence.

Sadly, capital punishment for apostasy is sometimes "justified" on the grounds of a range of Hadith, such as one that reports Muhammad as saying, "Whoever changes his religion, kill him!" One might wish to point out that this is a very general remark, and could refer just as easily to a Christian, a Jew or an adherent of any other faith, and not just to Islam.[22] Given the many teachings in the Qur'ān about the importance of the freedom of religion and tolerance, we are well-advised to refer to the original text for guidance in this matter.

The Qur'ān's prohibition on consuming alcohol is well-known, and was also revealed in stages. The first mention of alcohol refers to the plant matter which the Arabians of Muhammad's time used to make intoxicating beverages:

---

21 Q.17:15; 18:29; 6:104.
22 Affi and Affi, 2014, 5-14.

> And from the fruit of date-palm and vines: from it you derive intoxicants as well as wholesome sustenance- in this, there is a message indeed for people who use their reason.[23]

Here, the Qur'ān compares intoxicating substances with the wholesome food that can be derived from the same natural sources, provided by God to humanity for their nourishment. Intoxicants are contrasted here with "wholesome sustenance", underlining the difference between the negative qualities and impact of alcohol with the life-giving properties of the natural foodstuffs. The second reference in the Qur'ān to alcohol refers to both the consumption of alcohol and gambling, saying:

> They will ask thee about intoxicants and games of chance, Say: "In both there is great evil as well as some benefit for man; but the evil which they cause is greater than the benefit which they bring."[24]

Here, we are told very clearly that while drinking and gambling may have some advantages, the evil they cause is far greater and therefore it is vastly preferable to stay away from both. This verse appeals to the reader's or listener's own powers of reason to understand that they should avoid engaging in both vices as they simply are not worth the trouble.[25]

Later on, the Qur'ān returns to the theme, addressing Muslims directly and saying: "O You who have attained to faith! Do not attempt to pray while you are in a state of drunkenness ... (but wait)) until you know what you are saying".[26] It is interesting to note that this revelation does not yet prohibit the consumption of alcohol absolutely. Rather, it bans Muslims from praying while drunk, suggesting that alcohol was forbidden only during and before praying. Consider, however, the fact that Muslims

---

23 Q. 16:67.
24 Q. 2:219.
25 Affi and Affi, 2014, 30.
26 Q. 4:43.

are required to pray five times a day. With this obligation to pray with a clear head, we can clearly see that the situation afforded very few chances for those who wished to drink to do so. The complete banning of alcohol is made clear in a later revelation, which leaves us in no doubt as to Qur'ānic ruling on the matter. The relevant verse states:

> O You who have attained to faith! Intoxicants and games of chance, and idolatrous practices, and the diving of the future are but a loathsome evil of Satan's doing; shun it, then, so that you might attain to a happy state. By means of intoxicants and games of chance Satan seeks only to sow enmity and hatred among you, and to turn you away from the remembrance of God and from prayer. Will you not then, desist?[27]

Perhaps the most extraordinary and far-reaching revelations, from a legal and sociological viewpoint, are the Qur'ān's teachings on the matters of women's and slaves' rights. Prior to Islam, Arab women were seen essentially as the property of their husbands or (if they were unmarried) the other senior males in their lives, and had minimal rights of any sort. The Qur'ān addressed this situation by making it clear from the outset that women are complete persons, just as men are.

Before Muhammad established Islam, women were allowed to engage only in the domestic sphere. They did not receive any education and had minimal access to responsibility outside the home. Islam addressed these gross inequalities by ensuring that women had access to the same rights and responsibilities as men and by underlining that both are equally human and beloved by God. Nowhere is this simple edict clearer than in the following verse:

> For Muslim men and women, for believing men and women, for devout men and women, for men and women who are patient and

---

27 Q. 5:90-1.

QUR'ĀNIC LEGISLATION

constant, for men and women who humble themselves, for men and women who give to charity, for men and women who fast (and deny themselves), for men and women who guard their chastity, and for men and women who engage much in God's praise; for them has God prepared forgiveness and great reward.[28]

Even during Muhammad's own lifetime, many women were active, enquiring Muslims. We see this in the example of his wife, Umm Salama, who is said to have asked why the Qur'ān addresses men and not women (showing, in the process, that even in early Islam, some women were thinking critically about the Qur'ān, including the use of language, in figuring out their place within this new way of living).[29] When the Qur'ān discusses issues that are of concern to both genders, it typically uses the male gender, linguistically speaking, to address both. But in response to Umm Salama, it revealed verses that spoke to both directly.

Just as the Qur'ān's teachings about usury and alcohol were introduced in increments, so too were those teachings that dealt with the matter of equality between the genders. In the profoundly unequal society of seventh century Arabia this was an important aspect of revelation, as too many changes introduced at once would have been impossible for society to integrate. Over the course of the period of revelation, women gained the right to be educated, to earn their own money, to hold positions of public office, to engage in acts to protect their country if it was attacked, and to act as witnesses in the eyes of the law. As a general principle, they were now allowed to give themselves in marriage without permission or help from a guardian; the categories of women who required a guardian to permit them to give their hand in marriage were minors, women of unsound mind or otherwise incapable, those with no experience in making decisions on their own, virgins, or members of the aristocracy.[30]

---

28 Q. 33:35.
29 Barlas, 2002, 20.
30 Affi and Affi, 2014, 115-124.

In general, the Qur'ān is very clear on the essential equality of women and men,[31] seeing them as each other's protectors, their origins located in a single self,[32] and equally obliged to command right and forbid wrong, as well as engaging in prayer, the giving of alms, and obedience to God and His messenger, Muhammad.[33]

Often, the reasoning behind a given command is not explicitly stated, but a detailed reading and an understanding of the context provides clarity. For instance, the verses about inheritance never say directly, "women should have the right to inherit property, just like men," although this is the clear implication. Prior to Islam, Arabian women had no right to inherit at all. In establishing the categories of family members who have the right to inherit, the Qur'ān clearly includes women while also establishing guidelines to the usefulness of possible heirs in their kinship groups. The relevant verse states: "As for your parents and your children – you know not which of them is more deserving of benefit from you (therefore this) ordinance from God. Verily, God is all-knowing, wise."[34] A daughter's share in the inheritance is less than her brother's. This in no way indicates that she is to be considered inferior, but rather reflects her position in society. According to Islamic law, a daughter is the full and only owner of any property given to her by her father and husband when she gets married, and she can decide when she receives it. However, regardless of how much personal wealth she has, her husband is responsible for supporting her for the rest of her life; effectively, half of what he has is used to support her. Thus, one can see that sons and daughters are ultimately treated equally, and that Islamic law enshrines this equality. Today's Muslim lawyers would do well to revisit the Qur'ān and consider the spirit of gender equality in which it lays out all the laws on inheritance![35]

---

31 Sonn, 2006, 11.
32 Barlas, 2006, 256.
33 Q. 9:71.
34 Q. 4:11.
35 Iqbal, 1989, 135.

QUR'ĀNIC LEGISLATION

Women and men in marriage are described as being "garments" for one another in the following verse that addresses Muslim men: "It is lawful for you to go in unto your wives during the night preceding the (day's) fast, they are as a garment for you and you are as a garment for them."[36] Thus, we can see that God's intention for men and women is that they complement each other, offering each other protection, comfort and perhaps even embellishment, and bringing their respective strengths and weaknesses to the relationship.[37] Although men may lead the family in certain ways (and very much did so in the context of the extremely patriarchal society that prevailed in Muhammad's time), in general a woman's rights within the marriage are equal to her husband's.[38] For example, in matters of divorce there is a waiting period during which the divorce is essentially provisional and sometimes the divorcing man may express the desire for the marriage to continue after all. In these cases, wives nonetheless have the right to refuse the resumption of marital relations with their husbands. The husband, of course, will be considered responsible for maintaining the family, which is why he is given the first option not to finalise the divorce during this waiting period.[39] The Qur'ān states that, on marrying, women should receive a dowry of a sum agreed upon between the bride and groom.[40] It refers to this sum as "women's wages" in recognition of the great value of the work that women carry out, and their need and right for fiscal compensation. Clearly, in Islam marriage is not just an arrangement about the provision of services. The relationship between husband and wife must be one of "love and mercy".[41]

In today's world, there are sometimes cases in which the wife actually earns a larger salary than her husband, or in which the woman cares for her husband because he is ill or disabled. In these cases, women can be given a

---

36 Q. 2:187.
37 Q. 9:71.
38 Q. 2:228.
39 Asad, 2003, 50, note 216.
40 Q. 4:25.
41 Q. 30:22.

degree of precedence over their husbands, as they are essentially acting as the head of the family. In this author's experience, this is the current reality for many Muslim families and an example of how the timeless relevance of the Qur'ān continues today. Lamentably, later generations of Muslims tended to step away from the Qur'ān's progressive views on women, and many reverted to the belief that women are inherently inferior to men, that they are defective from a moral and intellectual standpoint, and in no position to understand or interpret God's law and much less to judge the religious knowledge generated by males. Even within Muhammad's own lifetime some of his contemporaries tried to undo the progressive rules of the Qur'ān, notably the teaching that women had the right to own property, by wilfully choosing to misunderstand some of the verses.[42] In this way, they excluded women from the public sphere and, for the thousand or so years of the Muslim empire, from all educational and intellectual endeavour. To this day, the unfortunate reality is that some Muslim societies are rife with discrimination towards women, and even misogyny.[43] In some Muslim societies, even the state has colluded with the wholly un-Qur'ānic oppression of women. For example, under the 'Abbāsid rule, "female slavery and subordination to men" were institutionalised, including the presence of harems in which women were entirely at the mercy of the men who owned them.[44] In this social context, even very exceptional women, who managed against the odds to acquire an education and some standing in society, were generally excluded from public life in every way. The twentieth century Islamic scholar Rahman fulminated against the oppression of women in the modern Islamic world, and pointed out that, if its teachings were truly followed, the Qur'ān would be an agent of women's liberation in society, saying:

---

42 Mernissi, 1991.
43 Barlas, 2006, 255.
44 Barlas, 2006, 257.

The Qur'ān insistently forbids the male (from) exploit(ing) the female on the strength of his stronger position in society, and Islam set(s) into motion the whole complex of measures – legal and moral – whereby sex discrimination would be completely eradicated. It forbad[e] the recourse to polygamy under normal circumstances, allowed the woman to own and earn wealth, declared her to be an equal partner in society: noting and allowing for the disadvantages she had in the society of that age.[45]

Some women scholars of Islam have highlighted the traditional practice of interpreting the Qur'ān through the medium of the Hadith as problematic, insofar as this tends to lead scholarship away from the fundamental teaching on women of the Qur'ān, which makes it very clear that they are in no way inferior to men. In turn, because women have tended to be excluded from the opportunity to develop the skills of critical thinking, few have been in a position to challenge the status quo.[46] This is a problem not just for women but for men too, as denying women's experience and voice prevents everyone from benefitting from understanding the whole of the Muslim experience,[47] and even from understanding (as much as is possible) the nature of God, Who is beyond gender or sex.[48] Despite God's intention that women should be accepted as equals, later Muslims often did not follow the Qur'ān's rules on this matter and even upended them at times; for example, interpreting a particular verse as permitting men to beat their wives when it can more accurately be interpreted as prohibiting domestic violence![49]

Polygamy was a feature of the social organisation of seventh century Arabia. Islam did not rule out polygamy as a valid form of marriage, but it appended numerous regulations and stipulations, including an absolute

---

45 Saeed, 2006, 224.
46 Hassan, 2000, 235.
47 Barlas, 2006, 261.
48 Barlas, 2006, 261-2.
49 Wadud, 1999, 26; 77.

maximum number of four wives. Furthermore, any man who was not completely confident of being able to be fair to several wives was only to marry one, within the umbrella of the general guideline that, "you shall never be able to do justice among wives no matter how desirous you are to do so".[50]

Exploring the Qur'ān with care, it quickly becomes apparent that polygamy was accepted in early Islam on a legal basis, with the understanding that monogamy would be introduced when society had changed and become more favourable to it (for instance, in a warlike society like seventh century Arabia, young men tend to die in larger numbers than young women, resulting in an imbalance between the genders; in such a situation, without polygamy many women would never have had the chance to marry and have children at all).

As mentioned above, divorce is permitted in Islam. However, it is not taken lightly. Couples whose marriages have run into trouble may divorce after two trial separations, during which time people from each family work with them to try to find a way to keep the marriage together.[51] If this does not work, the couple is allowed to go their separate ways, although the husband must provide his former wife with financial support, an obligation that is described as being for those who are "righteous".[52] Women can precipitate divorce when they and their husbands have agreed the financial side of things.[53]

Closely related to the low status of women in pre-Islamic Arabian society was the matter of female infanticide. This occurred when families were very poor and felt that a female baby would be a useless mouth to feed, when the birth of a female was considered a dishonour to the family, or because of the perceived risk that a girl could be captured by an enemy tribe and come to prefer them to her own people. Some dissenting voices had been raised prior to Islam, notably by Zayd ibn Amr ibn Nufayil, who

---

50 Q. 4:129.
51 Q. 4:35; 4:129.
52 Q. 2:241.
53 Q. 2:229.

QUR'ĀNIC LEGISLATION

can be seen as a precursor of Muhammad in some ways, and who died not long before Muhammad started to receive revelations.[54]

The Qur'ān ruled that the appalling act of infanticide was never acceptable, saying, "And when the girl-child that was buried alive is made to ask, for what crime she had been slain".[55] Elsewhere, it also refers to the practice of slaughtering baby girls, saying:

> When one of them is given news of the birth of a baby girl, his face darkens and he is filled with gloom. In his shame he hides himself away from his people because of the bad news he has been given. Should he keep her and suffer contempt or bury her in the dust?[56]

This passage clearly condemns female infanticide, but it also makes it clear that it is despicable to let the girl live only for her to be treated badly because of her sex; women are creations of God and should be honoured, just as men are. The Qur'ān's denunciation of the way women were treated in Arabia prior to the advent of Islam is clear. Either of these alternatives is evil: to keep the child as an object of perpetual contempt, or to bury her alive, as was sometimes done by the pagan Arabs. This passage contains an utter condemnation of men's attitude towards women in pre-Islamic Arabia. The Qur'ān deplores the very notion of God despising women as many Arabs did, and the practice of associating with God ideas about women that are repugnant to Him. It urges His people to trust in Him, reassuring them that there will always be a way to raise their families and stating, "Do not kill your children for fear of poverty, it is We who shall provide sustenance for them as well as for you. Verily, killing them is a great sin."[57] While these teachings have a clear historical context, they continue to be valid to this day. Consider, for example, parents who are con-

---

54 Al-'Asqalāni, 1929, 112.
55 Q. 81:8-9.
56 Q. 16:58-9.
57 Q. 17:31.

sidering an abortion because of financial concerns. Just as in the days of Muhammad, God promises that there will be a way.[58]

The matter of adultery is covered in detail in the Qur'ān, and the punishment is outlined in the following verse:

> As for the adulteress and the adulterer – flog each of them with a hundred stripes, and let not compassion with them keep you from (carrying out) this law of God, if you believe in God and the Last Day; and let a group of the believers witness their chastisement.[59]

The Arabic term used here to denote adultery is "zina", which refers to sexual intercourse between a man and a woman who are not married to one another, whether or not either of them is married to someone else. Thus, unlike the current use of the term "adultery" in the west, it does not distinguish between "cheating on" one's spouse, or engaging in intercourse before or outside marriage, which can be termed "fornication".[60] Whereas the original punishment for women who committed adultery was house arrest for the remainder of her life, this was changed to flogging.[61]

Why does the Qur'ān emphasise the importance of penalising adultery? The fact is that sexual purity for both genders, before and during marriage, and after divorce, is considered enormously important in Islam, and those who engage in illicit behaviours are removed from the community of chaste men and women.

Today, in much of the world, chastity is no longer respected as a virtue, and as a result adultery is not considered a serious offence. Possibly the husband receives the payment of damages, but that is all. In Islam, however, adultery is seen as a breach of trust, and recognised as a factor that destroys families and peace within the home, and that can even result in children

---

58 Al-'Asqalāni, 1929, 423.
59 Q. 24:2.
60 Asad, 2003, 532.
61 Q. 4:15.

being deprived of the loving care of their mothers. Clearly, there is a big disconnect and, indeed, most Westerners find Islam's punishment by flogging far too severe a punishment for adultery.

A number of points need to be made. Firstly, stoning to death is not prescribed by Islam but is, instead, an earlier law that derives from Judaism. The Qur'ān itself clarifies that stoning is not an appropriate punishment, both explicitly and in context.[62] In the relevant verse, it clarifies that married slave-girls who committed adultery should be punished with half the severity of married free women. As there is no way to "half" stone someone to death, this ruling clearly states that they should receive half as many lashes.[63]

The Qur'ān provides detailed rulings about how to deal with accusations of adultery within a marriage. For instance:

> And as for those who accuse their own wives (of adultery), but have no witnesses except themselves, let each of these (accusers) call God four times to witness that he is indeed telling the truth, and the fifth time, that God's curse be upon him if he is telling a lie. But (as for the wife, all) chastisement shall be averted from her by her calling God four times to witness that he is indeed telling a lie, and the fifth (time), that God's curse be upon her if he is telling the truth.[64]

Here we can see that a husband's accusation is seen as proven if his wife refuses to swear an oath vouching for her innocence, but disproven if she takes an oath of condemnation. While oath-swearing cannot legally prove guilt or innocence, in this scenario, both husband and wife are absolved of legal consequences, although there remains the option of divorce.[65]

---

62 Q. 4:25.
63 Ali, 1992, 698.
64 Q. 24:6-9.
65 Asad, 2003, 534.

The Qur'ān also deals with the matter of discord within the family. It says:

> And as for those women whose ill-will you have reason to fear, admonish them (first); then leave them alone in bed; then beat them; and if thereupon they pay you heed, do not seek to harm them. Behold, God is indeed most high, great.[66]

In this context, "ill-will" refers to the wife's mistreatment of her husband or vice-versa, including what today would be referred to as "mental cruelty". In the case of men, it also denotes mistreatment of their wives in the physical sense. When we mistreat our spouses, we are engaging in a serious breach of our marriage vows. From a wide range of authenticated traditions, we know that Muhammad was fiercely opposed to domestic violence. On more than one occasion he is depicted as saying, "Could any of you beat his wife as he would beat a slave, and then lie with her in the evening?" and in another tradition, we see him forbidding the beating of any women, saying, "Never beat God's handmaidens."[67]

The term "daraba" which is translated here as "beat" is used in diverse parts of the Qur'ān to mean different things. For example: "Go forth (to war) in God's cause"[68]; "Strike the rock with thy staff"[69]; "We veiled their ears in the cave"[70]; "Do not coin any similitudes for God";[71] "God propounds the parable of two men"[72] and "God sets forth a parable".[73] Given this great diversity of meaning, my feeling is that the above verse does not refer to "beating" people in the literal sense, but should be interpreted as

---

66 Q. 4:34.
67 Asad, 2003, 109-10.
68 Q. 4:94.
69 Q. 2:60.
70 Q. 18:11.
71 Q. 16:74; 36:78; 43:17.
72 Q. 16:75.
73 Q. 14:24, 39:29.

indicating "separate from them", as in the following Qur'anic verse: "(O You who deny the truth) Should We, perchance, withdraw this reminder from you altogether, seeing that you are people bent on wasting your own selves?"[74]

How are we to interpret these teachings in the context of our modern families and the challenges we face? Perhaps we can considered three steps: Ideally, in the case of problems between the spouses verbal advice or chastisement is enough; if not, there is the option of suspending marital relations. In case of conflict between spouses four steps are mentioned, to be taken in that order: (1) verbal advice or admonition may be sufficient; (2) if not, sex relations may be suspended; (3) if neither of the above works, perhaps one might consider a slight physical prompt, so long as this does not degenerate into cruelty.[75]

The Qur'ān considers happy, faithful marriage to be an exalted state, and warns against anyone preventing others from attaining it. Reflecting the presence of slavery in the Arabic culture of the day, it says: "And do not, in order to gain some of the fleeting pleasures of this worldly life, coerce your (slave) maidens into whoredom if they happen to be desirous of marriage".[76] Clearly, Islam respects the right of every man or woman to enter into marriage, and decries inferior relationships as "whoredom".

The Qur'ān also dealt with the issue of slavery and, as with other cases, adopted an incremental approach to legislation. As the system of slavery was integral to the Arabian way of life in the seventh century, abolishing it in one fell swoop would have been impossible. Thus, for the time being, the Qur'ān accepted that the existence of slavery was legal. However, it exerted great efforts to ensure that God's people would do everything in their power to free slaves, creating a social environment in which slavery was bound to disappear. Freeing slaves, which is referred to in the Qur'ān as "liberating the neck" is described categorically and praised as a virtue,

---

74 Q. 43:5.
75 Ali, 1934, 220.
76 Q. 24:33.

and together with providing for the poor and for orphans, described as an "uphill path" upon which every virtuous person should walk.[77] The reference to the neck refers to the release of slaves from bondage, and should also be read as referring to the release of captives. In general, the Qur'ān makes it clear that freeing people from bondage is one of the obligations of Islam and indeed one of the finest acts that any Muslim can carry out and particularly pleasing to God.[78]

Another way in which Muslims can help slaves to become free is to support their own efforts to gain their liberty. The Qur'ān states that slaves who offer to buy their own freedom in instalments should be facilitated in this by agreeing a sum that is consistent with their situation with the owner. All slave owners are obliged to accept this bid for freedom.[79] Furthermore, all slaves are entitled by law to do whatever work they can to lawfully obtain the money they need to earn their own freedom. When they have achieved this, no slave owner can refuse them, with the only conditions being confirmation from an unbiased source of their good character, and their ability to fulfil their obligations.[80] Furthermore, owners are obliged to do whatever they can to assist slaves in their efforts to earn what they need in order to become independent, or even by providing some of the compensation themselves. This is consistent with the Qur'ānic teaching that revenues obtained through taxes should be used for the purpose of freeing slaves, among other things.[81]

The Qur'ān also makes numerous rulings intended to lead the Arabs towards the gradual abolition of slavery. For instance, it states that only captives in a "just war" may be used as slaves (with the understanding that most laws are not just),[82] and that freeing slaves can also be seen as a way

---

77 Q. 90:11-16.
78 Asad, 2003, 36, note 146.
79 Rahman, 1979, 39.
80 Q. 24:33; Asad, 2003, 540.
81 Q. 9:60; Asad, 2003, 540.
82 Q. 8:67.

of doing penance for a wide range of sins.[83] It states that there should be no restrictions on marriage between the free and the slaves, stating, "And (you ought to) marry the single from among you as well as such of your male and female slaves as are fit (for marriage)."[84] This verse refers to the community as a whole; to all unmarried men and women. As well as indicating the fundamental equality of all human beings, it also underlines the frequently enunciated advice from Muhammad that marriage is preferable in a range of ways, including the ethical and the social, to being celibate.[85]

Islam makes special provisions for the care and support of minorities and the poor and, above all, for the care of orphans. There are orphans in all societies, and in the past, when many more parents died of disease and other causes, large numbers of children were left without parents and guardians. Muslims are under a strong moral obligation to do whatever they can to make orphans' lives better, including investing in their education, welfare, health and financial status. People who are specifically given the responsibility of caring for orphans must treat them as part of their own family rather than considering them different in any way.[86] The Qur'ān states:

> And they will ask thee about (how to deal with) orphans, Say: to improve their conditions is best. And if you share their life, they are your brethren: for God distinguishes between him who spoils and him who improves.[87]

The Qur'ān also teaches that orphans' possessions should be protected so that they are cared for in later life, and that those who take orphans' property for themselves will be punished in the afterlife.[88] Guardians cannot

---

83 For example, Q. 4:92; 5:89; 58:3.
84 Q. 24:32.
85 Asad, 2003, 539, note 42.
86 Affi and Affi, 2014, 155.
87 Q. 2:220.
88 Knysh, 2006, 216.

do anything to orphans' possessions other than acting to improve them. Thus, a guardian might invest orphans' possessions with the intention of increasing them, provided that they transfer all these possessions to them when they come of age and are in a position to manage their own affairs. In the case of orphans who are still minors, the Qur'ān very clearly directs guardians that they may not make use of orphans' belongings,[89] and states:

> And test the orphans (in your charge) until they reach a marriageable age; then, if you find them to be mature of mind, hand over to them their possessions, and do not consume them by wasteful spending, and in haste, ere they grow up. And let him who is rich abstain entirely (from his ward's property); and let him who is poor partake thereof in a fair manner. And when you hand over to them their possessions, let there be witnesses on their behalf-although none can take count as God does.[90]

The Qur'ān considers murder to be a crime against all of society, and not just the victim. It states:

> ... whosoever kills a person unrightfully or without a mischief (i.e., a war) on the earth, it is as though he has killed all humanity; while he who saves one person, it is as though he has saved all humanity.[91]

In recognising the offence of murder as a heinous crime against all of society, the Qur'an affords the next of kin of the murder victim the opportunity of requesting either the death penalty or forgoing the death penalty in favour of settlement by means of a payment of "blood money", both of which are in line with pre-Islamic customs; however, the Qur'an goes

---

[89] Asad, 2003, 156.
[90] Q. 4:6.
[91] Q. 5:32; Rahman, 1984, 144.

further by introducing forgiveness as an additional choice which the next of kin can also exercise and which the Qur'an regards as the most preferable.

Theft is also dealt with in the Qur'an. At the time of revelation, robbers were often punished for their crimes with having their hands amputated, which was widespread throughout Arabia. This has to be seen in the context of the nomadic, Bedouin society that prevailed then. While there were settled areas like Mecca and Medina, society was dominated by nomadic people who travelled the country with their tents and camels. In this context, there was no practical way in which to imprison thieves; prisons require a stable, settled society with the infrastructure necessary to build a jail and care for inmates. In the absence of this, and with the need to protect society from the predations of thieves, amputation provided a way to dissuade would-be criminals, while also marking offenders permanently so that the public was warned of their predilections, and making it harder for them to steal again.[92] Since there were no protective barriers to safeguard the property of people, society could not afford to tolerate the proliferation of theft. Moreover, before the arrival of Islam, Arabian society had no centrally recognised form of government. There was no authority that oversaw a legal system and there were few ways in which the nomadic peoples could protect the livestock that were their primary property and the source of their income. In this social context, the harsh punishment of amputation was appropriate in a way that it is not today;[93] now we have complex societies and the capacity to contain criminals within an effective and compassionate prison system.

The Qur'an makes relatively few specific rulings on how theft should be dealt with. There is no discussion about how many witnesses are required in order to convict someone, of mitigating circumstances that might reduce the punishment (unlike, for instance, teaching on the breaking of the dietary regulations, in which the lack of other available food is accepted as a mitigating circumstance). While the Qur'an does not reject the practice

---

92 Kamali, 2008, 130-1.
93 Affi and Affi, 2014, 83-4.

of amputating a hand, nor does it give instructions on how this should be carried out, or under what circumstances, with the clear message that it does not recommend this as a form of punishment outside the context of seventh century Arabia.

Accepting that mutilation was a context-appropriate approach to the punishment of theft in pre-Islamic Arabic society, how are we to interpret the Qur'ān's teachings in this area today? Given the large number of unanswered questions around this matter, I believe that we are bound to accept the idea of amputation as metaphoric rather than legalistic. This is supported by the Qur'ān's account of an event involving the prophet Joseph, which relates:

> When she heard of their malicious talk, she sent for them, and prepared for them a sumptuous repast, and handed each of them a knife and said (to Joseph): "Come out and show thyself to them. And when the women saw him they were greatly amazed at his beauty, and they cut their hands (with their knives), exclaiming, "God save us! This is no mortal man! This is nought but a noble angel.[94]

In this context, the term "to cut" (qatt'ana) does not refer to the amputation of the hand but to making a small cut to the fingertips. This reference adds to our contention that references in the Qur'ān to the cutting of hands should be read as a metaphor. Moreover, while the Qur'ān has relatively little to say on the matter of punishment for theft, it has a great deal to say on dealing with the underlying causes of it. For example, when it is demonstrated that poverty or addiction contributed to theft, society has an obligation to tackle the root cause of it. In this way, by identifying the causes of crime and developing solutions to deal with them, the vices that contribute to theft are, as it were, "cut off". In various locations in the Qur'ān the term "qatta" is used to denote cutting or severance in a

---

[94] Q. 12:31.

metaphoric way. It is used to indicate the afterlife, when human beings are "severed" from their past life,[95] while to this day the same term is used in everyday Arabic to indicate a variety of meanings that have nothing to do with the amputation of hands, such as "qatta an-nahra", which means, "he crossed the river", and "qatta haqahu", which means, "he denied him his rights".[96]

Muhammad Ashmawi, a contemporary scholar of law, has expressed the contradictions inherent in Qur'ānic teaching on the punishment for crime very well. While the Qur'ān does not forbid the Arabian custom of amputating thieves' hands, there are so many conditions that have to be met before a punishment can be carried out that such harsh penalties are effectively inapplicable. In the case of theft, for instance, the object that is stolen has to be marked with the owner's seal and to have been stolen from a well-guarded place (thus excluding pilfering, plundering, and the picking of pockets); it must have a monetary value and the robber must not be in dire need. Moreover, if the robber has any degree of ownership over the goods stolen (such as in the case of public goods), amputation cannot be applied.[97] Thieves could also avoid punishment if they were truly repentant. The Qur'ān states: "But as for him who repent after having thus done wrong, and makes amends, behold, God will accept his repentance, verily, God is much–forgiving, and dispenser of grace."[98] They could also avoid punishment by returning the stolen goods before the theft was discovered by the authorities.

Historic precedence shows that Islamic rulers recognised that there were many circumstances in which the amputation of hands was inappropriate, even in times gone by. For example, the great Caliph 'Umar, who reigned in Arabia during a period of famine, waived the ruling completely during that time, when so many people were in truly desperate straits.

---

95 Q. 6:94.
96 Affi and Affi, 2014, 86-8.
97 Saeed, 2006, 136.
98 Q. 5:39.

In summary, the evidence is abundant that hand-cutting can only ever be seen as an appropriate punishment for theft within a society that has a robust, integrated social welfare system and in no other circumstances whatsoever.

Today, there is a vast degree of variation between how law is applied in the diverse Muslim lands and an urgent need for scholars, legal experts and lay people to explore and understand how the Qur'ān's teachings continue to be relevant in the modern world. The great question that must be asked (especially in the current fraught ideological climate) is whether Islam is a way of life that can adapt to the rapidly changing circumstances of modern society. Does the Qur'ān's eternal validity mean that *nothing* must ever change, or can the fundamental rules it espouses adapt to our changing social and legal needs without being unduly compromised? Can we embrace aspects of the liberalisation of society, while also not losing sight of God's fundamental plan for us, and His teachings on the correct way to live?

At the time of writing, some Muslim nations have been much more successful than others in finding values and meaning in the Qur'ān that guide the lives of their people, and the legislation they live by,[99] without ignoring the simple fact that society has changed greatly since the seventh century, with the corresponding need for understandings of God's law, as revealed through His prophet, Muhammad, to be considered in this fresh light.

---

99 Iqbal, 1989, 129.

CHAPTER 14

MECCA AND MEDINA SURAHS

THE TWO GREAT Arabian cities of Mecca and Medina are hugely important to the development of Islam, and this importance – historical, theological and spiritual – is reflected throughout the Qur'ān, which is composed of Surahs that were received by Muhammad in these two cities.

After arriving in Medina and establishing himself and his followers, Muhammad had to set about establishing a new political and social order that would accommodate everyone in the city, and not just the small (but determined and growing) Muslim community, in an atmosphere of peace and cooperation. The situation was vastly different to Mecca, and offered both opportunities and challenges to Muhammad and his people: In Mecca, most of the permanent residents belonged to the Quraysh tribe (as did Muhammad himself), as well as their slaves and their various dependants. While people from many different ethnic groups visited Mecca for reasons of trade and pilgrimage, the full-time citizenry was relatively homogenous. The dominant culture was Quraysh, and this fact quite simply influenced every single aspect of Meccan life.

The situation was much more complex in Medina. The city was dominated by two powerful tribes that had been in a state of feud for generations. Weary of the constant turmoil and, no doubt, looking for a way out that would allow them to cease the internecine violence while leaving everyone's honour intact, many of them looked to Muhammad as a new leader who might be able to bring peace to the city at last. As well as these two large tribes, Medina was home to a sizeable Jewish minority which, like the Arab majority, was divided into tribes and clans that did not always get along very well. The Hijra, or the movement of Muhammad with his followers into Medina, added to the diversity and complexity of what was already a city with a fascinating and often very challenging mosaic of cultural difference.

Muhammad's initial concern was to secure the safety and security of the Muslim community and to create a sense of unity that would allow it to grow and flourish, spiritually and in every other way, in the context of the Muslims' new home. To this end, shortly after arriving in Medina, he began constructing a mosque that would be the focal point of the Muslim community, and he worked hard to establish a pact of brotherhood between the Muslims who had fled Mecca as refugees and the Ansar (the helpers). This was especially important because the Muslim community was quite diverse; converts came from rich and poor backgrounds alike, and included men, women and children. Without a sense of common purpose it would have been hard for him to achieve the result he was looking for. A common place of worship would help to foster a sense of togetherness, would provide a location to which those curious to learn more about Islam could travel, and would signal to the wider world that the new Islamic faith and way of life, together with its prophet, was something that could and should be taken seriously.

While Muhammad was preoccupied by practical matters, he was also frequently in receipt of revelations from God, with many additions to the Qur'ān being received after his relocation to Medina. Intriguingly, the material received in Medina can generally be distinguished by Qur'ānic scholars from the revelations received in Mecca, both in terms of style and content, providing generations with a rich seam of research and investigation. These differences, and the implications of them, have long been the topic of spirited debate.

The reason why scholars of the Qur'ān are so interested in understanding which Surahs were received in Mecca and which in Medina is simple:

By understanding the historical context of any particular Surah better, we can understand its message more completely,[1] and by understanding its message more completely, we are in a better position to know its implications for us as we go about our daily lives. For example, the Surahs that come from Mecca often feature arguments with the polytheists of Mecca, who so strongly resisted God's message as revealed to His prophet Muhammad. While this is clearly rooted in historical context, it is also relevant in modern times, as it pre-empts any objections or arguments against the Qur'ān that might be proffered by unbelievers.

While early Muslims recognised a general difference between Surahs revealed in Mecca and those revealed in Medina, this did not always take into consideration the precise timing of the revelation, or the fact that some of the Surahs in the Qur'ān contain verses from both periods. For the sake of categorisation, they decided to consider chapters that were begun in Mecca to be Meccan, and those that began in Medina to be Medinan, and determined in this way that the Qur'ān contains 85 Surahs from Mecca and 29 from Medina. While this is useful as a general guide to how revelation occurred, it suggests a much greater degree of simplicity than was in fact the case. There are also a number of elements that were revealed outside both Meccan and Medina, and others that are a composite of Meccan and Medinan verses. In general, a too-rigid stance in this area has tended to be problematic in terms of scholarship, and this should be borne in mind in any discussion of the two broad categories of Surahs.

Having said that, there are certain stylistic differences that tend to be associated with the two categories: Surahs that contain the word "kalla" are invariably from Mecca, for instance, as are those that begin with the words "O Mankind". Moreover, all the Surahs that begin with the mysterious letters discussed in Chapter Nine are from Mecca, with the exception of Surah two and Surah three.[2] Other differences can revolve around the length of the verses, the sort of issues discussed, the language used in ad-

---

1 al-Zurqani, 2012, 185,
2 al-Zurqani, 2012, 185,

dressing people and the categories of people and events discussed (including Jews, Christians, pagans, Hypocrites and various historical events associated with the two respective cities). Meccan texts tend to be quite short and concise, reflecting the fact that at this point Muhammad did not have scribes, and the Surahs had therefore to be committed to memory. They do not shy away from making their point forcefully, and they frequently invoke earlier prophets, including Noah, Abraham, Jonah and Jesus, and the various ways in which these had to struggle with their people in times gone by. In this, they lead the listener (or reader) to draw a direct comparison with Muhammad and the many trials and tribulations he had to face as he worked hard to bring his message to the people of Mecca. Muhammad and his message are placed firmly within the context of the monotheistic faiths of the region.

As well as frequently opening verses by saying "O mankind," the Surahs from Mecca often have recourse to oath-making, commonly using a sequence of oaths to underline a point (as discussed in considerable detail in Chapter Eight) and to frequent references to the afterlife – heaven and hell – to earlier holy scriptures, to the creation of a new and moral way of life, and to the many ways in which the new Muslim community suffered at the hands of those who would not believe the life-changing message that Muhammad had brought.[3] In summary, the Meccan Surahs tend to revolved around common themes, including the call to worship the one true God (the same God as worshipped by the other monotheists) in a pure way, the rejection of idol-worship and the worship of false Gods as carried out by the pagan Arabs of Mecca for countless generations, and the elaborations of stories of earlier prophets. The Meccan Surahs provide detailed descriptions of the afterlife, heaven and hell, and how the good will be rewarded, and they discuss the nature of good behaviour, including factors such as not committing infanticide and caring for orphaned children while also respecting their property rights.

---

3   Salah, 2007, 182-9.

As well as providing clear information about God and His plan for humanity, Meccan Surahs also seem to reflect the probable ethnic composition of Mecca at the time of Muhammad's revelations. Although a few scholars have posited the permanent presence of large Christian and/or Jewish communities in the city, there is no evidence of such a thing[4] (unlike the situation in Medina, as we shall see).

As stated above, Mecca was relatively homogeneous in ethnic terms; inhabited by a large tribal group, the Quraysh, that dominated commerce and government, administered justice according to local norms, and oversaw the ingress and egress of visitors to the city. However, this does not mean that all the Arabs of Mecca had the same or even similar religious views, or that they had no or few opportunities to learn about different faiths. In fact, the picture is relatively varied. Most followed their forefathers in worshipping idols while some others appear to have at least been interested in and intrigued by exploring the idea of a monotheistic religion, and a few had even embraced Christianity, reflecting the fact that some of the Christians in the area had engaged in evangelising behaviours.[5] That many of the Meccan Arabs were familiar with at least some of the precepts of Christianity is made very clear in the following verse, which references the Christian belief in resurrection and an afterlife and is, at the very least, indicative of the probability that Christians and, presumably, Jews had been attempting to gain converts among the Arabs for a while:

> And the disbelievers say, Shall we be resurrected after we and our forefathers have been turned to dust? We and our forefathers before us have been promised this—but this is nothing but legends of the communities of the past.[6]

---

4 Rahman, 1989, 150-1.
5 Rahman, 1989, 151.
6 Q. 27:67-8.

Elsewhere in the Qur'ān we find a limited number of verses addressed to Jews in the Meccan period,[7] suggestive of a small community of Jews in Mecca, presumably augmented periodically by others – friends, relatives and business acquaintances – visiting for purpose of trade and/or pilgrimage. There are also suggestions in the Qur'ān, again from the Meccan period, that some Jews and Muslims may have hoped for the arrival of a new Messiah, or at least a prophet, within their lifetimes, and were hopeful, when Muhammad arrived on the scene, that he might be the one they had been waiting for. The Qur'ān itself suggests that some of the Jews accepted Muhammad as God's messenger, and addresses the people of Mecca, when they demanded proof, directly by saying: "Was it not a sign for them that the learned men of the children of Israel recognise him?"[8]

Despite these exhortations, the Meccan Surahs are clear on the issue that the vast majority of the people of Mecca rejected Muhammad's message and were determined to continue worshipping idols and false gods, as their ancestors had always done, while most Jews and Christians would not recognise him as a new prophet. The Qur'ān criticises the Arab pagans for their failure to listen to Muhammad and his life-changing message, saying that if they are visited by misfortune, they certainly cannot claim that they were never given any warning by God, for not only had He sent His messenger Muhammad, but He had also sent them His word by way of His prophet Moses, and in those earlier times too, His message had been rejected.[9]

Morality per se is only discussed in broad strokes in the Surahs from Mecca, which is to say that while the verses from this period do give a clear indication of what God wants from His people, they do not give detailed instructions relating to every aspect of behaviour, and according punishments and rewards. There are various types of Surahs, including relatively simple exhortations from God, or from God through the medium of

---

7 Rahman, 1989, 152.
8 Q. 26:197.
9 Q. 28:47-8.

Muhammad, those that bring together a series of oaths,[10] and others that affirm the Qur'ān as the Word of God and stress its huge importance as God's ultimate and final message to mankind.[11] They appear to some extent to reflect the way in which they were received, and Neuwirth[12] speculates that they reference the fact that they were initially discussed in a public setting in Mecca, probably near the Ka'ba, a physical site associated with Abraham and thus a tangible reminder of Muhammad's position as the heir and successor of the prophets who had gone before. Bear in mind that during this period the Surahs were committed to memory rather than written down by scribes. Their relative brevity would have facilitated this process. However, while Meccan Surahs share certain qualities that tend to distinguish them from the Surahs that came later, there is also movement and development within the Meccan period. Despite the fact that at this time the Surahs were committed to memory, with the passage of time numerous references to the Qur'ān refer to it as a "book", either in the context of an oath,[13] or when its importance is confirmed.[14] Later Meccan Surahs often also lead the listeners' mind away from their immediate surroundings and banal, everyday concerns to the site of the earlier revelations and the wider world, framing their message in a broader context and stressing the centrality of the monotheistic doctrine. This message is often provided in three parts, beginning by addressing the listener directly, delivering the message, and then affirming the importance and validity of the revelation, although in the later Meccan Surahs this straightforward structure is often replaced by longer, discursive elements.[15]

While the Meccan elements of the Qur'ān are very clear in terms of accepting the early revelations and much of the teachings they contain, they do not shy away from criticising Jews and Christians when these refuse to

---

10 For example, Q. 92:1-3.
11 For example, Q. 74:49-56.
12 2006, 110.
13 For example, Q. 36:2; 37:3; 38:1; 43:2; 44:2; 50:1.
14 For example, Q. 2:2; 10:1; 12:1; 13:1.
15 Neuwirth, 2006, 111.

listen to the message of Muhammad. For example, the Qur'ān criticises some of the Jewish scribes, saying:

> And before it (the Qur'ān) you were not given to reciting any scripture, nor did you write it down with your right hand- for in that case those who disbelieve in you would have reason to doubt.[16]

The Qur'ān also asserts itself as an authority on the subject of the various matters on which Jews and Christians disagreed.[17] It thus represents a way in which these two peoples should have been able to set aside their differences and accept God's ultimate Covenant with humanity.

While the Meccan Surahs do describe a population under duress and in difficulty, they do not seem to show the Muslims in dire straits and without options. While persecution was certainly a real problem, extending even to torture at times, it does not seem to have been approached systematically.[18] In sending the most vulnerable members of his congregation to refuge in Abyssinia, and in moving with his followers to Medina, Muhammad is not depicted as abjectly fleeing in fear of his life, but rather as quite calmly making the assessment that Medina would be a better place for Islam to flourish in, with the full expectation that Mecca could be claimed for Islam in the fullness of time.[19] In fact, during the latter part of their period in Mecca, Muslims seem to have been in a stronger position than they had been in before, and the Qur'ān describes them as being permitted to fight back when they are attacked,[20] which at the very least is suggestive of a growing degree of confidence.

Some scholars have looked for a decisive break between the Meccan and the Medinan Surahs and there certainly are differences in terms of both style and content. Since the very early days of Islamic scholarship,

---

16 Q. 29:48.
17 Q. 27:76.
18 Rahman, 1989, 157.
19 Rahman, 1989, 158.
20 Q. 16:126.

most had agreed that some of the earlier verses were later repealed, and that this is evident in the later verses.[21] The twentieth century scholar Mahmud Muhammad Taha created a model that, if correct, appeared to show radical differences between the Surahs revealed in Mecca and those revealed in Medina. He deduced that Meccan revelations represent the Qur'ān's core message, while Medinan revelations were strictly relevant to people at a specific place and time. According to this schema, Meccan Surahs are "the primary, timelessly valid revelation addressed to all humankind" while the Medinan Surahs, which were revealed after the establishment of the Muslim society in their new home, reflected the Muslims' need to "compromise with existing socio-political circumstances and were not binding for all future societies."[22] If we accept Taha's contention (and it is a big and very controversial one), the implications for Islam are enormous because, according to him, the Meccan Surahs teach:

> ... the complete equality of the sexes, the command to use exclusively peaceful means to spread the Muslim message, and the equality of all social groups, e.g. the abolishment of slavery and the freedom of physical punishment such as the amputation of hands.[23]

This daring act of revisionism has not been generally accepted (quite the reverse) and in fact, despite certain differences as discussed in this chapter, between the Meccan and the Medinan Surahs there is also a high degree of continuity and cohesion, and no departure on the part of the Qur'ān from its core messages.

Surahs from Medina tend to be rather longer than those received in Mecca, with text that "flows" and that is less sophisticated in terms of

---

21 Wild, 2006, 283.
22 Wild, 2006, 283-4.
23 Wild, 2006, 284.

structure than earlier revelations. Neuwirth[24] has identified a number of distinct types among the Medinan Surahs. One she terms "rhetorical" and compares to a sermon in structure, in which the community is directly addressed in a rather formulaic way, often using formulae that, in a stylistic sense, are reminiscent of the psalms that we find in the Bible. They often address the community directly,[25] and sometimes present Muhammad not "just" as the person who receives and transmits God's message,[26] but as someone who is frequently addressed directly by God or even as God's agent on earth.[27] They often refer to specific historical events rooted in Medina, such as the struggles between the Jews and the Muslims in the city, and the various battles between Muslims and non-Muslims along with rules about how war should be conducted, the behaviour of the Hypocrites, and a wide range of rulings about behaviours that are pleasing or not pleasing to God, in concert with details of how misdeeds should be punished. Historical events that are referenced include the Battle of Badar (discussed in Chapter Six)[28] Uhud,[29] the siege of Khaybar[30] and the expedition to Tabuk.[31]

As the Medinan verses are so much more intimately related to the historical events of the time, we find references to important events that impacted the Muslim community and even relatively mundane matters to do with the daily lives of the Muslims of Medina found cheek by jowl with divine rulings from God.[32] Topics that related to forbidden behaviours and resulting punishments, including adultery, theft, slander, the spoils of war, marriage, divorce, and how to deal with the custody of children are all

---

24 2006b, 155.
25 For example, Q. 22:24; 33:47-9.
26 Q. 33:28.
27 Q. 33:21.
28 Q. 3:123.
29 Q. 3:155-74.
30 Q. 48:15.
31 Q. 9:29.
32 Neuwirth, 2006 b, 155.

discussed in detail and provide a comprehensive guide to how to behave in accordance with God's wishes that remains relevant today.

Verses in the Medinan Surahs typically open with "O You who believe," or "O People of the Book" and are thus addressed to Muslims and the other monotheists, the Christians and Jews. The latter two groups are urged to accept Islam and its messenger, Muhammad, and the story of the Hypocrites is told, warning the Muslims that they should never succumb to evil behaviours such as those they displayed.[33]

In Surahs from Medina, the Qur'ān urges believers to give up their properties and give themselves over to God's path, which means that they should pray according to God's rule, give to charity, and command right and forbid evil. In its first reference to war, revealed to Muhammad very shortly after his flight from Mecca to Medina, Muslims are also told that they have the right to fight in self-defence.[34] This established the principle that war should only ever be waged in self-defence. It is interesting to note that mention of war could only have come after the Muslims left Mecca; there they had been a tiny, persecuted minority and standing up for themselves physically would inevitably have led to their slaughter. Things were different in Medina.[35] While the term "jihad" is mentioned in the earlier Meccan Surahs, there it refers to the idea of defending oneself from attack. In the Medinan Surahs, we start to see this term being used in the sense of an integrated community effort up to and including war, if absolutely necessary.[36] (This is a complex topic that will be discussed in some detail in Chapter Eighteen.)

The relative simplicity of the Medinan Surahs in purely stylistic terms is not reflected in simple content; quite the reverse. The lengthier texts in particular are often extremely complex, rich in content, and often assume a considerable degree of knowledge on the part of the listener of the earlier

---

33 Saeed, 2008, 187-8.
34 Q. 22:39-40.
35 Rahman, 1979, 37.
36 Rahman, 1989, 160.

Surahs, revealed in Mecca, which have already established a range of certitudes about the divine nature of the revelations, and the importance of Muhammad as God's messenger.

Another interesting feature of the Medinan Surahs is that they reflect the higher degree of ethnic diversity in the city as compared to Mecca. Because the Muslim community had to negotiate the new space they inhabited with a much wider range of people, the Qur'ān responded by providing detailed and complex rules regarding how they should interact with them, while also exalting God's word as revealed in the Qur'ān and affirming Muhammad's position as the "absolute and divinely guided leader of the Muslim community."[37] Muhammad's role in the emerging Muslim community is compared to that of Abraham in earlier times, and the Qur'ān acts to cement the importance of Abraham to Islam by underlining the great significance of the hajj pilgrimage in his honour. Carefully, the Qur'ān outlines the dual juxtapositions of tradition and innovation. While Islam was a new religion, and Muhammad its prophet, it also rests on the shoulders of the prophets who have gone before and is thus intimately linked with the long history of monotheism that had its origins in the area we know today as the Middle East:

> The new community that follows the Abrahamic cred is portrayed as now having a religion of its own, expressed by the word dīn in the sense of reckoning, or divine judgement to be held on the "last day." A visible symbol of this new religion is not least the fast of Ramadan that commemorates the crucial privilege of the community to be receivers of a scripture of their own.[38]

The holy obligation of pilgrimage to Mecca was established in this time and was essential for "Those who can afford it," which meant those who could afford to pay for their pilgrimage and also ensure that their families

---
37 Wild, 2006, 273.
38 Neuwirth, 2006b, 157.

were taken care of while they were away. This holy obligation stands to this day and is an important element of Islamic belief and practice. As well as being pleasing to God, pilgrimage served then, as it does now, to grow a sense of unity and brotherhood among all Muslims, regardless of social class, ethnicity, and race.

While there are clear differences between the Surahs from Mecca and those from Medina, it should not be inferred from this that the theological message that was being received by Muhammad had actually changed. Rather, the rules and messages received in revelation in Mecca are assumed and are ever-present as material that has been memorised by the Muslims, and that now provides the context for the new instructions on the nature of prayer, self-defence, and so forth.[39] In this way, the Meccan and Medinan revelations together provide us with a complete picture of how to live as a devout and faithful Muslim.

---

39 Neuwirth, 2006, 109.

CHAPTER 15

THE QUR'ĀN AND OTHER HOLY SCRIPTURES

THE QUR'ĀN IS very clear in stating that it, and it alone, is God's definitive and final word, while also recognising the great value and importance of the messages received by the earlier prophets and the importance of respecting those of other faiths: "God is greater and wider than to be confined to one particular creed to the exclusion of others. For God says: 'Wherever you turn, there is the face of God'."[1]

Moreover, the Qur'ān states that it is one in a line of revelations from God, with earlier revelations including the Torah, Psalms, and Gospel.[2] For this reason, Jews and Christians are designated as "People of the Book," and the fact that they share so much with Muslims makes it permissible for the latter to marry them and share meals with them.[3]

Many Muslims argue, and hold it a mark of faith to believe, that the scriptures that Jews and Christians hold dear have been corrupted and therefore no longer represent the Word of God. This belief is widely held among "ordinary" Muslims, but Islamic scholars tend to have a more nuanced view of the matter.[4]

The Qur'ān itself states that, "They distort the meaning of (revealed) words and have forgotten some what they were told to remember."[5] An

---

1 Q. 2:115.
2 Q. 3:3; 4:163.
3 Q. 5:5.
4 Saeed, 2008, 147.
5 Cited in Saeed, 2008, 147.

issue that various scholars have suggested was the subject of deliberate distortion is that of prophecies foretelling the arrival of Muhammad as a prophet. There are suggestions, supported by a number of Surahs in the Qur'ān, that some Jews and Christians who were his contemporaries may have hidden the relevant scriptures from the Torah and the Gospel.[6]

Important scholars of Islam have tended to maintain that the sacred texts themselves were not distorted, but that the meaning given to them became so, over time.[7] This seems to be supported by a verse in the Qur'ān which refers to teachings being distorted "with the tongues," which is likely to refer to the inevitable confusions and distortions (deliberate and otherwise) that can result from repeated oral iterations of a message.[8] A careful reading of the Qur'ān suggests that only some groups within the "People of the Book" distorted scripture, misrepresented the messages it contains, and appended lies that served their ungodly purposes. An example of the lies in question include the claim by some Jews and Christians that only they will be permitted to enter heaven.[9] The Qur'ān rejects this idea strongly and instead states that "any who direct themselves wholly to God and do good deeds, and believe hereafter" will be permitted to enter heaven after the Day of Judgement.[10]

In the early days of Islam, particularly after they had moved to Medina, which had a large Jewish population, Muhammad and his followers expected that many of the Jews, who shared their monotheistic beliefs, would harken to the message of God as received by Muhammad and quickly join the growing religion. They were disappointed when they realised that this was not the case, and that many of the Jews saw their own religion as an inheritance specific to them as an ethnic unit, and that they had no interest in the idea of a new revelation that opened up God's promise to all of humankind. The Qur'ān laments:

---

6   Saeed, 2008, 149.
7   Saeed, 2008, 147-8.
8   Saeed, 2008, 148.
9   Q. 2:111.
10 Khalil, 2012, 7-8.

Can You, then, hope that they will believe in what you are preaching – seeing that a good many of them were wont to listen to the word of God and then, after having understood it, to pervert it knowingly.[11]

This is bolstered by a remark in the Torah which says, "Ye have perverted the words of the living God".[12]

And what of the Christians? The Qur'ān speaks with admiration of the spiritual values of many of Christianity's priests and monks, and makes important assertions underlining the many factors shared by Christianity and Islam. Firstly, it notes that Christians are the people whose beliefs and way of life come closest to Islam, and secondly that the aforementioned priests and monks recognise God's holy truth when they hear it, and shed tears of humble gratitude for His guidance.[13] It states:

> For, when they come to understand what has been bestowed from on high upon this Apostle, thou canst see their eyes overflow with tears, because they recognize something of its truth.[14]

Another important quality shared by Christianity and Islam is that both are universal faiths. This means that, unlike Judaism and certain other faiths, they do not apply simply to people with particular racial or ethnic qualities, but that they are relevant to all of humanity, without exception.

Prior to Islam, Christianity had done great work in the area of helping people out of the metaphoric darkness in which they had been living, and ending awful practices including human sacrifice, infanticide, paganism, and polygamy, while also striving to meet the various educational, social and material needs of the people. With reference to this, the Qur'ān states:

---

11   Q. 2:75.
12   Jeremiah 23:26.
13   Ayoub, 2004, 313-4.
14   Q. 5:83.

THE QUR'ĀN AND OTHER HOLY SCRIPTURES

And do not argue with the followers of the earlier revelation otherwise than in a most kindly manner – unless it be such of them as are bent on evildoing and say: "We believe in that which has been bestowed from on high upon us, as well as that which has been bestowed upon you; for our God and your God is one and the same, and it is unto Him that we all surrender ourselves."[15]

Islam picked up the baton from Christianity and continued this work. It introduced major social reform, which included granting women more rights, especially in the areas of marriage and inheritance, giving them greater visibility in public life, and making the situations of the poor and orphans (among others) better. As Islam expanded beyond Arabia, these reforms were brought to Africa, Asia, and parts of Europe. At the same time, Muslim scholars made great breakthroughs in the areas of medicine, mathematics, architecture, culture and the arts. This movement of expansion and cultural flourishing was brought to a halt in some parts of the south of Europe. The last five hundred years have seen the stagnation of discovery in the Islamic world and the potential for important development within Islam has been hindered.

Neither the Qur'ān nor Muhammad demanded that Jews and Christians abandon their faiths in return for living in peace. In Islam, all humans are recognised as one in substance, even if they are racially and ethnically diverse. Islam was born when one man meditated in the cave of Mount Hira in the sole company of His Lord God. Christianity had brought a call to the people to live in a moral way, and a message of truth. Similarly, Islam was born at a time when many Arabs had realised that their ancient religious practices were futile, and were looking for meaning and truth.[16]

---

15 Q. 29:46.
16 Ayoub, 2007, 10.

The Qur'ān issues a direct invitation to the People of the Book (Jews and Christians) to come into communion with the followers of Islam, saying:

> Say "O followers of earlier revelation! Come unto that tenet which we and you hold in common: that we shall worship none but God, and that we shall not ascribe divinity to aught beside Him, and that we shall not take human beings for our lords beside God".[17]

Looking at the broader implications of this message, we can see that it applies not just to the Christians, who believe that Jesus is divine and even attribute some divine qualities to their saints, but also to the Jews, who similarly appointed Ezra and some of the great scholars of the Talmud with quasi-divine authorities.[18] Most of the scholars of the Qur'ān in classical times were in agreement that the fiercest accusations against the Jews were levelled at a historic group living in Arabia at the time of Muhammad and not at all Jews throughout history. For example, the Qur'ān reports that some of the Medinan Jews asked Muhammad, "How could we follow thee when thou hast forsaken our qibla and dost not consider Ezra a son of God?" Of course, it is important to observe that Ezra is hugely esteemed by all Jews, and that he has always attracted their highest praise as the one who restored and codified the Torah after it was lost while the Jews were in exile in Babylon. It is thanks to Ezra that the Torah is in the essential form it has today. In this way, Ezra, "promoted the establishment of an exclusive, legalistic type of religion that became dominant in later Judaism".[19] Since those days, Ezra has been venerated to the extent that his pronouncements on the Law of Moses are regarded by many Talmudists as almost as important as the law itself. In Islam, this sort of thinking is seen as deeply sinful, insofar as it suggests that an ordinary human being, no matter how accom-

---

17 Q. 3:64,
18 Q. 9:30-1.
19 Encyclopedia Britannica, 1963, Vol. IX, p. 15.

plished and important to the history of a particular group, is being raised to semi-divine status, with the blasphemous suggestion (even if it is just metaphorical) that he is a "son" of God. For this reason, the Qur'ān objects[20] to remarks such as "Israel is My son"[21] and "I am a father to Israel."[22]

From the very earliest days of revelation, Muhammad was in no doubt whatsoever that the messages he was receiving from God continued or revived those from the prophets who had gone before him. This is confirmed in the Qur'ān itself, which speaks of the revelations of Abraham and Moses in one of the earlier Surahs received in Mecca.[23] However, it is important to recognise that the respect and deference paid in the Qur'ān to the earlier prophets and their scriptures does not translate to a general acceptance of how all the "People of the Book" were actually practising their faith at the time of revelation. There has often been a great deal of confusion in attempting to marry the Qur'ān's veneration of important prophets of the past, including Abraham, Moses and Jesus, and the way in which it deals with the Jews and Christians living at the time of Muhammad. In this area, there are two major factors at play: On the one hand, Muhammad and his followers had numerous dealings with the Jewish populations living in Arabia at the time, and the Qur'ān discusses various incidents around these dealings, including political pacts that were made at the time, and what happened when these were violated. These are historical matters. Theologically speaking, we actually know very little about how much Muhammad was aware of the teachings and sacred documents of Judaism and Christianity.

On certain issues regarding how Muslims should perceive other "People of the Book", the Qur'ān is very clear and unambiguous. While respecting and acknowledging the importance of many of the earlier prophets, it unequivocally rejects the Christian claims for the divinity of Jesus, which is a

---

20 Asad, 2003, 263, note 44.
21 Exodus 4:22-3.
22 Jeremiah 31:9.
23 Q. 87:18-19.

doctrine that lies at the heart of Christianity, and it does this from the early days of revelation in Mecca.[24] Many Christian scholars of Islam have argued that this "misapprehension", as they see it, results from Muhammad's Christian contemporaries portraying Christ to him as a "son of god" in a physical sense, and that if he had been presented with a more sophisticated, spiritual view of Christ's divinity, he would not have rejected it. This argument is unconvincing on a number of levels. First of all, while the Qur'ān was mediated through Muhammad as messenger, he is not the author of it, but God is. Moreover, even the Meccans' polytheism, as we know it from the Qur'ān, cannot be considered as merely unsophisticated, crude and physical. While the Qur'ān does, as we have discussed above, accuse the pagans of venerating goddesses whom they referred to as "daughters of God," the term was not used in a simple literal sense, because these deities were considered by the Meccans to be "parts" of God.[25]

Some might argue that perhaps there was a distinct Christian sect in Arabia at the time that had developed independently, and did not subscribe to the belief in the Trinity, and that this group could have been the one that influenced Muhammad. But if such a group *had* existed (and there is no evidence that it did), then why would the Qur'ān have so firmly rejected the doctrine of the Trinity, both in the Meccan and the Medinan Surahs, along with the divinity of Jesus?[26] On this matter, the Qur'ān is remarkably clear:

> Verily, those who have attained to faith (in this divine writ), as well as those who follow the Jewish faith, and the Christians, and the Sabians – all who believe in God and the Last Day and do righteous deeds – shall have their reward with their Sustainer; and no fear need they have, and neither shall they grieve.[27]

---

24 Q. 19:16-36.
25 Q. 43:15.
26 Rahman, 1979, 26.
27 Q. 2:62; 5:69.

THE QUR'ĀN AND OTHER HOLY SCRIPTURES

This passage, which is cited several times in the Qur'ān, is in fact central to Islam. Here, it is made clear that human beings can be saved for all eternity when they are faithful to three central elements: they must believe in God, believe in the Day of Judgement, and live righteously according to God's teachings. This is in conflict with the Jewish doctrine that the historic fact of their descent from Abraham means that they are "God's chosen people" even if they are not living consistently with these three simple elements of faith.[28] Elsewhere in the Qur'an it is even clearer on this matter, where it says:

> Thou wilt surely find that, of all people, the most hostile to those who believe (in this divine writ) are the Jews as well as those who are bent on ascribing divinity to aught beside God; and thou wilt surely find that, of all people, they who say, "Behold, we are Christians," come closest to feeling affection for those who believe (in this divine writ): this is so because there are priests and monks among them, and because these are not given arrogance.[29]

In this passage, the Qur'an states that those who do not believe that God sends revelations exclusively to the Jews (who believed themselves to be His "chosen people") know that humility is the central element of all true faith. In this context, it does not include Christians among those who "are bent on ascribing divinity to aught beside God" despite the fact that they are guilty of such by considering Jesus to be God. Even considering this sinful view, the Christians do not deliberately or consciously worship a plethora of deities because their doctrine subscribes to a belief in the One True God, whom they consider to be manifested in a trinity of persons, including Jesus. While this teaching is anathema to Islam, it does not result from

---

28 Asad, 2003, 14, note 50.
29 Q. 5:82.

deliberate sin[30] but from a sort of overenthusiasm, an "overstepping the bounds of truth"[31] in their veneration of the prophet Jesus.[32]

The Qur'ān praises many qualities of the "People of the Book" (Jews and Christians) while condemning others, and inviting them to heed not just the Qur'ān itself, but also their own holy books, the Torah and the Gospel. It says:

> If they would but truly observe the Torah and the Gospel and all (the revelation) that has been bestowed from on high upon them by their Sustainer, they would indeed partake of all the blessings of heaven and earth. Some of them do pursue a right course, but as for most of them vile is what they do.[33]

Consider the implication that "If they would but truly observe the Torah and Gospel", they would listen to and obey these scriptures in the spirit in which they were originally meant, without the "wishful thinking" which led the Jews and Christians to believe, respectively, in their status as a chosen people and in the divinity of Jesus and "vicarious redemption" of his followers,[34] they would actually be following the Word of God. The Qur'ān states that a result of this wishful thinking has been God's anger towards them for not following His teaching. It says:

> Having broken their solemn pledge, We rejected them and caused their hearts to harden, they distort the meaning of the (revealed) words, taking them out of their context.[35]

Similarly, of the Christians the Qur'ān states:

---

30 Asad, 2003, 160, note 97.
31 Q. 4:171; 5:77.
32 Asad, 2003, 160, note 97.
33 Q. 5:66.
34 Asad, 2003, 158, note 54.
35 Q. 5:13. Similar accusations are made of the Jews in Q. 4:46.

THE QUR'ĀN AND OTHER HOLY SCRIPTURES

> And from those who say "behold, we are Christians, We have accepted a solemn pledge: and they too, have forgotten much of what they had been told to bear in mind, whereof We have given rise among them to enmity and hatred.[36]

The Qur'ān cites the fact that the Christians departed from Jesus's real teachings, and therefore from God's sacred truth, as the fundamental reason for the hatred that has led so often to allegedly Christian nations fighting each other; a situation that has led to endless war and internecine persecution.[37] It also laments the state of affairs that led to the Christians and Jews, both in theory worshippers of the One True God, rejecting each other as kindred, saying: "The Jews assert, the Christians have no valid ground for their beliefs, while the Christians assert: the Jews have no valid ground for their beliefs, and both quote the divine writ."[38]

While the Qur'ān reserves extreme respect and reverence towards those scriptures it considers earlier revelations, as discussed above, it does not demur from criticising those, above all the People of the Book, who have not remained faithful to the messages of their prophets, which are described as containing "wisdom, guidance, and light".[39] It says:

> Verily, it is We who bestowed from on high the Torah, wherein there was guidance and light. On its strength did the prophets, who had surrendered themselves unto God, deliver judgement unto those who followed the Jewish faith, and so did the (early) men of God and the rabbis.[40]

There is nothing to stop Muslims dining with and eating food prepared by "People of the Book", so long as the foodstuffs they consume are consistent

---

36 Q. 5:14. Also Q.2:59; 2:159,174; 3:78.
37 Asad, 2003, 144, note 27.
38 Q. 2:113,
39 Saeed, 2008, 146.
40 Q. 5:44.

with Shari'a law.⁴¹ This means that they cannot consume, for example, the forbidden categories of meat such as:

> … carrion, blood, the flesh of swine, and that over which any name other than God's has been invoked, and the animal that has been strangled, or beaten to death, or killed by fall, or gored to death, or savaged by a beast of prey, save that which you may have slaughtered while it was still alive, and (forbidden to you is) all that has been slaughtered on idolatrous altars.⁴²

The Qur'ān proceeds to disassociate the great prophet Abraham from both the Jews and the Christians, stating that those who can most convincingly lay claim to him are those who follow his teachings,⁴³ and presenting itself as "the determinant factor" when it comes to deciding what in the earlier scriptures is genuine and what is false in the earlier scriptures.⁴⁴

Scholars have sometimes been surprised to realise just how much Islam shares with the other Abrahamic religions, particularly Christianity. For example, there are many sites throughout the Middle East and the Levant area that are considered sacred sites of pilgrimage by Christians and Muslims alike. This was even truer in the case of early Christian history, before the devastation of the Crusades and the ensuing colonisation of the area.

It is interesting to note that Muslims who live as minorities in developed Western countries are often much freer to experiment with ideas and actions than their brothers in faith in their original homelands. It is intriguing to note that Muhammad himself said, long ago in seventh century Arabia, that:

---

41   Affi and Affi, 2014, 9.
42   Q. 5:3.
43   Q. 3:67-8.
44   Abduh, 1999, 410 ff.

> ... there will be a time when your religion will be like a hot piece of coal in palm of your hand; you will not be able to hold it. They asked him: would this mean there would be very few Muslims? "No", replied the Prophet, "They will be large in numbers, more than ever before, but powerless like the foam on the ocean waves."[45]

Some commentators have remarked that nowadays Muhammad's prediction looks remarkably prescient. Although today there are more Muslims than ever before, with Islam being practiced all over the world, for many their faith really has become "as hot as a piece of coal". Everywhere one looks, Muslim societies appear to be in turmoil, while Muslims themselves often feel that they are being constantly judged, as if in a court of law, and accused of being "terrorists", "fanatics" and of belonging to an "extremist religion". The young Muslims who are prepared to kill themselves for their beliefs attract the greatest hatred and fear, and many in the west assume that their fervour comes from hatred of the west, its lifestyle, and of democracy.[46]

Everyone, Muslim and non-Muslim alike, should be aware that God has made it clear that He created religious diversity and, as such, it is a matter of divine ordination.[47] God Himself, in His infinite wisdom, has created us in our diversity, each with our own racial, ethnic and religious identity. This is not something to fight against, but to embrace as part of God's grand plan for humanity.[48] The Qur'ān makes it clear that this very diversity is an important tool against corruption among humanity. Without other groups to limit their aspirations and ambitions for expansion, individuals or communities would be vulnerable to becoming obsessed with the idea of domination,[49] and humility is an essential aspect of faith.

---

45 Jami 'at Tirmidhi, 2007, Hadith 2260.
46 Ahmed, 2003, 1-12.
47 Q. 5:48.
48 Ramadan, 2004, 202.
49 Ramadan, 2004, 202.

While difference can lead to conflict (as it sadly often has throughout history), it also offers an opportunity for immense growth and learning.[50] For this reason, true Muslims are obliged to respect and strive to understand the spiritual paths of others, not just because this is in the interest of justice, peace and social harmony, but because it is an integral aspect of seeking God's divine truth.

Today above all, in our globalised world with its intricately interlinked economies and its multiple religions, we all need to strive to find a sense of the sacred, to reject the notion that religion itself is a cause of division, and to seek out and apply the principles of ecumenism and ethics that were gifted to us by all the great prophets. This goes beyond merely respecting religious difference to recovering the simple spiritual wisdoms that unite us. We need to open our hearts to God – metaphorically speaking, to open the door – because if we do not, He will only continue to knock more loudly. Above all we must never try to enforce with war; "One cannot reduce terror by holding over the world the threat of what one most fears".[51]

The Qur'ān tells us that, "God does not change the condition of people until they change that which is within their inner selves"[52] and urges all Muslims everywhere as follows:

> As for such (of the unbelievers) as do not fight against you on account of (your) faith, and neither drive you forth from your homeland, God does not forbid you to show them kindness and to behave towards them with full equity. God only forbids you to turn in friendship towards such as fight against you because of (your) faith, and drive you forth from you homelands, or aid (others) in driving you forth; and as for those (from among you) who turn towards them in friendship, it is they who are truly wrongdoers.[53]

---

50 Ramadan, 2004, 203.
51 Berry, cited in Boase, 2005, 2-3.
52 Q. 13:11.
53 Q. 60:8-9.

THE QUR'ĀN AND OTHER HOLY SCRIPTURES

While the Qur'ān often urges that there should be understanding and good relations between Muslims and other People of the Book, it also urges peace and kindness towards other groups. For example, Muslims should always deal kindly and fairly with pagan believers, unless they are actually trying to destroy Muslims and their faith. In this, all Muslims should follow Muhammad's own example. In the Qur'ān, God instructs Muslims to:

> Call Thou (all mankind) unto thy Sustainer's path with wisdom and goodly exhortation, and argue with them in the most kindly manner: for, behold, thy Sustainer knows best as to who strays from His path, and best knows He as to who are the right-guided.[54]
>
> And with respect to dealings with Jews and Christians: "… do not argue with followers of earlier revelation otherwise than in the most kindly manner".[55]

Islam's consistent emphasis on dealing with kindness, tact and reason in all religious discussions with individuals of other faiths is completely consistent with the Qur'ān's overarching instruction that "there shall be no coercion in matters of faith".[56]

Throughout history, those who have engaged in positive interreligious dialogue, with a view to enhancing mutual understanding and respect, have found this an intensely rewarding experience. There has never been a point in time at which this has been more important than today. One problem is that there is often a considerable disconnect between the people involved directly in the dialogue and those who practice the various religions on the ground. In general, there has been a failure to engage ordinary men and women in the process, and this is an enormous shortcoming.[57] Today, sadly, Muslims and non-Muslims often regard each other with sus-

---

54 Q. 16:125.
55 Q. 29:46.
56 Asad, 2003, 416, note 149.
57 Ramadan, 2004, 201.

picion and even enmity. The task of reducing these negative emotions, while also bringing the two groups close together, seems immense, but I believe that it is not insurmountable.

Inevitably, dialogue between members of the great Abrahamic faiths of Judaism, Christianity and Islam offers more points of common reference, as adherents of these faiths believe in the essential nature of monotheism, but it is also very important to engage in respectful dialogue with those of other faiths, and to use as a basis for discussion any common ground in the area of values and teachings.[58] It is from our faith that we derive our ethics and our values, but these things are meaningless unless they can be translated to useful, productive dialogue in this complex, challenging, wonderful social world that God has created for us all to share.

---

58 Ramadan, 2004, 203.

CHAPTER 16

ABROGATION IN THE QUR'ĀN

THE TERM "ABROGATION" refers to the repeal of a custom, institution, or law. Because so many claims about abrogation in the Qur'ān have been made in so many quarters, an understanding of this issue is very relevant to any discussion of the Qur'ān, which changed the world, starting in Arabia, in so many dramatic and fundamental ways.

Although formal Islamic scholars rarely discuss the notion of abrogation in much detail, there remain parts of the Islamic world in which these ideas are still widespread and popular. From the outset, it is essential to note that they are ideas that were first expressed generations after Muhammad's death and that they have absolutely no foundation in either the Qur'ān or the Hadith (and therefore no genuine foundation in Islam itself). A range of criteria are used in support of the concept, but none of them hold up to even relatively superficial scrutiny.

The concept of abrogation is a topic seldom discussed in Islamic studies, but one which is vigorously championed, along with an intense interest in the chronology of the Qur'ān[1] within some quarters of the Islamic world, prompting some scholars of Islamic law to devote a lot of attention to the matter of early Muslim history.[2] This concept was founded long after the death of the Prophet and has no true basis in Islam, but those who champion the notion of abrogation do so on various tenuous grounds.

---

1 Firestone, 2006, 317.
2 Knysh, 2006, 217.

They insist that there are several forms of abrogation. The first is when one Qur'ānic ruling replaces another. Those who believe in abrogation provide "evidence" in the form of a range of Qur'ānic verses that they believe to have been abrogated by others. In some cases, the abrogation is considered to have an impact on the ruling as well as the recitation of the verse in question. In these cases, they maintain, the whole verse should be considered to be withdrawn from the Qur'ān, and its ruling considered invalid and inapplicable to Muslim teaching.

One example of the wording and the ruling of a verse being abrogated is found in the following Hadith, which provides a ruling on breastfeeding (it is not permitted, according to the ruling, for a woman who has breastfed a male child who is not her biological infant to subsequently marry him when he grows up), and which is alleged to be an abrogated verse:

> Ā'ishah, may God be pleased with her, reported that it had been revealed in the Holy Qur'an that ten clear breast-feedings made the marriage unlawful. This was abrogated (and substituted) by five breast-feedings and God's Messenger, may peace be upon him, died (while this was recited as part of the Qur'an). Before (the death of the Messenger), it was found in the Holy Qur'an.

In fact, this verse simply does not exist in the Qur'ān, although the implication of this Hadith is that it was present in the Holy Book at one point and was subsequently removed. If this contention were true, it would have the worrying implication of calling the Qur'ān's very authenticity into question, as well as God's promise that He would protect the Qur'ān from corruption. We are bound to ask who would dare to assume that they had the authority to high-handedly remove a verse from the Qur'ān which was sent to humanity by God Himself. For this reason, most Islamic scholars reject the authenticity of this Hadith and the notion that it once formed part of the Qur'ān.

A second example of so-called abrogation is seen when a Qur'ānic ruling is said to be replaced by a Sunnah, or one of Muhammad's own sayings. This notion is easy to dismiss because, whatever the value of extra-Qur'ānic teachings, they can never replace the Qur'ān itself, even when they were originally uttered by Muhammad. This simple fact is acknowledged even by many scholars who subscribe to the idea that abrogation per se is reasonable. As no teaching can ever reach the status of the Qur'ān, no teaching can ever be equal.

The first form of abrogation is said to refer to a verse's wording but not to its ruling. In other words, the verse itself is no longer considered to be part of the Qur'ān, but its ruling should be held to be valid nonetheless. Lest anyone think that this is a matter purely of academic interest, consider the erroneous belief that married adulterers should be punished by being stoned to death. Those who believe in abrogation are prone to argue that the wording of the verse that is the source of this idea has been abrogated, but that the ruling is still God's law. They claim that the relevant verse, although it is no longer in the Qur'ān, is preserved in a Hadith that states: "'(As for the) elderly person, whether male or female, if they commit unlawful sexual intercourse, stone them (to death)'."[3] At a glance, we can see that this alleged one-time verse makes no sense whatsoever and therefore has no basis in the Qur'ān or in legitimate Islamic teaching. The Qur'ān clearly states that intercourse is only permitted within the context of lawful marriage, and therefore that anyone who engages in intercourse in another setting has committed adultery. It gives as punishment the penalty of receiving a hundred lashes, regardless of the marital status of the adulterer in question.

While the idea that this Hadith was abrogated from the Qur'ān can quickly be dismissed, a more detailed exploration reveals many problems with it. Linguistically, problems arise from the usage of the masculine term "shaikh" and its feminine equivalent, "shaikha", referring to the elderly. "Shaikh" is used three times in the Qur'ān. When the Prophet Jacob's sons

---

3 Saeed, 2006, 79-81.

are depicted as describing him, they refer to him as a very elderly man, or "shaikh kabīran".[4] Elsewhere, the Prophet Shu'aib's daughters describe their father similarly in the context of explaining to Moses why there was no man to help them to water their cattle.[5] In our third example, when the aged Abraham and his wife, Sarah, are told that they are going to have a child, Sarah is shocked and asks, "Shall I give birth when I am an old woman and this husband of mine an old man? This is a wonderful thing!"[6] In this verse, the Qur'ān uses the term "shaikh" to mean "old man" and "ajūz" to mean "old woman". "Ajūz" is used on two other occasions in the Qur'ān, with reference to the wife of the Prophet Lot.[7] It seems clear, therefore, that while the Qur'ān does use the term "shaikh" to mean "old man", it never uses the term "shaikha", but rather "ajūz".[8] This makes it more than clear that the Qur'ān could never have been the origin of this Hadith, but we are forced to ask, furthermore, why it singled out the elderly when this is a group that generally has a very limited libido and is presumably the least likely to engage in adultery. Are we supposed to assume that the adulterous who are *not* elderly should not face the same punishments for their misdeeds?

Why, despite all the evidence to the contrary, is the doctrine of abrogation so persistent in so many parts of the Islamic world? One reason is the fact that some verses seem at first glance to be very difficult to reconcile with one another. Rather than teasing out the logic and meaning behind them, it seems easier to state that one "abrogates" another, and thus put an end to the matter. This contention, problematic from the start, leads to further and further complications as there is no consensus among those who subscribe to the "doctrine of abrogation" as to which verses are subjected to it, which abrogate others, and whether the abrogation refers to the complete cancellation of the verse in question, along with the teaching

---

4 Q. 12:78.
5 Q. 28:23.
6 Q. 11:72.
7 Q. 26:171; 37:135.
8 Fatoohi, 2013, 172-3.

it contains, or merely to an element of it. Should it be removed from the Qur'ān, or left as part of the whole, with the understanding that it no longer applies? While some point to just five verses, others maintain that the doctrine applies to hundreds! When one commentator found himself unable to reconcile two verses, he would claim that the second abrogated the first, while another commentator, seeing no conflict between them, would reject this contention – and so on and so forth! Over the years, this has been a very thorny issue for this group of people.[9]

Commentators of the Qur'ān who have erroneously interpreted these verses as outlined above are stating their opinion, which is in no way based on anything Muhammad ever said. We should bear in mind that only Muhammad, who was the agent of revelation, can be seen as having the requisite authority to state whether or not a given verse should be accepted as part of the Qur'ān. Thus, he was the only one who had any authority to speak of matters of abrogation. Yet, despite this, there is not even one Hadith in which Muhammad addresses this issue.

The first verse in the Qur'ān states:

> Neither those from among the followers of earlier revelation who are bent on denying the truth, nor those who ascribe divinity to other beings beside God, would like to see any good ever bestowed upon you from on high by your sustainer; but God singles out for His grace whom He wills – for God is limitless in His great bounty.[10]

And the second, "Any message which We annul or consign to oblivion We replace with a better or a similar one. Dost thou not know that God has the power to will anything?"[11]

---

9 Ali, 1992, 51.
10 Q. 2:105.
11 Q. 2:106.

These elements of the Qur'ān refer to the fact that it has superseded the earlier books of revelation, the Torah and the Gospel. These verses have often been misinterpreted by a range of Islamic scholars, who have taken the term "ayah", which is translated here as "message", to imply its narrowest possible meaning, which is simply a verse, because each of the verses in the Qur'ān contains a message. From this starting point, they have leapt to the conclusion that some of the Qur'ān's own verses were abrogated, or changed, prior to the completion of the Holy Book. This notion summons the idea of an ordinary person going through the rough draft of a document and marking it up, deleting certain passages and replacing them with others with his or her cut-and-paste function. However, nothing could be farther from the truth. In fact, there is absolutely no evidence of any sort to suggest that Muhammad ever intended a single verse of the Qur'ān to be "abrogated". Moreover, given that the Qur'ān itself stresses its perfection and inimitability, suggesting that God might need to revise His own text strikes one as more than a little blasphemous!

Any scholar or would-be scholar of the Qur'ān should listen to the Holy Book itself, which addresses the issue of its perfection (thus negating the possibility of abrogation of any of the verses very clearly), when it says, "Will they not, then, try to understand this Qur'an? Had it issued from any but God, they would surely have found in it many an inner contradiction!"[12]

Quite simply, the doctrine of abrogation makes no sense, has no basis in fact, and cannot be considered as a viable approach to understanding and interpreting the Qur'ān. How, then, are we to interpret the above verses?

If, instead of seeing the term "ayah" in its narrowest sense, as "message", we read it as "passage", and then understand the second verse quoted above in the context of the first, which refers very clearly to Jews and Christians refusing to accept Muhammad's teachings, which came after the Torah and the Gospels and replace them, it is abundantly clear that the

---

12 Q. 4:82.

concept of abrogation here applies to the earlier revelations from God, and not in any way to the Qur'ān.[13]

Reading verse Q. 2:106, Islamic scholar Maulana Muhammad Ali[14] states his view that it is perfectly clear that it addresses the Jews directly. This opinion is given further weight by the fact that the two preceding verses discuss one of the Jews' objections to Muhammad's teachings, which was that they felt themselves unable to accept revelations of God that were not sent down to one of them. They asked, "Why was another revelation sent down to Muhammad and why was a law containing new commandments promulgated?" This question is answered in verses Q. 2:105 and 106, which tell them that God, and not unappointed groups of people, chooses whomever He wishes to be the vehicle of His message to humanity and that if a law was abrogated, it is because God had given Muhammad a better one.

During Muhammad's lifetime, the Jews of Arabia are quoted as saying that, "Our hearts are repositories of knowledge."[15] This refers to their belief that, because they were already in receipt of revelations from God (in the form of the Torah), they do not require any further messages from Him. The Qur'ān address this contention, saying:

> Vile is that (false pride) for which they have sold their own selves by denying the truth of what God has bestowed from on high, out of envy that God should bestow aught of His favour upon whomever He wills of His servants.[16]

In other words, it is clear that the Jews were experiencing jealousy about the fact that a non-Jew, the Arabian prophet Muhammad, was in receipt of revelations from God.

---

13 Asad, 2003, 22, note 87.
14 1992.
15 Q. 2:88.
16 Q. 2:90.

As we have noted elsewhere, the Qur'ān is noteworthy, among many other qualities, for being much more comprehensive than the earlier books of revelation, while also resembling them in many aspects. This makes perfect sense. The laws revealed to Moses, while they represented God's intentions for humanity, are also context-bound in that they are of primary relevance to a specific group of people at a specific period of time. For this reason, they applied only to them. When God, instead, sent down a new series of revelations with messages that are universally applicable, they clearly replace, or abrogate, the earlier ones.[17] The new laws are, quite simply, better, and they should be understood as such. This is clarified in the Qur'ān which says:

> And now that We replace one message by another – since God is fully aware of what He bestows from on high, step by step – they (who deny the truth) are wont to say, "Thou but inventest it". Nay, but most of them do not understand it?[18]

In this verse, it is made abundantly clear that the Qur'ān is referring to the replacement of earlier revelations with the messages that it contains. While the Qur'ān acknowledges that God sent revelations to earlier prophets, such as Moses and Jesus, it also clarifies that it represents a new series of messages from God, which should be understood as replacing and overriding all those that went before.

Another verse that addresses this issue reads as follows: "No falsehood can ever attain to it openly, and neither in a stealthy manner, (since it is) bestowed from on high by One who is truly wise, ever to be praised."[19] This refers to the impossibility of making changes or omissions, "between its hands, nor from behind it", which means that the Qur'an should not be changed openly or covertly, by means of interpreting verses in a knowingly

---

17 Ali, 1992, 51.
18 Q. 16:101.
19 Q. 41:42.

confusing way, or in a hostile manner. The well-known Islamic scholar Abu Muslim al-Isfahani[20] bases his rejection of the concept of abrogation on this verse. Other scholars, too, have pointed to the inconsistency inherent in accepting the Qur'ān's teaching of its own inimitability. Accepting the abrogation of any verses in the Qur'ān would entail declaring, either overtly or implicitly, that this aspect of the Qur'ān should now be seen as void or as false within the context of the Qur'ān. This simply cannot be, as the Qur'ān itself (in the verse quoted above) states that, "no falsehood can ever attain to it."[21] It should be noted that there is a distinct difference between the incremental approach often used in the Qur'ān to introduce a new concept or rule for living over the lifetime of Muhammad (as in the cases of the legislation associated with alcohol consumption and slavery, as discussed elsewhere in this book), in which each successive ruling on a particular matter adds to and supplants the previous ruling[22] and with "true" abrogation in which later verses are thought to completely supplant or change those that came before.[23] While the former refers to the substitution of latter verses in the Qur'ān with incrementally more detailed instructions, abrogation in the legal, juristic sense was a later development in Islam, and one that arose in the man-made attempt to eliminate difference and simplify often very complex legal matters.[24]

Lest anyone wonder whether the discussion of abrogation is a purely academic one to be argued over by Islamic scholars in their ivory towers, think again. The examples given above, and particularly that pertaining to the rules on adultery, show that there are often enormous legal and sociological repercussions when ideas about abrogation are integrated into a society's legal system. For example, there have been proponents of the theory of abrogation who have maintained that the presence of one verse which states that Muslims should "slay the unbelievers wherever you find

---

20 al-Dīn ar-Razi, n.d.,132.
21 Asad, 2003, 736, note 35.
22 Reinhart, 2006, 436.
23 Firestone, 2006, 317.
24 Rahman, 1989, 89-90.

them"[25] essentially renders null and void 124 verses in the Qur'ān that do not suggest any such drastic action.[26] For this reason, and more, it is very important to understand the need to recognise the Qur'ān itself as the ultimate arbiter of God's will for humanity, and not subsequent, and inevitably subjective, assessments made by mere mortals.

---

25 Q. 9:5.
26 Knysh, 2006, 218.

CHAPTER 17

QUR'ĀNIC INIMITABILITY

THE EXTRAORDINARY BEAUTY of the language of the Qur'ān, with its unparalleled richness and powerful use of metaphor, has led to scholarly consensus on the issue of the document's unique quality.[1] Furthermore, Muslims everywhere uphold the Qur'ān as not just unique but inimitable, in the fullest sense of the term. In other words, in the past, present and future, no text will ever match or approach it, as it is already perfection itself.

During the early phase of revelation, when he was still in Mecca, Muhammad went often to the Ka'ba to recite the Word of God. As time passed, he attracted growing numbers of followers, who often prostrated themselves on the ground or wept as he recited the sacred book.[2] All of this was frequently overlooked by a crowd of those who did not like what Muhammad was doing, but who could not help but notice that his messages, and the way in which they were framed, were truly extraordinary. As the number of Muhammad's supporters grew, his opponents continued to reject his message of salvation for all the faithful, while feeling incrementally more threatened by it, and by the growing number of his followers. But *why* did they stay to listen? Could it be that they secretly wished to hear his message, while rejecting him in public? None were able to dismiss the power of the Qur'ān's words. All they could do was try to heap scorn on anyone who recited them. Some of the onlookers were poets who resented the fact that they could never match the Qur'ān in terms of its incredible literary qualities. How hard it must have been for them to witness the sup-

---

1 Fazlur, 1979, 104.
2 Q. 5:83; 32:15; 17:107-9.

porters of the prophet reciting the Qur'ān, each striving harder than the other to express their love for its words more completely in their recitation!³ At the same time, while poets were greatly respected throughout the Arabic world, none of them claimed to be a prophet of God. Among the things Muhammad was accused of was that he was "just" a poet; that he himself was composing the verses he recited.⁴

The Egyptian scholar, Mustafa Sadiq al-Rafi'I, has stated that no one who has listened to the Qur'ān in a true and complete way can reject its message, saying that for such a person:

> Every single part of his mind was touched by the pure sound of the language's music, and portion by portion, note by note, he embraced its harmony, the perfection of its pattern, its formal completion. It was not so much as if something was recited to him but rather as if something had burned itself into him.

Repeatedly, throughout history we hear tales of conversions that reflect this wisdom. Perhaps the most famous of all is that of 'Umar bin Al-Khattab, who was heir-in-waiting to the Caliph.

At first, 'Umar – a young and vigorous man – was a fierce opponent of Islam. When he heard that his sister Fatima and her husband Sa'id bin Zayd had become Muslims, he rushed to their house. As he stood outside the door, he could hear someone reciting the Qur'ān to them. Enraged, he blustered into the room. The person who had been reciting hid, and Fatima concealed the pages under her legs. Umar demanded to know what he had heard while Fatima and Sa'id tried to calm him down. Unabashed, they told him that they had become Muslims and that they believed in God and His apostle, Muhammad. They said that this would be true, regardless of what 'Umar decided to do.

---

3 Boullata, 2000, 257.
4 Kermani, 2000, 109.

On hearing his sister and brother in law's words, 'Umar calmed down. He asked Fatima to tell him more about the scriptures, and she took out the concealed pages and handed them to him. 'Umar start to read the Surah Taha aloud, and when he had finished, he remarked on the beauty and nobility of the language therein, and made his way straight to Muhammad to convert to Islam.

The ninth century scholar, 'Ali Rabbani al-Tabari, said that "Muhammad is the one whose tongue God has made into a sword, and this sword is clear Arabic," while scholar Rashid Rida states that the words of the Qur'ān, so extraordinary in scope and beauty, "have changed the souls of the Arabs, and the Arabs, on their part, have changed the foreign nations", and that reciting the Qur'ān often leads to "the strongest spiritual and social revolution in history".[5]

One of the most important tenets of Islam is the doctrine of "i'jaz-al Qur'ān", which upholds the Qur'ān's inimitability. This doctrine originates in the sacred book, in which the Qur'an describes itself unequivocally as the only miracle of God ever facilitated by Muhammad, although formal theological thought on the matter dates to the centuries after Muhammad.[6] Moreover, although the Qur'ān makes numerous references to the preceding Holy Scriptures, at no point does it describe any book other than itself as miraculous, and it challenges those who would doubt it to "bring forth one Surah" like those of the Qur'ān"[7] and to "call upon anyone other than God"[8] in order to do so, Although the Qur'ān has issued challenges to humanity to produce a book that is comparable to it, nobody at any period in history has ever managed to do so. In fact, linguists and scholars of Arabic, with their intimate knowledge of the language and its manifold complexities, are in general agreement about the exceptional beauty and high quality of the language used in the Qur'ān.[9] The concept of "i'jaz" is

---

5 Boullata, 2000, 258-271.
6 Rahman, 2000, 279.
7 Q. 2:23.
8 Q. 10:38.
9 Rahman, 1989, 104.

often very difficult for those from non-Arabic cultures to understand, as there are few similar ideas and no close equivalents whatsoever, particularly in Western cultures.

The Qur'ān remains the only book of revelations from God that has remained utterly uncorrupted by human interference since its inception. Even in Mecca in the days of Muhammad, a place then famed for its many orators, masters of the Arabic language, nobody could even come close to producing a document comparable to the Qur'ān.

Arabic scholars have discussed the issue of the i'jaz in detail, concluding that, "The best composition is the least in size but the greatest in semantic outcome".[10] This means that the length of the text or verse that needs to be considered in order to understand the message it contains is relevant. The Qur'ān states:

> Will they not, then, try to understand this Qur'an? Had it issued from any but God, they would surely have found in it many an inner contradiction. The fact that it is free of all inner contradictions—in spite of its having been revealed gradually over a period of twenty three years—should convince them that it has not been composed by Muhammad.[11]

Since the early ninth century (thus about two hundred years after the initial period of revelation), scholars of Islam have laboured to prove that the Holy Book could not have been authored by any human being. In the process, they have examined the Qur'ān in incredibly minute detail (and, in the process, have led to a lively school of Arabic literary studies).

The doctrine of inimitability is first referenced in the Qur'ān itself, which simply states that it is not comparable to any other writing, and can never be matched by any work carried out by human hands.[12] Subsequently,

---

10 Graham and Kermani, 2006, 128-30
11 Q. 4:82.
12 Q. 2:24; 11:13; 10:38.

and to this day, this matter has attracted huge attention from all scholars working in the field of Islam, from linguists and literary theorists to interpreters of the Qur'an. They can look to various verses, including some rooted in Islamic history. When Muhammad's critics in Mecca suggested that the prophet himself was the originator of the Qur'an rather than God, as he claimed, the Qur'an ripostes:

> Say: "Even if all humankind and *jinn* (imperceptible spirits)) came together to produce something like this Qur'an, they could not produce anything like it, however much they helped each other".[13]

Taking as a starting point the fact that the Qur'an is the miraculous word of God, as revealed to Muhammad, scholars have analysed the language of the Qur'an and compared it to a wide variety of other texts, including poetry. From the middle of the medieval period, scholars produced great tomes on the topic of Arabic poetry, many of which foresaw the debates that would be held in the future in the areas of linguistics and literature. They discussed both the Qur'an and the entire corpus of literature in Arabic, bringing together the rich strands of theology and the study of literature in a manner not matched by modern scholarship. Ordinary people often found it difficult to distinguish between the style of the Qur'an and that of poetry. A traditional story tells of the well-known poet 'Abdalla ibn Rawaha, said to have been caught by his wife in the process of leaving his mistress's rooms. Have long suspected him of adultery, his wife challenged him to recite from the Qur'an. She knew that her husband would never do so if he had been unfaithful, as he had sworn not to recite the Holy Book unless he was pure. Rawaha recited three verses from a poem that resembled the Qur'an and, tricked by this, his wife was convinced of his innocence.[14]

---

13 Q. 17:88.
14 Graham and Kermani, 2006, 128-30 and Rippen, 2006, 109.

However, by studying both literature and the Qur'ān intently, scholars could see the difference. Moreover, throughout Arabic history following the revelations received by Muhammad, the Qur'ān has been hugely influential not just in the areas of theology and spirituality, but in the development of a unique literature throughout the Arabic-speaking world, and even non-Muslim scholars recognise it as a singular work of literature. Although the Qur'ān both reports that Muhammad was sometimes referred to as a "poet" by those who stated that he himself was the author of the Qur'ān, and rejects the very notion that it should ever be referred to as poetry, the language it contains is comparable to the finest poetry in various ways, including its profound emotional depths of expression, and its extraordinary use of rhythm, which approaches musicality at times. When reciting the Qur'ān, faithful Muslims do so in such a way that the beauty of the language, as well as the content of the verses, is evident even to those who are not familiar with Arabic,[15] although, sadly, much of the Qur'ān's artistry, if not all of its content, is lost in translation. While the translation of complex, nuanced and poetic material also poses a tremendous challenge, the Qur'ān appears to represent the greatest challenge of all, even to the most gifted translator. At the time of Muhammad, Arabic-speakers were:

> ... the most poetically and linguistically sophisticated of peoples, the people who above all treasured and mastered the art of eloquence, and who could be convinced only by a literary miracle.[16]

In fact, at various periods throughout history, there have been debates about the matter of whether the Qur'ān should be translated at all, with some feeling that translation, even for the purpose of trying to bring the Qur'ān's message to the people, should be inadmissible.[17] For this reason,

---

15 Rahman, 2000, 41.
16 Graham and Kermani, 2006, 230.
17 Leemhuis, 2006, 155.

while there are many devout Muslims speaking a wide range of languages other than Arabic, without a knowledge of the language the full depth of meaning of the Qur'ān is bound to be lost on them. It is, therefore, much to their benefit to study Arabic as well as translations of the sacred text; a challenge that will enhance their lives in many ways.[18]

The noted scholar 'Abd al-Qahir al-Jurjani devoted himself to an exploration of poetic language in Arabic, both in the context of the Qur'ān and in poetry per se. In his book *Evidence of the Qur'ān's Miraculous Character* he explores and analyses certain stylistic turns of phrase in minute detail. We can clearly see that the Qur'ān had an immense and lasting impact on Arabic poetry. Prior to the Islamic period, while there was a thriving tradition of oratory and poetry, poets tended to work within a narrow range of genres. After the revelation of the Qur'ān, Arabic poets experienced a sort of renaissance, with the emergence of new ways of using imagery, poetic motifs, and the richness of the Arabic language. In fact, there is simply no way in which to discuss Arabic poetry without making constant reference to the Qur'ān which, apart from its own intrinsic poetic qualities, has influenced the development of Arabic literature from the early days of Islam. The well-known contemporary poet Adonis, an important figure in Arabic literature, views the Qur'ān as a decisive point in Arabic literature because of its aesthetic and literary qualities, and the fact that it represents a schism from the conventions of the time.[19]

We know from history that the Meccans, threatened by Muhammad's revelations, went to famous poets and experts to see how they should understand the things that Muhammad was saying. These experts told them in wonderment that the Qur'ān defied categorisation, as it was not rhyming prose, nor was it poetry.[20] For example one poet, Walīd bin Mughīra, was surprised and shocked by how different Muhammad's revelations were to the poetry that he was familiar with, saying: "I know many qasides and

---

18 Rahman, 1989, 105.
19 Graham and Kermani, 2006, 131.
20 Graham and Kermani, 2006, 127-131.

rajaz verses, and I am even familiar with the poems of the Jinee. But, by God, his recitation is like none of them."[21] In fact, the Qur'ān itself makes reference to its unusual and powerful use of language:

> God has been bestowing from on high the best of all teachings (ahsan al-hadith), in the shape of a divine writ fully consistent within itself, repeating each statement in manifold forms – (a divine writ) whereat shiver the skins of all who of their sustainer stand in awe (but) in the end their skins and their hearts do soften at the remembrance of (the grace of) God.[22]

When something unusual happens, our skin is typically the first part of the body to register its impact on us. When one has a spiritual experience, the first sensory reaction is typically the feeling of "goosebumps" on the skin. In the verse cited above, the Qur'ān cites the feeling of goosebumps as a reaction to the word of God, prior to the emergence of a new feeling of calm and readiness to receive God's message.

It is important to bear in mind the position that poets held in Arabian society at the time. While they were very important figures, they did not challenge societal conventions at all, but tended to occupy positions of leadership within their respective tribes. The Qur'ān, however, threatened the very nature of tribal society, and of the people's polytheistic practices, and posed an enormous threat to the status quo in its proclamation of the oneness of God and of His people.[23]

While the wider culture of poetry and oratory has resonance in the Qur'ān (and Muhammad was initially mistaken by many for a poet), the sacred book also displays many differences: "The norms of old Arabic poetry were strangely transformed, the subjects developed differently, and

---

21 Kermani, 2000, 109.
22 Q. 39:23.
23 Kermani, 2000, 109.

the meter was abandoned."[24] Try as they might, and regardless of how many experts they consulted, none of Muhammad's critics was able to even come close to reproducing the beautiful, transcendental language of the Qur'ān.[25]

As a side note, it is worth mentioning that the importance of Arabic to the Qur'ān actually has many aspects. Arabic, as stated elsewhere, was an important unifier among the peoples of the Arabian Peninsula. At the time of Muhammad, there was no concept of nationhood among these groups, which were often at war with one another. In many ways, their common language, Arabic, was the one thing that brought them all together. In everyday speech, there were many dialectal differences that would have made communication difficult at times, especially as the vast majority of people was illiterate. However, among the educated, and especially those who created, recited, and listened to poetry, formal Arabic was standard and relatively unchanging,[26] and "old Arabic poetry with its formal language, sophisticated techniques and extremely strict norms and standards was identical."[27] By using this language in such a perfect and transcendental way, the Qur'ān signals its eternal relevance to all peoples everywhere.

Another factor in proving the Qur'ān's inimitability is Muhammad's illiteracy. No matter how great his intelligence, he would simply have been unable to produce a document such as the Qur'ān. (It is important to note, however, that while the Qur'ān appears to support the idea of Muhammad being illiterate,[28] the word "ummiy", which is often translated as "illiterate", can also be translated as "gentile," in which case it would reflect the fact that Muhammad was Arabian rather than Jewish.)

It is noted that each of the prophets of God has been given a sign or proof from God to His people that He is speaking the truth. In each case, the miraculous sign has been especially relevant to the people and culture

---

24 Kermani, 2000, 108.
25 Graham and Kermani, 2006, 129.
26 Kermani, 2000, 107-8.
27 Kermani, 2000, 108.
28 Q. 7:157-8.

of the time and place in question. For example, Moses was given a staff that turned into a snake; a miracle perfectly adapted to the magical thinking of the people of his age. Jesus was given the capacity to cure lepers; a miraculous quality that resonated with an oppressed group, the Jews, in which sickness was ever-present. Muhammad, an illiterate man, was given the gift of eloquence in the medium of the holy Qur'ān. Again, in a culture and at a time in which the oratorical arts were greatly prized, this was the most effective way for God to signal to humanity that Muhammad really was bringing them His message.[29]

The Islamic scholar al-Bāqillāni, who dates from the eleventh century and first formalised the concept of i'jaz as we know it today, wrote that each prophet who brings God's message to man is given his own miracle. He wrote that:

> ... a prophet's mission is not authentic without his giving some evidence and legitimising himself through a sign. He does not distinguish himself from a liar by his features, nor by what he himself says, nor by anything else but by proof which has appeared for him so that through it he can prove the validity of his mission.[30]

For Muhammad, the fact that the language and expression of the Qur'ān was so perfect as to be inimitable was the proof, the miracle that the people needed to know that he was truly providing them with the Word of God:

> When the native speakers of (Arabic) saw that all of them were incapable of challenging, finding fault with, or imitating the Qur'ān, they found themselves in the same situation as those who had seen the white hand or the staff changing into a snake, which revealed their lies.[31]

---

29 Rahman, 2000, 279.
30 Graham and Kermani, 2006, 129.
31 Graham and Kermani, 2006, 129.

QUR'ĀNIC INIMITABILITY

At the time of the revelations, Arabic was a remarkably concise language. In its written form, parts of a sentence could be left out when they were clear from the context and this "elision", or "ellipsis", is a recurring feature throughout the document, and especially when it concerns oath-making, and comparing and contrasting.[32] This, of course, can lead to difficulties in translation. For example, in the Qur'ān, Heaven is often described as featuring streams of water. The relevant Arabic phrase, "tajri min tahtiha al-anhar", can be translated as "Under which rivers flow", which can suggest in translation that the Qur'ān is stating that there are underground rivers in the afterlife in Heaven. The reader with a good knowledge of Arabic understands that, instead, the words evoke a garden in the shade, through which many streams flow.[33] These ellipses occur in the context of an extraordinary range of literary techniques and methods, including the ample use of inversion, metaphor, abbreviation, idiom, repetition, and allusion.[34] In any language, the presence of so many very diverse and often very subtle techniques would render translation very difficult. The extremely nuanced quality of the Arabic language, with its propensity to put these linguistic techniques to frequent use, makes an effective, accurate translation of the Qur'ān all the more challenging. Some scholars, such as ibn Qutayba, consider these ellipses, identify eight discrete varieties among them, and discuss the ability to express complex and profound ideas in just a few words, as a crucial aspect of the Qur'ān. Ibn Qutayba states that:

> ... you see that not mentioning something is more eloquent than mentioning it, refraining from expression more informative than indulging in it, and you find yourself more articulate on something if you do not speak it, and the explanation more complete if you do not announce it.[35]

---

32 For example, Q.11:17, 50:1; 13:31; 38:9.
33 Haleen, 2010, xxx.
34 Rahman, 2000, 278.
35 Qatayba, in Rahman, 2000, 279.

Of the many examples of ellipsis, it is necessary to provide only a few here. In one verse, for example, the Qur'ān says, "Ask the city," by which it means, "Ask the people of the city",[36] while in another it states, "pilgrimage is the months best known," by which it means, "the period of pilgrimage is the months best-known."[37] Others forms of ellipsis involve invoking one half of a comparison, and allowing the reader's or listener's mind to "fill in" the missing element. For instance, the Qur'ān says, "Not all of them are alike. Some of the People of the Book are an upright community, rehearsing the signs of God all night long and they prostrate themselves."[38] Although it does not use words to compare this "upright community" to those who are less than upright, the comparison is implicit and can be made even in the absence of actual language.

Muslims, believing in the Qur'ān's inimitability, can point (among other things) to the complete lack of internal contradiction in the text, and the fact that it contains a large amount of historical data about preceding prophets and the people they lived amongst; information that Muhammad could never have known. Some recent scholarship of the Qur'ān also suggests that it contains descriptions of scientific data that were not known at the time of Muhammad, but discovered many centuries later.[39] For example, proponents of this theory claim that the following verse refers to the Big Bang:

> Are, then, they who are bent on denying the truth not aware that the heavens and the earth were (once) one single entity, which We then parted asunder?-and that We made out of water every living thing? Will they not, then, believe?[40]

---

36 Rahman, 2000, 280.
37 Rahman, 2000, 280.
38 Q. 3:113-4; 39:9.
39 Saeed, 2008, 53.
40 Q. 21:30.

When making bold claims of "evidence" for one scientific theory or another in the Qur'ān, it is important to bear in mind that scientific findings change all the time. What today's research indicates is the truth about something may well be disproven tomorrow. However, while it would be wise to hesitate before ascribing the above verse to a description of the "Big Bang", it is fair to say that it certainly does refer to the universe as a unified whole. In Muhammad's day, nobody knew that the entire universe originally derived from the element hydrogen which, through gravity, eventually became solar systems and galaxies, and moved into progressively smaller parts; stars and planets. In the statement that God made every living thing out of water, we find a simple but wonderful truth that all scientists recognise today. There are three major implications: Firstly, all living matter is known to have originated in the sea; secondly, water, and only water, possesses the specific qualities that are needed in order for life to appear and continue to develop; and thirdly, the building-block of every living cell, plant or animal, which is known as protoplasm, is largely made up of water. Thus, life is utterly dependent on water.[41] The Qur'ān was received and written down at a time in which there was no scientific understanding of the water cycle, and yet it describes it in terms that are perfectly consistent with what we know today.[42] It also describes the creation of the seas, and the relationship between them and the rivers that flow into them, often in the context of a discussion about navigation.[43] It describes such phenomena as changes to the air at altitude,[44] the presence of electricity in the atmosphere,[45] and the nature of shadow.[46] It discusses how the wind carries pollen to fecundate fruit-bearing trees, while the rain allows nature to flourish and grow, associating the wind and rain in a way

---

41 Asad, 2003, 491-2.
42 Q. 50: 9-11; 23:18-9; 15:22.
43 Q. 14:32; 16:14; 31:31; 41:44; 25:53; 35:12; 55:19-22.
44 Q. 6:125.
45 Q. 13:12-3.
46 Q. 16:48; 81; 25:45-6.

that would not be understood by science for many centuries.[47] While this matter is fascinating for the scientifically literate to read, it must also have been compelling for a society dependent on said trees for much of their sustenance.[48]

The Qur'ān also discusses the binary nature of the world, in which each thing has its natural opposite.[49] This can be seen everywhere in the natural world; in human sexuality, in animals and plants; and in natural qualities including heat and cold, positive and negative magnetism and charges, and more.[50]

Although the Qur'ān discusses the creation of earth and the heavens, it does not provide the details of a sequence for these events,[51] referring variously to the creation of earth and the creation of heaven.[52] In just one instance is a sequence referred to, where it says:

> Are you the harder to create or is it the Heaven that (Allah) built? He raised its canopy and fashioned it with harmony. He made dark the night and he brought out the forenoon. And after that He spread it out. Therefore he drew out its water and its pasture. And the mountains He fixed firmly. Goods for you and your cattle.[53]

The above verse indicates that earth must have been created before the heavens were made, and "spread out" and made arable and suitable to support humankind after the cycle of day and night had been established. At various points in the Qur'ān the wonders of creation are given as ample proof to humanity that God exists, and that His gifts to humankind are

---

47 Q. 15:22.
48 Ali, 1934, 713, note 1960.
49 Q. 36:36.
50 Asad, 2003, 676-7, note 18.
51 Bucaille, 1976, 147.
52 Q. 7:54; 41:9-12.
53 Q. 79:29-33.

all around us.⁵⁴ Intriguingly, the Qur'ān refers to the creation of *earths* and *heavens* in the plural,⁵⁵ suggesting that at some point in the future science might develop sufficiently to find other planets like ours elsewhere in the galaxy. It describes God as carrying out creation in six periods,⁵⁶ including "things in the heavens", "things on earth" and "things between the heaven and the earth".⁵⁷ The Qur'ān points out the beauty and perfection of the things we see all around us: the glory of the heavens⁵⁸ and God's dominion over what He has made.⁵⁹ It explains how celestial bodies, such as the sun and moon, appear to travel through the sky but are really following the trajectory of their own orbit;⁶⁰ a concept that was not understood at the time of revelation, but was uncovered by scientists centuries later.

As science grows in scope, and researchers become increasingly able to understand the intricacies of the universe, it is impossible not to note the remarkable ways in which the Qur'ān discussed scientific truths that we know now, but that were not known at the time when it was written down.

As stated elsewhere, one of the key qualities of the Qur'ān is the fact that provides a detailed guide to life in all its aspects, explaining everything we need to know in detail, including "commands, similitudes, examples, stories, parables, etc."⁶¹ rather than simply telling stories and giving vague suggestions. This guide to living occurs in the context of a document of extraordinary and unparalleled linguistic, scientific and literary complexity, to the extent that it is rightly considered to be miraculous, in and of itself.

---

54 Q. 21:30; 41:11; 2:29
55 Q. 2:29; 23:17; 67:3; 71:15-6; 87:12.
56 Q. 25:59; 32:4; 50:38.
57 Bucaille, 1976, 152.
58 Q. 50:6; 31:10; 13:2; 55:7; 22:65
59 Q. 23:86; 45:13; 55:5; 6:96; 14:33; 36:39; 16:1; 6:97; 16:16; 10:5.
60 Q. 21:33; 36:40
61 Yusuf, 1934, 805.

CHAPTER 18

QUR'ĀNIC JIHAD

The term "jihad" is commonly misused, perhaps particularly in the Western media. Literally speaking, it refers to striving hard, exerting ourselves to make the best effort possible and trying always to do our best to serve God and live according to His message as revealed to His prophet Muhammad. In other words, jihad means that God calls everyone to do as much as they can to live their lives according to God's holy law. Jihad can also be employed as a tool of deterrence to avoid potential wars and/or conflicts as the following Qur'anic verse attests: "Hence, make ready against them whatever force and war mounts you are able to muster, so that you might deter thereby the enemies of God, who are your enemies as well..."[1]

In the Qur'ān it says:

> "O You who have attained to faith! Shall I point out to you a bargain that will save you from grievous suffering. You are to believe in God and His Apostle, and to strive hard in God's cause with your possessions and your lives, this is for your own good – if you but knew it.[2]

We can therefore understand jihad to mean a Muslim's sacred religious and legal duty to strive against evil in all its manifold forms and to spread the word of God by using their hearts and tongues to command right and forbid wrong, as we have discussed in some detail in Chapter Eleven.

---
1 Q. 8:60.
2 Q. 61:10-11.

QUR'ĀNIC JIHAD

It is important to recognise from the outset that jihad emphatically does *not* mean "holy war"[3] although, as we shall see, in certain very limited and proscribed circumstances, it can at times incorporate violent action. To put it simply, jihad is not holy war, but occasionally holy war can be an element of jihad.

When we live in the service of God, violence can only be seen as an element of jihad in the context of self-defence. Moreover, it is only in self-defence that jihad is ever seen as a collective duty. When fighting is referenced in the Qur'ān specifically, the term generally used is "qital", whereas "jihad" is taken to refer to striving, and sometimes argumentation, as in the following verse: "Hence, do not defer to (the likes and dislikes of) those who deny the truth, but strive hard against them by means of this (divine writ), with utmost striving."[4]

Jihad takes for granted the fact that Muslims will have people and things to strive against, which might include an oppressive regime that restricts their religious freedom, parents, family members or friends who try to persuade them to ignore or leave their faith, or any inclinations they might personally have to act against God's law. In this respect, jihad can be seen as a daily endeavour in which every Muslim individually takes part, striving in a myriad of small and large ways to do their best to serve and please God.

Jihad also implies an adversary, or someone or something to struggle against in this continuous journey towards pleasing and exalting God in every way possible. Jihad, Firestone states:

> ... is exerting one's utmost efforts and abilities in relation to an "other," and that other is usually defined as "an object of disapprobation" that could range from a concrete human enemy to Satan or to the evil inclinations in one's own self.[5]

---

3 Firestone, 2006, 308.
4 Q. 25:52.
5 Firestone, 2006, 309.

In summary, jihad refers to each and every believer's responsibility to pray, to give to charity, to command good and forbid evil, and to strive to establish an Islamic system of moral and social norms in the society in which they live.

Jihad can be a tool, exercised at the individual level, towards establishing the sort of society that God has demanded we strive towards on earth.⁶ It is a nuanced term that can incorporate a wide range of behaviours and actions, ranging from simply being generally faithful and pious to taking part in or supporting a holy war⁷ (which, as we will shortly explore in detail, can only be engaged in in a very limited range of circumstances). Above all, it refers to a deeply individual relationship with God and with one's obligations and duties to Him. For example, with respect to the matter of remaining true to Islam even though our loved ones do their utmost to convince us to turn away from it, the Qur'ān states:

> If your fathers, your sons, your brothers, your spouses, your clans, the wealth which you have acquired, the trade whose decline you fear and your houses with which you are so pleased – if all these things are dearer to you than God, His Messenger, and struggling in His Cause, then wait till God brings down His judgement; God guides not an unrighteous people.⁸

In this context, we can engage in jihad by refusing to turn our backs on the one true faith, even if our very own parents try to persuade us to revert from Islam to paganism or another faith that is not of God.⁹ The text above is rooted in the situation in Mecca, in which many of the pagan Quraysh rejected Muhammad's message and strove to prevent others from joining the newly converted Muslims. However, it is just as applicable today when

---

6 Rahman, 1989, 63.
7 Firestone, 2006, 311.
8 Q. 9:24.
9 Rahman, 1991, 159.

family members and friends, or even the messages we receive from the media, or our own imperfect hearts, might try to dissuade Muslims from remaining true to their faith.

The Qur'ān uses the term "shir'ah", which means "the way to a watering place" to indicate the sort of legal system that is required in order for a community to thrive both socially and spiritually. Striving to establish such a legal system, one in which Islam can flourish and the many rules for living provided by the Qur'ān can be followed, can be part of jihad. Consider for a moment the climate of Arabia, in which the Qur'ān was both received and written down. In this context, a watering-place or oasis, where animals and people alike find the very substance that they need to survive, is the key to life; a very vivid metaphor to use in an arid, desert land in which the physical environment itself could sometimes be a threat to existence. Similarly, without an adequate social and moral code, ideally the perfect social and moral code provided to us by the Qur'ān, no community can truly thrive. Such a code is the "watering-place" or oasis of the spirit.

Of course, the specific nature of jihad in each case will inevitably be impacted by the particular characteristics of the historic period in question. Life is very different today to how it was in the seventh century, and the challenges that we face now are often different too. In the very earliest days of Islam, Muslims were a tiny and persecuted minority, and in this context there was no way they could have considered organising themselves to spread Islam on a grand scale. Moreover, Muhammad had been born into, and the early Muslims lived in, a time and place that were particularly bellicose.[10]

Revelations from God are rare events and when God makes His voice known directly to humanity, we are forced to assume that this is because He intends for us (the human race in general) to make a dramatic change to how we live in order to please and serve Him better. In each case of revelation, initially only a small number of people have listened to the Word

---

10 Firestone, 2006, 312.

of God and, in so doing, have made it incumbent upon themselves to share His message with the world.[11] The early Muslims found themselves in this position within a cultural setting in which war and physical violence were never far away. Arabia was a tribal society based on commerce, and tribal conflict was a simple fact of life. Whereas the followers of Christ lived at a time when the local population was dominated by the might of the Roman Empire, and thus would never have been able to spread their word through military action, even if they had tried, both the Old Testament and the Qur'ān were revealed in the context of tribal cultures that were more or less constantly in a state of warfare and were, broadly speaking, evenly matched, meaning that a resolution was never likely. In this historical context, we have to accept that the newly emerging Muslim community would have had no choice but to engage with the local norm of militancy merely in order to survive. As Muhammad and his followers had been tasked by God with the much greater task of also bringing God's message to Arabia and the world, some violence was inevitable,[12] and every member of the Muslim community, whatever their position and station in life, was required to engage in jihad, up to and including engaging in violence within the limits and proscriptions provided by God.[13] Thus, while jihad does not mean or necessarily imply violence or war, there are times when violence and war can be part of jihad.

While the very earliest Muslims were a very weak community, after their relocation to Medina and the growth in the number of converts and the strength of the group, Muhammad started to receive more revelations urging the Muslims to stand up for themselves in the face of the frequent difficulties they faced, and not to accept aggression and intimidation from those who would silence them and refuse to listen to God's message for humanity as revealed to His prophet. This was in contrast to the earlier revelations, received

---

11 Firestone, 2006, 312.
12 Firestone, 2006, 313.
13 Firestone, 2006, 314.

QUR'ĀNIC JIHAD

by Muhammad while he was still in Mecca.[14] While some critics have considered the Qur'ān's teachings on this matter to be inconsistent, in fact they reflect the changing circumstances in which Muhammad and his followers found themselves. Had they insisted on fighting back against their aggressors in Mecca, they would have been wiped out, and an opportunity to bring God's word to the people would have been lost. In Medina, from a stronger position, they were better able to defend themselves against those who wished them ill, and more able to engage in what Rahman describes as "a positive participation in the direct entry into and changing of the state of affairs."[15] With each stride forward and advance in numbers, the Muslim community was in a better position to work towards a greater degree of influence in the world of men in terms of spreading God's message far and wide.

While spreading God's word is a fundamental aspect of jihad, this should never be mistaken with the idea that it is appropriate to force others to adopt the faith. Early Islamic leader Abu Hanifa stated that jihad should never entail going to war with non-Muslims simply because of their lack of faith. Conversely, Islamic teaching has consistently maintained that Muslims should be extremely tolerant towards those who do not believe, in particular the Christians and Jews with whom they share so much; the People of the Book.[16] At no point does the Qur'ān state, suggest or intimate that Muslims should go to war so as to change others' religion. In fact, it states the precise opposite, saying:

> There shall be no coercion in matters of faith, Distinct has now become the right way from (the way of) error: hence, he who rejects the powers of evil, and believe in God has indeed taken hold of a support most unfailing, which shall never give way: for God is all-hearing, all-knowing.[17]

---

14 Firestone, 2006, 316-7.
15 Rahman, 1979, 260.
16 Khadduri, 1984, 164-5.
17 Q. 2:256.

The Qur'ān clearly states that forcible conversation is strictly prohibited in Islam. Therefore, anyone who "converts" under such circumstances is not really a Muslim at all because they have not actually entered a Covenant with God; they have simply pretended to do so because they are afraid, or because it seems expedient. Moreover, any Muslim who tries to force or coerce a non-believer to convert to Islam is actually committing a terrible sin in the eyes of God. This flies in the face of the widespread and grievously misinformed view that maintains that Islam offers those who do not believe the choice between converting or accepting a violent death.[18] Because religion rests upon true faith and free will, a forcible conversion is meaningless, and attempting to compel people to change their religion is an offence to God. The Qur'ān states that, "Unto every one of you have We appointed a (different) law and way of life".[19] In this verse, we can read the phrase "every one of you" as indicating the various tribes and communities that make up humanity which, as we have seen elsewhere in this text, was created in this way by God Himself.

As mentioned briefly above, Islam permits for war only in a very limited range of scenarios. In this respect, it shares the view with most other world religions, including Christianity, that there are some circumstances in which war can be justified, and even seen as holy. Historically, Islamic scholars have not always been in perfect consensus on the issue of which wars can be considered holy, but all agree that the Qur'ān is the ultimate authority on this matter.[20]

While recognising that war is very occasionally the lesser evil, the Qur'ān reiterates its message of peace in many instances. It states, "Fight in God's cause against those who wage war against you, but do not commit aggression, for, verily, God does not love aggressors,"[21] and, "If they do not let you be, and do not offer you peace, and do not stay their hands, seize

---

18 Asad, 2003, 58, note 249.
19 Q. 5:48.
20 Firestone, 2006, 308.
21 Q. 2:190.

QUR'ĀNIC JIHAD

them and slay them whenever you come upon them: and it is against these that We have clearly empowered you (to make war).²²

These verses make it abundantly clear that the *only* violence permitted to Muslims is self-defence. God adds that when aggressors cease with their acts of violence, God will yet forgive them²³ and that, when they do, Muslims should immediately cease fighting them.²⁴ The Qur'ān states, "And fight in God's cause against those who wage war against you, but do not commit aggression – for, verily God does not love aggressors."²⁵ Here, the Qur'ān uses the term, "la ta'tadu", which means here, "do not commit aggression" and "al-mu'tadun" to indicate "those who commit aggression". The fact that only self-defence is a permissible reason to have recourse to violence is underlined in the Qur'ān's reference to "those who wage war against you".²⁶

After Muhammad and his followers had left Mecca for Medina, the few Muslims who had no choice but to remain were sorely persecuted. At this time, the following Qur'ānic verse was received:

> Permission (to fight) is given to those against whom war is being wrongfully waged – and, verily, God has indeed the power to succour them, those who have been driven from their homelands against all right for no other reason than their saying "Our Sustainer is God".²⁷

God's promise here ties in with His promise to help the faithful by warding off evil.²⁸ Here we see God dealing with a situation in which a small group of people has been driven from their home and persecuted, simply because of

---

22 Q. 4:91.
23 Q. 2:192.
24 Q. 2:193.
25 Q. 2:190.
26 Asad, 2003, 41, note 167.
27 Q. 22:39-40.
28 Q. 22:38.

their sincerely held faith in Him. The case of the Muslims who fled Mecca is the first instance of when fighting for the cause of self-defence was permitted and, in this context, we see God's true believers fighting back against a larger, stronger group that was mistreating it. Indeed, the nascent Muslim community was fighting at the time for its very existence and thus for the existence of the faith in the One True God. Although they had every right to live in Mecca and worship at its holy sites, they were sent into exile. Moreover, the principle of religious freedom for which they fought did not apply just to them, but also to the Christian and Jewish minorities.[29]

Prior to the emergence of Islam throughout Arabia certain months, known as Muharram, Rajab, Dhu'l-Qa'dah and Dhu-l-Hijjah, were considered "sacred". During these periods, all violence between the various tribes that lived in the area had to come to a halt. For the people who made up these tribes, these periods of truce were literally the only times they knew when war was not underway in one way or another. Whereas the Qur'ān revoked many of the local customs and traditions, it confirmed this one, with the idea of maintaining these periods of truce between the very bellicose tribal groups that characterised the area, and thus promoting peace throughout Arabia, in which warfare had long been a way of life.[30]

What are the other circumstances in which it is permitted for Muslims to go to war? In fact, there are a few. One such is in the cause of defending the oppressed. The Qur'ān orders its people to stand up for those who are unable to do so for themselves, saying:

> What is amiss with you that you do not fight in the cause of God and of the utterly helpless men and women and children who are crying "O our Sustainer! Lead us forth out of this land whose people are oppressors, and raise for us, out of Thy grace, a protector, and raise for us, out of Thy grace, one who will bring us succour.[31]

---

29 Ali, 1991, 961-2.
30 Asad, 2003. 256; Q. 9:5.
31 Q. 4:75.

QUR'ĀNIC JIHAD

As we have already seen, during the period of revelation the Muslims themselves were oppressed. They suffered terrible sanctions and discomforts, up to and including threats to their lives, being beaten, insulted and belittled, losing business and the ability to interact with their peers in a normal way, the ability to carry out their religious obligations, and even the right to purchase the basic necessities of life. As bad as all of this was, for those Muslims left behind after Muhammad's Hijra to Medina, including slaves who had converted to Islam, and women and children who were unable to leave Mecca because they depended on a Meccan man for their sustenance, it was all that much worse. For these people, who faced such a terribly difficult situation, God gave the Muslims permission to fight on their behalf.[32]

A large number of Qur'ānic verses refer to the pagans' long-held hostility towards the Muslims, and it is worth referring to a number of them to provide some background and historical context. In one, fighting is described as an "awesome thing" but that, "turning men away from the path of God and denying Him, and (turning them away from) the Inviolable House of Worship and expelling its people therefrom (all this) is yet more awesome in the sight of God," and the Muslims are warned that they have enemies who will seek to fight against them until they have renounced their faith, unless the Muslims hold strong.[33] Another warns Muhammad that those who deny the truth (the pagans and other unbelievers) schemed against him to stop him from preaching or spreading God's word, but that God is "above all schemers".[34] Another verse urges Muslims to fight back against those who had broken their promise, tried to expel Muhammad, and were eager to attack them,"[35] while another warns that Muslims' enemies would not treat them well if they overcame them, stating, "They seek to please you with their mouths, the while their hearts remain averse (to you), and most of them are iniquitous.[36] Yet another states, "But if they

---

32 Yusuf, 1934, 234, note 593.
33 Q. 2:217.
34 Q. 8:30.
35 Q. 9:13.
36 Q. 9:8.

incline to peace, incline thou to it as well, and place thy trust in God.[37] Here, the Qur'ān states that even when Muslims' enemies proffer peace as a trick, with no intention of following it through, this offer must always be accepted. We should only judge others' intentions on the basis of the most visible evidence, and suspecting that intentions are genuine does not give us just cause to turn down an offer of peace,[38] and another urges, "And fight against them until there is no more oppression and all worship is devoted to God alone."[39] This refers to self-defence, in a rather broad sense, as the only justification for war that God will accept.

The Qur'ān also states that there are occasions when it is permissible to go to war in order to protect religious freedoms, which is seen as falling within the remit of self-defence. A relevant verse states:

> But as for those who have come to believe without having migrated (to your country) – you are in no wise responsible for their protection until such a time as they migrate (to you). Yet, if they ask you for succour against religious persecution, it is your duty to give (them) this succour – except against a people between whom and yourselves there is a covenant: for God sees all that you do.[40]

When those who are persecuted for expressing and practicing their religious faith turn to the Muslim community for help, Muslims are obliged to provide it (unless they have a specific alliance with the people who are carrying out the persecution).

Even though wars of self-defence are permitted in a limited range of circumstances, the Qur'ān continues to limit the extent of violence that is allowed, even in wartime, in teachings including, "do not overstep the limits," and "God does not love those who overstep the limits," and "He

---

37 Q. 8:61.
38 Asad, 2003, 249, note 67.
39 Q. 8:39; 2:193.
40 Q. 8:72.

QUR'ĀNIC JIHAD

loves those who are mindful of Him". Six verses provide four prohibitions, six restrictions, and a number of cautions including, "in the way of God", "be conscious of God", "God does not like those who overstep the limits", "God is with those who are conscious of Him", "with those who do good deeds" and "God is Forgiving, Merciful".[41] Every time the Qur'an discusses war, it provides detailed reasoning and justifications for why any violent action should be taken.

Accepting that war is sometimes inevitable, the Qur'an provides for the proper treatment of prisoners of war. With reference to Muhammad himself, it states that:

> It does not behove a prophet to keep captives unless he has battled strenuously on earth. You may desire the fleeting gains of this world, but God desires (or you the good of) the life to come and God is almighty, wise.[42]

In general, when the Qur'ān addresses Muhammad directly it also addresses its rulings to his followers. The verse above makes it abundantly clear that nobody can be taken or kept as a prisoner of war unless he was taken in the context of a jihad, which is a holy war of self-defence, or to obtain freedom. In other words, nobody may acquire or keep a slave, and even captives of a just war must be freed as soon as the hostilities have come to an end. The Qur'an states:

> When you meet (in war) those who are bent on denying the truth, smite their necks until you overcome them fully, and then tighten their bonds, but thereafter (set them free), either by an act of grace or against ransom, so that the burden of war may be lifted thus (shall it be).[43]

---

41 Haleem, 2011, 65-6.
42 Q. 8:67.
43 Q. 47:4.

This verse should be read in the context of a just war, falling within the definition of jihad, when Muslims rose up in defence of social, political and religious freedom. As we have seen above, these are the only circumstances in which it is allowed for Muslims to engage in violence. The verse above relates also to a war that was already underway, and Islamic scholars believe that it was revealed after the first reference in the Qur'ān to physical warfare.[44]

Throughout the period of captivity of anyone taken prisoner, the Qur'ān makes it clear that they should be treated well and cared for. It states, "And who give food – however great be their own want of it – unto the needy, and the orphan, and the captive."[45] The term that is used here to denote "captive" is "asir". While this literally means "captive", it can also be used in a figurative sense to indicate someone who is made helpless by his circumstances for one reason or another. Debt is given as one of the things that can make someone helpless, and Muhammad is cited as saying, "Thy debtor is thy captive; be, therefore, truly kind to thy captive."[46] All believers are thus told that they must invariably be kind towards those who are in need of help (and thus "captive" in a sense). This injunction applies to both believers and non-believers alike, and even to domestic animals, which depend on human beings to stay alive.

The certain aim of jihad, as described in numerous instances throughout the Qur'ān, is to "make God's cause succeed"[47] with all the resources available to us individually. Historically, there have been cases when social-political groups have attempted to apply the principle of jihad to interventions that cannot be described as self-defence.[48] As Rahman states, "jihad was often misused by later Muslims whose primary aim was territorial expansion and not the ideology they were asked to establish."[49]

---

44 Q. 22:39-40. Asad, 2003, 778, note 4.
45 Q. 76:8.
46 al-Dīn al-Razi, n.d. Vol. 30, p. 245.
47 Q. 9:40.
48 Sachedina, 2006, 298.
49 Rahman, 1989, 43; 63.

QUR'ĀNIC JIHAD

For all pious Muslims, anxious to adhere to both the spirit and the letter of God's message, it is essential that they acquire clarity around the true nature of the concept, and understand that the true jihad is rooted in God's eternal laws of justice, charity and the use of violence only as a last resort, only as self-defence, and even then only within a very curtailed set of circumstances as outlined by God through the medium of His messenger, Muhammad.

CHAPTER 19

QUR'ĀNIC COMPILATION

THE QUR'ĀN WAS received by Muhammad in a series of revelations in the seventh century, and the content has been unaffected by changes, additions, or deletions ever since, thanks to the quick intervention of early Caliphs and scribes who acted promptly to ensure that the full message sent by God to His prophet would be accessible to His people for all time. In this respect, the Qur'ān is strikingly unlike other books of revelation, or indeed any early manuscripts, none of which have been preserved with such integrity for such a long time. In the very few cases of minor variations in spelling of a small number of words, these refer merely to accents on certain sounds, or references to pronunciation, and have no impact on the meaning of the words, phrases or passages in question.[1] (We will look at these cases in some more detail presently.)

It is a staple of Muslim belief and scholarship that the Qur'ān is the Word of God as it was revealed to Muhammad by the Angel Gabriel over a revelatory period starting when he was about forty, and coming to an end with his death after the dramatic events that we have described above. As we have seen, even in Muhammad's lifetime this hypothesis attracted more than a few critics, including those who suggested that Muhammad was insane and/or that the Qur'ān was simply the fruit of an over-active imagination. We have already discussed Muhammad's direct detractors in some detail and do not have to repeat this material in any significant detail. As we have seen, none of Muhammad's critics were able to produce verses of a similar calibre, proving that the Qur'ān was emphatically not the work

---

1 Asad, 2004, 383, note 10.

QUR'ĀNIC COMPILATION

of an insane person. If those who accused Muhammad of insanity were themselves mentally well, surely they should have been able to create equal or even better work than he? And yet they could not.

The utter perfection of the Qur'ān is referenced in various verses, including, "Behold, it is We Ourselves who have bestowed from on high, step by step, this reminder, and, it is We who shall truly guard it (from all corruption),"[2] while elsewhere it states, "Nay, but this (divine writ which they reject) is a discourse sublime. Upon a well-guarded tablet."[3] This latter verse is the only succinct description of the Qur'an in the whole document. Some scholars take it literally and interpret it to mean that there is a "heavenly tablet" on which the Qur'ān has been eternally inscribed by God, while others maintain that the verse should be read metaphorically to indicate the fact that God's Divine Word is imperishable, timeless and eternally valid for all mankind. Scholars Tabari, Razi and ibn Kathir generally agree that the second interpretation is the relevant one that should be taken to heart, and that the words "upon a well-guarded tablet" mean that God has promised us, His people, that the Qur'an will never be corrupted, which means that it has never, and will never, be subjected to additions, reductions, or changes to the text.[4] This means that we can always count on the Qur'ān to reveal God's intentions for us, and His rules for how we can live in a way that is pleasing to him.

The fulfilment of this prophecy has always been, and shall always be, evidence of the Holy Qur'ān's sacred truth; that it will always remain impervious to attempts to destroy it, or to corrupt its text and message to mankind. Even Western writers who are generally hostile to Islam recognise that at no point in the history of civilisation has there been any other book that has remained unaltered from the original text, making the Qur'ān unique among all books of revelation and, indeed, all other important books throughout time.

---

2 Q. 15:9.
3 Q. 85:21-2.
4 Razi, Vol. 30, 125.

The Qur'ān's integrity and fidelity to the Sacred Word received by Muhammad is particularly remarkable considering the historical context in which he and his earlier followers lived, and considering the prophet's own illiteracy (as was common at the time). During his lifetime, neither Muhammad nor his followers compiled the Qur'ān as a book in the everyday sense of the word, although various pieces of evidence suggest that individual Surahs may have been written down using diverse local materials including "leafless palm-branches and stumps of palm-branches"[5] as well as other objects available locally. At that point in time there was no real need to compile the Qur'ān as a book, as so many of the new Muslims had actually memorised extensive portions of the Qur'ān and could recite it from memory, and because Islam still revolved around the physical presence of the prophet himself who was, in any case, continuing to receive messages from God. The term "jama'a," which is often used in historical accounts of the early days of Islam, can refer to both collecting material physically and committing it to memory.[6] Moreover, as the Qur'ān was not revealed all at once, but over a period of time, it could not have been put together as a book in the earliest stages of Islam, before the entire text had been received.[7] The Qur'ān states[8] that God Himself had assumed the responsibility of ensuring that the Holy Book would remain forever perfectly as He had given it to Muhammad. It also makes it clear that the responsibility of maintaining early books of revelation (in other words, the sacred scriptures of Judaism and Christianity) in a state of purity had been that of the people. This is elucidated in the following verse:

> Verily, it is We who bestowed from on high the Torah, wherein there was guidance and light. On its strength did the prophets, who had surrendered themselves unto God, deliver judgement unto those

---

5 Gilliot, 2006, 44.
6 Gilliot, 2006, 44.
7 Affi Ali, 2003, 6-7.
8 Q. 15:9.

who followed the Jewish faith; and so did the (early) men of God and the rabbis, inasmuch as some of God's writ had been entrusted to their care; and they (all) bore witness to its truth.[9]

Another implication of this verse is that the Torah, which records the Law of Moses, was written specifically for the Jewish people, and was never intended to be applied to humanity in general, unlike the Qur'ān, with its universal applicability. A further implication is that there was yet more that God would reveal in the fullness of time. We find this further revelation in the Qur'ān.

We know that Muhammad himself was illiterate, so who actually carried out the work of writing down the revelations he received? Various scribes wrote down elements of the book during his lifetime. According to Muslim tradition, Abu Bakr, the first Islamic Caliph, instructed Zayd ibn Thabit, who was one of Muhammad's most important scribes, to bring all the revelations together to form a single volume, after Muhammad's death. This, of course, would have included the revelations that had been written down using a diverse range of materials, as mentioned above, and those which had been painstakingly committed to memory by Muhammad's followers. A number of Muhammad's other close companions provided assistance. Apparently, the many fatalities of Muslim soldiers, particularly in the Battle of Yamāma in 633,[10] included a large number of men who had inscribed the Qur'ān in their memories, and there was concern that if many more died, parts of the Qur'ān might be lost forever, or there might be disagreements about whether or not certain elements were authentic. As these were difficult, bellicose times, this was a reasonable fear to entertain. To prevent any of this from happening, it was essential that the whole Qur'ān be written down, and Zayd collated all the written down sources that were available to him, together with materials that had been

---

9 Q. 5:44.
10 Gilliot, 2006, 45.

committed to memory, and wrote them up as a single document.[11] Zayd had already been involved in committing some of the revelations received by Muhammad to concrete form, and is said to have been ordered by the prophet himself to record some of the verses of the Qur'ān on the shoulder blade of a camel immediately after they were received.[12] The immense work of writing up the Qur'ān took place during the reign of Abu Bakr, and history records that he kept the first entire copy with him at all times until he died. At that point it was passed on to the second Caliph, and entrusted by him to his daughter Hafsa, who had been one of Muhammad's wives.[13]

The third Caliph, Uthman, decided that it was imperative to create a standardised Qur'ān that could be widely spread throughout the growing Muslim territories, for Muslims of long-standing and new converts alike. While sources indicate that the texts of the Qur'ān had already been gathered together during the time of Abu Bakr, the need for a standardized text was based on advice received by Uthman that disputes about the Qur'an and its recitations were emerging throughout the newly expanding Muslim caliphate and that various unauthorised codices were in circulation, possibly containing errors and deviations from the original text, with no guarantee as to their accuracy. At this point in history, most Muslims still heard the Qur'ān in the context of oral recitations and, as is the nature of material transmitted orally, inconsistencies were creeping in and giving rise to disputes. The codices in question are described as "manuscript books in which the individual leaves were collected between two boards".[14] It is not difficult to imagine how, unchecked, this situation would inevitably have led to further inaccuracies creeping in and the steady dilution of God's message. As this was a time at which the Islamic Caliphate was expanding and growing, the potential for confusion would have been con-

---

11 Gilliot, 2006, 45.
12 Leemhuis, 2006, 145.
13 Saeed, 2008, 43.
14 Leemhuis, 2006, 145.

siderable. Thus, Uthman instructed Zayd and several other companions of Muhammad's to use the first collation of the Qur'an to compile a single authoritative text,[15] that would be a faithful record for all times. In creating a definitive Qur'an, he and his colleagues painstakingly committed to writing the verses received by Muhammad in the context of revelation, adding nothing and taking nothing away, with the only editorial input (if we can even call it that) being decisions made as to the order in which the Surahs would appear within the complete volume.[16] The compilers of the Qur'an make no claims that any special significance should be given to the order in which the Surahs appear, but present the book as a selection of writings (described by Neuwirth as a "heterogeneous ensemble",[17] sometimes with Surahs appearing to be without context) preserved in their original form as received by Muhammad himself, and not necessarily in a particular order.

Because reciters of the Qur'an came from diverse dialectal backgrounds, Uthman told Zayd and the men helping him with this important task to prioritise the Quraysh dialect of Arabic, as spoken in Mecca, whenever there was any dispute over how a particular verse should be read. This was a logical decision based on the fact that Muhammad was a member of the Quraysh tribe and that the Qur'an had been received by him in this particular dialect.[18] Since every divine writ was meant to be understood by humankind, it is obvious that each had to be formulated in the language of the people whom the particular prophet was addressing in the first instance, and the Qur'an, notwithstanding its universal application and importance, is no exception in this respect. It was also backed up with instructions from the Qur'an itself, which states: "And Never have we sent forth any apostle otherwise than (with a message) in his own people's tongue, so that might make (the truth) clear unto them."[19] In this way, the Quraysh dialect has become enshrined as the mode of communication of

---

15 Salid, 2007, 369.
16 Neuwirth, 2000, 144.
17 Neuwirth, 2000, 144.
18 Asad, 2003, 370.
19 Q. 14:4.

the Qur'ān, despite a multiplicity of dialects and variations in everyday use among the Arab peoples.

Having completed a definitive text of the Qur'ān, Zayd and his associates sent copies to all of the provincial centres of the caliphate, after which Uthman instructed the authorities to destroy all the unauthorised editions that were being used at the time, and to use the authorised version that had been provided.[20] To the present day the Uthman Codex, as this definitive edition is known, is the authoritative text of the Qur'ān, used by all Muslims everywhere, and one of the many important factors that make a community of a very disparate selection of people. While the removal of flawed versions of the Qur'ān from circulation was not immediate, within two generations or fewer the Uthman Codex was the standardised version, used throughout the Islamic world, in which a general tendency towards the codification of materials other than the sacred could also be observed.[21]

While the content and order of the material has remained unchanged since Uthman's day, a number of linguistic issues continued to be standardised subsequently, including, "distinguishing between consonants with a similar shape, marking of long vowels, marking of short vowels, as well as certain other matters, such as the doubling of consonants, etc."[22] Some development was also seen in the area of presentation. Whereas the very earliest versions seem to have been written down very plainly, with the passage of time elements such as the transitions between Surahs came to be marked with "ever more elaborate and colourful headings",[23] introducing an element of decoration, and echoed over the years in the rich tradition of decorative art that characterises Islam. Over the years that followed the compilation of the Uthman Codex, the trend among Islamic scholars was to accept it as the "pure and complete revealed version of the Qur'ān",[24]

---

20 Gilliot, 2006, 45.
21 Gilliot, 2006, 49.
22 Gilliot, 2000, 48.
23 Leemhuis, 2006, 147.
24 Shnizer, 2006, 170.

despite a few voices that, for a while, clung to the use of earlier, imperfect codices.

While many scholars are in general agreement about the history of Qur'ānic compilation, there have been some Western scholars who have been critical of both the document itself and the manner of its compilation, and who have looked at the origins of Islam in a different way. Among these scholars we can count Richard Bell, Montgomery Watt, John Wansbrough, Michael Cook and Patricia Crone. For example, in *Hagarism: The Making of the Islamic World*,[25] Cook and Crone suggest that Islam was actually a messianic Arab movement allied at the time with Judaism, and not a religion emerging from true revelation. In "*Qur'anic Studies*"[26] Wansbrough posited the notion that the Qur'ān was a literary work rather than God's revelation as committed to memory by Muhammad and recorded in permanent form by his scribes; in other words, that it was entirely man-made. In the process, he claimed that it is more accurate to see early Islam as a sect that emerged from the local Judaeo-Christian tradition at a historical period of intense debate between contemporary Christian and Jewish populations in the area.[27]

While some Western scholars have carried out remarkable work in the field of Islamic studies (and quite a few are cited extensively throughout this work), Western scholarship of Islamic history and theology is not without its problems at times. Little independent research has been carried out by Westerners on the matter of the early sources and origins of the Qur'ān, resulting in a situation whereby they are obliged to rely very heavily on early work carried out by Muslim scholars in this area. This has exposed them to criticism that they avoided exploring early Islamic sources in depth because they were afraid that they would upset or offend Muslims. In part because of these issues, many Western scholars exploring the area of early Islamic sources moved steadily away from a dependence on Islamic scholars in this

---

25 1977.
26 1977.
27 Saeed, 2008, 47-8.

area, and began to examine work carried out by non-Muslims from a range of linguistic and cultural backgrounds. This body of research has led some of them to attribute a Jewish and Christian origin to Islam and the Qur'an, and to a series of arguments that maintain that many of the elements of the Qur'ān are also seen in early scriptures from the Judaic and Christian traditions, making it essentially derivative. Building on this theory, some have maintained that Muhammad must have been intimately familiar with the teachings of the Jews and Christians, and that he borrowed from these teachings, localised them for the purpose of an Arabic listenership, and transformed them into what we know as Islam today.

Wansbrough controversially argued that the Qur'ān, far from containing the divine word of God, was in actual fact a redaction of Judaeo-Christian scriptures and that Islam was a continuation of a Judaeo-Christian sect at that time trying to spread in Arab lands. He argued that much of what we know today as Islamic history was simply invented by later generations of Muslims who wished to create a unique group identity, and that even the figure of Muhammad was simply an invention, intended to provide a figure around whom Arabs could rally, as Jesus had been "invented" by the Christian peoples for a similar purpose. In his efforts to promote this extraordinary hypothesis, Wansbrough, whose book contains serious linguistic errors,[28] claims that the Qur'ān was originally put into writing in Mesopotamia almost three centuries after the period in which Muhammad was said to have lived, and that it continued to evolve, change, and adapt for many centuries again after this period. He points to the fact that there are instances within the Qur'ān of the same story being told in various locations of the book, and argues that this indicates that it had many authors rather than just one.

Crone and Cook point to Qur'ānic inscriptions in the Dome of the Rock[29] that differ from the authorised Qur'ān as further evidence of their hypothesis. Crone and Cook, whose book was published at around the

---

28 Rahman, 1989, 55.
29 An important Islamic shrine on the Temple Mount in Jerusalem.

same time as Wansbrough's, maintain that the archaeological evidence, as well as some contemporary works in languages including Armenian, Greek, Arabic, Coptic, Latin, Aramaic, Hebrew and Syriac, suggest that the growing Muslim community was an Arab movement that was inspired by Jewish Messianism. Like Wansbrough, they insist that Muhammad was not a real person but a mythologised invention.

Crone and Cook's work was poorly received by other scholars and, many years after their original publication, Crone conceded that extensive scholarship in the field of Islamic studies has resulted in the fact that we know much more about the historical Muhammad than we do about Jesus.

Wansbrough's work – published by Oxford University Press, no less – is clearly very challenging and controversial, and it has been influential in some areas. Some other scholars have built on his argument to claim multiple authors and the lack of an original divine authority as the source of the book. It is more than reasonable to conclude that Wansbrough's work, riven with a similar catalogue of errors to Crone and Cook's, should also be seen today as discredited. Indeed, if anyone were to accept Wansbrough's assumption that both Muhammad and Jesus were mythological rather than historical characters, we can only conclude that all three of the monotheistic faiths (including Wansbrough's own Judaism) were constructed on false foundations.

Wansbrough's insistence on the idea that the Qur'ān was written by many authors and that this is evidenced in variations in spelling, has been categorically disproven by American researcher Estelle Whelan, who has demonstrated that the variations witnessed in the inscriptions at the Dome of the Rock are there to ensure that the inscription could "flow" as a single text. Furthermore, as noted above, while the content of the Uthman Codex has remained consistent over time, there have been some changes in orthography and presentation. It should also be noted that for many years Arabic was written without either vowels or accents, which resulted in a situation whereby the same word could be correctly written more than one way (note too that standardised spelling in most languages, including English, is a relatively recent phenomenon).³⁰ The evidence indicates clearly that the text inscribed on the Dome of the Rock is actually consistent with an orthographic style that was briefly in use for a period in the areas of Ḥijāz and Yemen; "… early Qur'ān manuscripts with the same method of punctuation date roughly from the same period".³¹ Four surviving manuscripts reflecting the Uthman Codex but written using this style of orthography survive to this day.³² Moreover, the discovery in 2015 at the University of Birmingham of a Qur'ānic manuscript that dates to Muhammad's time clearly demonstrates that the Qur'ān certainly was not, as Wansbrough suggests, written by many authors long after the time in which a fictional Muhammad was supposed to have lived. The document has been subjected to radiocarbon analysis, which is considered to be 95% accurate, and indicates a creation date very close to Muhammad's time, which is reckoned to be from 570 to 632.

Yet more proof of the existence of the historical Muhammad is found in a range of Biblical and Qur'ānic passages, which talk of a Prophet entrusted with the task of bringing God's message to mankind. For example, the Gospel of St. John to the Paráklētos (a corrupted spelling of the designation Periklytos, which means "the much praised"), foretold the coming of another Messenger, a prophet, after Jesus. The term "Periklytos" is a precise translation into Greek of the Aramaic name "Mawhamana", and both names have the same meaning of "Muhammad" and "Ahmad", which derive from the verb "hamida", which means "he praised". The Gospel of St Barnabas, which was declared heretical by Pope Gelasius in 496, also provides further prophecy.³³

How then should we approach the work of Wansbrough and others who query the most fundamental elements of Islamic scholarship? There is a well-known proverb that maintains that a centipede does not limp when

---

30 Gilliot, 2006, 47.
31 Leemhuis, 2006, 147-8.
32 Leemhuis, 2006, 148.
33 Asad, 2003, 861, note 6.

it loses a leg. In other words, while losing a leg would be a big problem for many living creatures, as the centipede has so many of them, the loss of one makes little difference. Even if many authors such as Wansbrough were to publish books challenging the veracity and very nature of the Qur'ān, it will make no difference to it, as such is its reputation that it can withstand all that its critics throw at it.

CHAPTER 20

THE AESTHETIC POWER OF THE QUR'ĀN

THE QUR'ĀN STATES:

Had We bestowed this Qur'an from on high upon a mountain, thou would indeed see it humbling itself, breaking asunder for awe of God. ….And such parable We propound unto men, so that they might (learn to) think.[1]

This verse indicates that those who remain oblivious to God and the moral imperatives that derive from Him are deader, spiritually speaking, than a mountain, which is completely inert.

The human mind associates two main ideas with mountains; they are high, and they are rocky and hard. In the verse above, we learn that God is so sublime that even the highest mountains are humbled before His revelation. The Qur'ān is so powerful and filled with conviction that even hard rock splits in two before it. How, in these circumstances, can mere human beings display the arrogance that prompts them to consider themselves superior to the Qur'ān's message? How can they be so hard-hearted to resist its message? Humans who are open to God's message, and who are unspoilt, are not arrogant and do not consider themselves superior, but those who have allowed sin to destroy them are considered vile by God.[2]

---

1 Q. 59:21.
2 Ali, 1934, 1724, 5398.

THE AESTHETIC POWER OF THE QUR'ĀN

Scholars and lay people alike have often noted that the Qur'ān, as well as being the divine Word of God and a comprehensive guide to living righteously, is an impressive work of art, with astonishing aesthetic qualities that are unmatched in any other work of literature to have come before or after. Although the ultimate aim of the Qur'ān is to show humankind how to live well and serve God, its powerful aesthetic properties lay the groundwork and prepare us to receive His message. To this day, an essential element of the religious tradition of all Muslims is a certain fascination with the Qur'ān's awe-inspiring aesthetic qualities.[3]

The fact of the Qur'ān's remarkable aesthetic qualities is noted within the text of the Qur'ān itself, which states:

> God has sent down the most beautiful word; a scripture consistent in its repetition, at which the skins of those who fear their Lord crawl, but then their skins and their hearts are softened for the remembrance of God.[4]

In this verse we clearly encounter the expectation that readers or listeners will have an aesthetic reaction to the Qur'ān as well as an intellectual and spiritual one and that this reaction will come first in the form of particular physical sensations and experiences.

This effect of the Qur'ān was changing the hearts and minds of many Arabs at the time of revelation. The Non-Muslim Arabs at that time had realized its power and had tried to lessen the effect by shouting, clapping, singing and engaging in loud chatter. Abu-Zahra comments on this reality:

> The greatest among Muhammad's enemies feared that the Qur'an would have a strong effect on them, while they preferred lack of faith to faith and aberration to right guidance. Thus, they agreed not to listen to this Qur'an. They knew that everyone listening

---

[3] Kermani, 2006, 111.
[4] Q. 39:23.

was moved by its solemn expressive force that exceeded human strength. They saw that the people – even great personalities, the notables and mighty – one after another believed it, that Islam grew stronger, that the faithful became more numerous, polytheism became weaker, and their supporters became less.

As we have already discussed, in the early days of revelation, when Muhammad faced many critics and detractors, he was often accused of being a poet rather than a prophet of God.[5] In the context of seventh century Arabian society, in which poets and poetry were so highly prized, this reflects the fact that even the pagans who so vociferously rejected Muhammad's message could see that the Qur'ān was an impressive work with many fine aesthetic qualities. To them, not believing that it was truly the Word of God, this suggested that Muhammad himself was blessed with the gift of poetry. In fact, prior to the emergence of Islam, there appears to have been some concept of poets being inspired or possibly even possessed by some form of spirit when they created poetry:

> Many Arabs believed a poet to be invaded by a spirt when he delivered poetry; the precise nature of that spirit is not known, but it most probably involved some disturbance of consciousness or the supervening of a supernatural consciousness.[6]

The Qur'an addressed this idea and dismissed it in the strongest possible terms. It even suggests that those who believe themselves to be under the influence of spiritual guidance when they produce poetry may, unwittingly or not, be inspired by the devil, saying:

> Shall I inform you of those upon whom Satans descend? They descend upon every sinful liar. They listen carefully (to their inspiring

---

5 Q. 36:69; 21:5; 37:36; 52:30; 69:41.
6 Rahman, 1989, 93.

Satans) but most of them tell falsehoods. Poets are followed by us wayward ones. Do you not see that they wander aimlessly in every valley and that they say what they do not do—except those who believe and who do good deeds.[7]

As we have discussed in Chapter Seventeen, although Muhammad's critics were challenged with the task of producing verses comparable to those revealed to Muhammad, none of them were able to do so, or even to come remotely close. It has been argued that if they *had* been able to produce a work that matched the Qur'ān's exceptional aesthetic power, Muhammad's claims to be a prophet would have been invalidated, and they would simply have continued their lives unchallenged, as before. Instead, by their lack of response to the challenge they spoke louder than words, and Muhammad's message continued to spread.

Another important aspect of the Qur'ān's aesthetic qualities is one inextricably bound to the society in which Muhammad lived, and in which he had been instructed by God to commence spreading His message: Arabia, as we have discussed in various instances, was in those days a territory inhabited by a large number of tribes, which were frequently in a state of ongoing feud among each other to the extent that warfare was a simple fact of everyday life. There was no concept of nationhood among these scattered and belligerent tribes, and little sense of being a people with much in common. The one thing that the inhabitants of Arabia did share in those days was a language, together with a rich appreciation of the use of that language in a range of formal and informal settings, through the exposition of poetry and oratory. While everyday language was often dialectal and largely mutually incomprehensible, formal, poetic language was the same throughout the Arabian Peninsula and could easily be understood by any educated person. The Qur'ān's intimate relationship with the Arabic language is expounded where it says, "If We had made It a non-Arabic Qur'ān, they would assuredly have said: 'Why are its verses not

---

7 Q. 26:221-7.

clear? What? A non-Arabic Qur'ān and an Arabic messenger?'"[8] In the Qur'ān, which was revealed in the formal Arabic that they knew from the poetic tradition, the diverse peoples of Arabia could find something that would bind them together and give them a sense of unity, not just in terms of a common faith, but also in terms of their mutual love and appreciation of fine language and the complexities of literature in that most nuanced of languages.

In ancient Arabia, becoming known and respected as a poet was no small feat: "… the vocabulary, grammatical idiosyncrasies and strict norms were passed down from generation to generation and only the most gifted students fully mastered the language."[9] Typically, would-be poets studied for many years and had mastered the complex use of language before they were accepted as such. As one might expect from such a tradition-bound practice, even the best poetry never challenged ordinary Arabians' assumptions and ideas about society; the themes and topics covered by the poets were typically discussed in a very conservative way,[10] and while the poetry was often masterful and inspiring, it did not prompt Arabians to look critically at their society or themselves, or to contemplate a new approach to living and understanding the Divine.

The image of Muhammad speaking to his followers and to interested sceptics alike is evoked by what we know from the Qur'ān and historic sources, leading to the impression that the accusations of being a poet were considered a viable threat to the growth of Islam in these very early days.[11] If people had accepted that Muhammad was a poet, rather than a prophet of God, the revolutionary aspect of the Qur'ān's message would have been lost, and there simply would have been no spread of Islam beyond his very immediate followers.

---

8   Kermani, 2006, 107.
9   Kermani, 2006, 108.
10 Kermani, 2006, 108.
11 Graham and Kermani, 2006, 125.

THE AESTHETIC POWER OF THE QUR'ĀN

The Qur'ān revealed that Muhammad became very angry whenever anyone suggested that he was a poet,[12] and in general this anger seems to have been reciprocated by the established poets of the day. Poets were powerful, respected men in Arabian society, and they would have experienced Muhammad as a rival.[13] It must have been infuriating for them to see this relatively ordinary businessman reciting verses with a degree of beauty and complexity that they themselves had never been able to master.

The Qur'ān, a revolutionary document in every way, threatened the very fundamentals of the tribal society in which Muhammad lived, its social and religious practices, and the status and privileges accorded to the lucky few at the top of the social hierarchy. There must have been resentment that an illiterate man such as Muhammad, who had never studied poetry or gone through the arduous process that poets had experienced in order to attain the respected positions they held in Arabic society, was suddenly able to recite verses that were more impressive than any poetry, and also different from known forms of poetry and prose: "The norms of old Arab poetry were strangely transformed, the subjects developed differently, and the meter was abandoned."[14] Moreover, while Arabic poetry had always been very traditional in its themes and topics, the content of those extraordinary verses was revolutionary in content and scope;[15] as we have seen, the spread of Islam resulted in dramatic social change everywhere it occurred.

Because of the high status held by poets and poetry in Arabia, as news of Muhammad's recitations spread, curious locals and visitors from faraway places started to visit to hear Muhammad speak, even if they had no belief in him as a prophet and spokesman of God, or interest in hearing God's message. The Qur'ān mentions the great lengths the hostile Quraysh went to, to dissuade people from coming to listen to him.[16] Presumably,

---

12 Q. 21:5; Kermani, 2006, 108.
13 Kermani, 2006, 109.
14 Kermani, 2006, 108.
15 Kermani, 2006, 108.
16 Graham and Kermani, 2006, 127.

having heard some of the Qur'ān for themselves during Muhammad's regular recitations, they were aware of its awesome power to attract and fascinate even those listeners who believed themselves content with their old ways of worship and living.

In general, Muslim scholars agree that the profound aesthetic qualities of the Qur'ān are an aspect of its miraculous nature and, as we have discussed at some length in Chapter Seventeen, its inimitable nature. The Qur'ān itself, as well as a number of external sources, often references its aesthetic qualities, and early Islamic scholarship devoted a great deal of attention to this matter; many of the texts from the early centuries of Islam speak of the dramatic impact that listening to or reciting the Qur'ān can have on the individual in question.[17] Later scholars too, up to and including those working at the present time, have given considerable focus to the document's important aesthetic qualities and its properties as a work of literature as well as revelation. Historians from Islamic backgrounds generally agree that the key factors underlying the rapid spread of Islam throughout the Arabian Peninsula and beyond were not Muhammad's charisma and military prowess (although these were important) but the extraordinary literary qualities of the Qur'ān, with its ability to reach out and touch people's hearts, changing their lives forever. In this respect, their findings often diverge from those of Western historians, who tend to focus more closely on sociological elements.

Islamic history offers many examples of sceptics, and even those who bitterly opposed Muhammad's message, hearing God's voice through the Qur'ān and finding themselves so deeply moved by its aesthetic qualities that they converted to Islam then and there. Kermani cites various examples, among them the following dramatic story of the conversation of a poet:

> One story tells of the story of the poet and nobleman al Tufayl b. Amr al Dawsī. When he arrived at Mecca some men of the

---
17 Graham and Kermani, 2006, 126.

Quraysh called on him, warning him about Muhammad's magic speeches. They urgently advised him not to listen to his recitations. "By God, they were so persistent that I indeed decided neither to listen to anything he said nor speak to him," al-Tufayl is quoted as saying… The poet even stuffed wool in his ears, "fearing that some of his words might still get through, whereas I did not want to hear any of it!"

Eventually, when he met Muhammad, the poet took the wool out of his ears, followed him to his house, and asked him to recite something. When Muhammad recited to him from the Qur'ān, such was the power and beauty of his words that he converted to Islam on the spot.[18]

While the Meccans initially rejected both the message and the literary importance of the Qur'ān, as the Islamic community grew during the lifetime of Muhammad and after his death, awareness of the sacred book's literary and aesthetic aspects grew, and accounts of the extraordinary effects that reciting the Qur'ān could have on people began to be recorded in ever greater detail.[19] More and more, people are described as listening to the Qur'ān and feeling moved to convert instantly, as in the story of the poet above, simply because of the transcendental beauty of its verses and the dramatic emotional impact it had on them.[20] In this, Islam is markedly different to the other Abrahamic faiths; while there are important aesthetic qualities to Jewish and Christian scripture and practice, in neither faith are the literary and aesthetic qualities of revelation itself awarded such prominence. In fact, there is no linear relationship between them at all, and there are many other vast differences. In this respect, the closest parallel found in other faith traditions is Buddhism, in which certain sutras are venerated as "sublime expressions of the Buddha-word". Even here, however, there is simply no comparison to the vast weight given to the aesthetic quality

---

18   Kermani, 2006, 110-1.
19   Graham and Kermani, 2006, 126.
20   Graham and Kermani, 2006, 128.

and power of the Qur'ān. In Western tradition, there simply are no close parallels at all.[21]

One of the things that Muhammad's contemporaries found extraordinary about the Qur'ān was the fact that although they (and he) lived in an environment steeped in poetry and oratory, the Holy Book was very different to any of the works of literature they were familiar with. When they consulted local experts, the latter informed them that it bore no resemblance at all to other works of literature, and that it was neither poetry nor prose.[22] In other words, it defied categorisation and set a new standard for poets and artists to aspire towards.

While language in all its richness and diversity was certainly a central aspect of cultural life in Arabia at the time of Muhammad, a body of work in the area of literary studies was lacking until after the Qur'ān was revealed, and scholarly consensus is that the Qur'ān itself, and the research and debate that it led to, ultimately created a school of literary studies in Arabian culture. Certainly, after the revelation of the Qur'ān the poetic tradition, which was already very rich, became even more so. Whereas before poetry had been confined within rather narrow parameters, now it was freer to flourish and to seek out new forms of expression and thought. For example:

> The imagery of the Qur'ān and its stylistic departures from the strict formal rules of poetry inspired "modernists" such as ibn al-Mu'tazz to introduce new rhetorical devices and to replaces traditional norms.[23]

Poetry in the Arabic tradition also tended to become more concerned with secular themes after the spread of Islam. Because the Qur'ān covered everything in the spiritual realm, Arabic poets were free to discuss

---

21 Graham and Kermani, 2006, 129.
22 Graham and Kermani, 2006, 127.
23 Graham and Kermani, 2006, 131.

matters of daily living, urban life, and so on and so forth, and they were also inspired to strive ever harder to reach towards, if never achieve, the sublime qualities of the verses in the Holy Book. Also, for fear of being seen as blasphemous if they attempted to discuss sacred matters, most poets in the Islamic period preferred to address the affairs of man, rather than of God.[24]

Although music is generally restricted within Islam, and scholars have been loath to recognise any musicality in Qur'ānic recitations because of the need to avoid confusion between the Holy Book and any songs written or performed by mere mortals, there is a sense in which the melodic and rhythmic qualities of the Qur'ān can at times have something in common with music. Reciters of the Qur'ān often use techniques that are shared by some musical performers in other traditions. A revealing story from the early Islamic period tells of a man who was accused of engaging in loud singing inside a mosque and was duly arrested. A nobleman who had been praying told the police that the arrested man had simply been reciting the Qur'ān but told him afterwards, "Had you not sung so well, I would not have protected you."[25] While this story may well be apocryphal, it does reveal the idea that recitations of the Qur'ān could easily be confused with music and singing by those who were not expertly acquainted with the Holy Book.

To this day, modern Muslims are keenly aware of the aesthetic qualities of the Qur'ān, and in Islamic countries recitations, which can be given in theatres and other venues that are not specifically associated with religious practice, are often considered not just religious and spiritual, but artistic events that can be (and are) attended and appreciated by Muslims and non-Muslims alike. As Graham and Kermani say:

> ... the aesthetic power of the melodically recited scripture has been, so far as we can judge, an undeniable fact of Muslim piety

---

24 Kermani, 2006, 112.
25 Graham and Kermani, 2005, 132.

and practice from the earliest days of Islam to the present moment. The recited Qur'ān is and has ever been the epitome of aesthetic as well as spiritual perfection for the faithful.[26]

---

26 Graham and Kermani, 2006, 132-3.

BIBLIOGRAPHY AND FURTHER READING

Abduh, Muhammad. *Tafsīr al-Manār*, Vol. 6, Dar al-Kotob al-Ilmiyah. 1999.

Affi, Ahmed and Affi, Hassan. *Contemporary Interpretation of Islamic Law*, Matador. 2014.

Affi Ali, Ahmed, *Laqbaynta iyo sharaxa*. juska 28d oo Quraanka. Zaytun. 2003.

Ahmed, Ahbar S. *Islam Under Siege*. Polity Press. 2003.

Al-'Asqalāni, ibn Hajar. *Fath al-Bārī bi Sharh Sahīh al-Bukhāri*, Cairo, 1348 H/1929.

al-Dīn al-Razi, Fakhr. *At-Tafsīr al-kabīr*, Vol. 2, p5, Dar Hiya, Beirut, n.d.

Al Dhubyani, Nābigha. *Diwan*. Ed. S. Faysal. Beirut. 1968.

al-Kalbi, ibn. *Jamharad al-Nasab*. Ed. N. Hasan. Beirut. 1986.

al-Zurqāni, Muhammad. *Manāhil al-irfāni fi ulum al-Qur'ān*, Vol.1, Maktaba al-Assrya. 2012.

Al-Bukhari, Muhammad ibn Ismail. *Sahīh al-Bukhāri*, translated by Muhammad Muhsin Khan, Riyadh, Dar us-Salam Publications. 1996.

Ali, Abdullahi Yusuf. *The Holy Qur'an: English Translation and Commentary*, King Fahd Holy Qur'an Printing Complex. 1934.

Ali, Maulana Muhammad. *Introduction to the Study of the Holy Qur'an*, Columbus. 1992.

Al-Tufi, Najm al-Din. *'Alam al-Jadhal fi 'Ilmi al-Jadal* (w. Heinrichs, ed.), Franz Steiner Verlag. 1987.

Al-Zarkashi, Badr al-Din. *al-Burhan fi 'Ulum al-Qurān*, Isa al-Babi al-Halabi, Cairo. 1957.

Armstrong, Karen. *Muhammad: Prophet for our Time*, Harper–Collins. 2006.

Asad, Mohammad. *The Message of the Qurān*. The Book Foundation. 2003.

Ashamawi, Muhammad. "Shari'a: The Codification of Islamic Law", in *Liberal Islam, a Sourcebook,* Charles Kurzman, Oxford University Press. 1998.

Aquinas, Thomas. *Summa Theologiae*, Blackfriars. 1964.

Ayoub, Mahmoud. *The Qurān and its Interpreters*. Vol. 1. Suny. 1984.

Ayoub, Mahmoud. "Christian-Muslim Dialogue," *The Muslims' World*, Vol. 94. July 2004.

Ayoub, Mahmoud. *A Muslim View of Christianity*. Orbis Books. 2007.

Babylonian Talmud. *Ketubbet*, Chapter XIII, folio 105b.

Barlas, Alma. "Believing Women" in *Islam: Unreading Patriarchal Interpretations of the Qurān*. (ed. Barlas). University of Texas Press. 2002.

BIBLIOGRAPHY AND FURTHER READING

Barlas, Alma. "Women's Readings of the Qur'ān." In Damman McAuliffe, 2006, 255-71.

Boase, Roger. *Islam and Global Dialogue*. Ashgate Publishing. 2005.

Boullata, Issa J. *Literary Structures of Religious Meaning in the Qur'ān*, Routledge. 2000.

Bucaille, Maurice. *The Bible, the Qur'ān and Science, the Holy Qur'ān Examined in the Light of Science*, Seghers. 1976.

Bucaille, Maurice. *What is the Origin of Man?* Seghers. 1983.

Cook, Michael. *Commanding Right and Forbidding Wrong in Islamic Thought,* Cambridge University Press. 2000.

Cook, Michael. *Forbidding Wrong in Islam*, Cambridge University Press. 2003.

Cragg, Kenneth. *The Mind of the Qur'ān*, George Allens Unwin. 1973.

Crollius, Roest. "Mission and Morality." Vol. 27, *Missionalia,* Universita Georgiana Editrice. 1978.

Crone, P. *Meccan Trade and the Rise of Islam*. Princeton University Press. 1987.

Crone, Patricia and Cook, Michael, *Hagarism: The Making of the Islam World*, Cambridge University Press, 1977.

Dammen McAulifffe, Jane. *The Cambridge Companion to the Qur'ān*. Cambridge University Press. 2006.

Dammen McAuliffe, Jane. "Text and Texuality; Q. 3:7 as a Point of Intersection." In Boullata. 2000, 50-76.

Dammen McAuliffe, Jane. "Exegetical Sciences." In Dammen McAuliffe. 2006, 403-19.

Donner, Fred M. "The Historical Context." In Dammen McAulifffe. 2006, 23-41.

Encyclopaedia Britannica, 1963.

Esack, Farid. *Qur'ān, Liberation and Pluralism*, Oneworld. 1997.

Esposito, John. *Islam: The Straight Path*, Oxford University Press. 1998.

Farāhī, Hamid al- al-Dīn. *A Study of the Qur'anic Oaths: An English translation of: Im'ān Fi Aqsām al-Qur'ān*. 2008.

Farāhī, Hamid al-Din. *Exordium to Coherence in the Qur'ān,* Al-Mawid. 2013.

Fatoohi, Louay. *Abrogation in the Qur'an and Islamic Law*, Routledge. 2013.

Firestone, Reuven. "Jihad." In Rippen. 2006, 308-320.

Gabriel, Richard A. *Muhammad: Islam's First Great General.* University of Oklahoma Press. 2007.

Gaje, Helmut. *The Qur'ān and its Exegesis*, trans. Alford T.Welch, University of California Press. 1976.

BIBLIOGRAPHY AND FURTHER READING

Gilliot, Claude." Creation of a Fixed Text." In Dammen McAuliffe. 2006, 41-58.

Graham, William A. and Kermani, Navid. "Recitation and Aesthetic Reception." In Dammen McAuliffe. 2006, 115.

Gwynne, Rosalind W. "Patterns of Address." In Rippen. 2006, 73-97.

Gwynne, Rosalind W. *Logic, Rhetoric, and Legal Reasoning in the Qur'ān*. Routledge. 2009.

Haleen, Abdel. *Understanding the Qur'an; Themes and Style*. I. T. Tauris. 2011.

Haleem, M.A.S. *The Qur'ān*, Oxford University Press. 2010.

Hallaq, Wael B. *The Formation of Islamic Law*, Ashgate. 2004.

Hamidullah, Muhammad. *Battlefield of the Prophet*, Paris. 1939.

Hammudah, Abd al-Ati. *The Family Structure in Islam,* American Trust Publications. 1977.

Hassan, R. "Is Family Planning Permitted by Islam?" in G Webb (ed.) *Windows of Faith: Muslim Women Scholar-Activists in North America*. Syracuse University Press. 2000.

Hodgson, Marshall. *The Venture of Islam*, University Chicago Press. 1974.

Hudbaliyyin, Sharh Asli'ar. *ed 'al Farrāj*, Cairo. 1965.

Ibn al-Muthanna, Abu Ubayda Ma'mar. *Majaz al-Qur'ān*, ed. Sezgin, 2 Vols, Cairo. 1962.

Kermani, Navid. "Poetry and Language." In Rippen. 2006, 107-119.

Ishaq, ibn. *The Life of Muhammad*. Translated by A. Guillaume, Oxford University Press. 1967.

Iqbal, Muhammad. *The Reconstruction of Religious Thought in Islam*, Institute of Islamic Culture. 1989.

Izutsu, Toshihiko. *God and Man in the Qur'an*. The Keio Institute of Cultural and Linguistic Studies. 1964.

Jami 'at Tirmidhi. *Hadith 2260*, Vol. 4, Book 7, Dar us Salam. 2007.

Kamali, Mohammad Hashim. *Shari'a Law; an Introduction*. Oneworld. 2008.

Kamali, Muhammad Hashim. *Principles of Islamic Jurisprudence*, the Islamic Text Society. 1991.

Khaledd Anou El-Fadli. *Speaking in God's Name*, Oneworld. 2003.

Khalil, Muhammad Hussan. *Islam and the Fate of Others*, Oxford University Press. 2012.

Kennedy, Hugh. *The Prophet and the Ages of the Caliphates*, Routledge. 2004.

Kermani, Navid. "Poetry and Language." In Rippen. 2006, 107-119.

Khadduri, Majid. *The Islamic Conception of Justice*, John Hopkins University Press. 1984.

Khalidi, Tarif. *The Qur'an: A New Translation*. 2008.

Khalil, Khalil Ahmed. *Jadāliyat al-Qur'an*, Dar al-Tali'a, Beirut. 1977.

Knysh, Alexander. "Multiple Areas of Influence." In Dammen McAuliffe. 2006, 211-33.

Leemhuis, Fred. "From Palm Leaves to the Internet." In Dammen McAuliffe. 2006, 145-61.

Mahmasani, Subhi. *Falsafat al-Tashri' fi al-Islam*. E.J. Brill, Netherlands, 1961, citing *Sarakhsi,* Mabsut, XV11, 30. Brill, E.J. 1961, 190.

Manzur, ibn. *Lisan al-Arab*. Vol. 4, Dar Sader, Beirut, Lebanon. 1997.

Marlowe, L. *Hierarchy and Egalitarianism in Islamic Thought*. Cambridge University Press. 1997.

McAuliffe, Jane. *Qur'ānic Christians*, Cambridge University Press. 1991.

Mcgrath, Alister, E. *An Introduction to the History of Christian Thought*, Blackwell. 1998.

Mernisi, Fatima. *The Veil and the Male Elite*, Trans. Mary Jo Lakeland, Perseus. 1991.

Neusner et al. *The Talmud of the Land of Israel*, University of Chicago Press. 1982.

Neuwirth, Angelika. "Referentiality and Textuality in Sūrat al-Hijr. Some Observations on the Qur'ānic 'Canonical Process' and the Emergence of a Community." In Boullata. 2000, 143-72.

Neuwirth, Angelika. "Structural, Linguistic, and Literary Features." In Dammen McAuliffe. 2006, 97-113.

Neuwirth, Angelika (b). "Structure and the Emergence of Community." In Rippen. 2006, 140-158.

Qattān, Manā'. *Mabahīth fi ulum al-Qur'ān*, Muasasat al-Risalat. 1983.

Qurtubi, Abu Abd Allah Muhammad, *Al-Jami' li Ahkam al-Qur'ān,* Dar al-Kutub al-'Ilmiya. 1993.

Rahman, Fazlur. *Islam*, 2nd Edition, University of Chicago Press. 1979.

Rahman, Fazlur. *Islam and Modernity.* The University of Chicago Press. 1984.

Rahman, Fazlur, *Major Themes of the Qur'ān*, Bibliotheca Islamica. 1989.

Rahman, Fazlur, "Ellipsis in the Qur'ān; a Study of ibn Qutayba's Ta'ufil lUfushkil al Qur'ān." In Boullata. 2000, 277-288.

Ramadan, Tariq. *Western Muslims and the Future of Islam*. Oxford University Press. 2004.

Reinhart, A. Kevin. "Jurisprudence." In Dammen McAuliffe. 2006, 434-49.

Rida, Rashid. Tafsīr al-Manār, Vol. 6, 382, Dar al-Kotob al-Ilmiyah. 1999.

Rippen, Andrew. *The Blackwell Companion to the Qur'ān*. Wiley-Blackwell. 2006.

Rodinson, Maxime. *Muhammad*. New Press, 2002.

Rubin, Uri. "Prophets and Prophethood." In Rippen, 2006. 234-248.

Sachedina, A. "The Qur'ān and Other Religions." In Dammen McAuliffe, 2006, 291-309.

Saeed, Abdullah. *Interpreting the Qur'an*, Routledge. 2006.

Saeed, Abdullah. "Contextualising." In Andrew Rippen, The Blackwell Companion to the Qur'ān. Blackwell. 2006, 18-36.

Saeed, Abdullah. *The Qur'ān, an Introduction*. Routledge. 2008.

Salih, Subhi. *Mabahith fi ulum al-Qur'an*, Dar al'Ilmi. 2007.

Shahîd, Irfan. "Fawātih al-Suwar: The Mysterious Letters of the Qur'an," in Boullata. 2000, 125-39.

Shaltūt, Mahmūd. 'Al-Islām, 'Aqīdah wa Shari'ah, Dar Al-Sharūq. 1992.

Shnizer, Aliza. "Sacrality and Collection." In Rippen. 2006, 159-71.

Sonn, Tamara. "Introducing." In Rippen. 2006, 4-17.

Wadud-Muhsin, Amina. *Qur'ān and Women, Rereading the Sacred Text from a Woman's Perspective,* Oxford University Press. 1998.

Watt, W. Montgomery. *Muhammad at Medina.* Oxford University Press. 1956.

Wild, Stefan (ed.), *The Qur'ān as Text,* Brill. 1996.

Wild, Stefan. "Political Interpretation of the Qur'ān." In Dammen McAuliffe, 2006, 274-289.

Zahir, al-Alma'i A., *Manāhij al-Jadal fi al-Qur'ān al-Karim,* Matabi al-Farazdaq al-Tijariya. 1984.

Zebiri, Kate. "Argumentation." In Rippen. 2006. 266-81.

INDEX

'Amir, Abu 78
'Umar, Caliph 189
A
Aaron 32
Abbreviated letters 104
Abi Sulma, Zuhayr..134
Abraham .... xiii, 4, 20, 30, 61, 62, 85, 118, 194, 197, 202, 209, 211, 214, 222
Abrogation .... x, xx, 219, 220, 221, 223, 224, 225, 227
Abul-Faraj 86
Abyssinia 18, 19, 108, 198
Adam 26, 27, 31, 125, 161
Addiction 188
Adonis...235
Adultery 146, 180, 181, 200, 221, 222, 227, 233
Aesthetic qualities.................. xxi, 235, 271, 272, 273, 276, 277, 279, 280
Afterlife, The................ xix, 6, 16, 36, 38, 57, 89, 120, 131, 132, 185, 189, 194, 195, 239
Agriculture...5
Al-'Uzzā 124
Al-Bāqillāni...238
Alcohol........................... 119, 142, 144, 145, 170, 171, 172, 173, 227
Al-Dhubyani, Nābigha...134
Al-Din al-Razi, Fakhr 87

Al-Dīn al-Tawfi, Najm 153
Al-Fārābi 155
Al-Farsi, Salman 69
Al-Hudaybiyyah, Plain of 71
Al-Kindi 154, 155
Al-Lāt 124
Al-Muzzammil 107, 108
Al-Qahir al-Jurjani, 'Abd 235
Al-Qushayri 96
Al-Tabari, Jarir 83
Al-Tabari, Ali Rabbani 231
Altitude 241
Ambiguous verses .... xx, 83
Amputation .... xvi, 187, 188, 189, 199
Analogy .... xix, 25, 28
Anatolia 7
Angels 15, 49, 67, 84, 126, 155
Animism 41
Ansar, The 60, 76, 192
Apostasy 167, 168, 169, 170
Aquinas, Thomas 136, 137, 150
Arabia ...xv, xvi, xix, 1, 3, 6, 7, 8, 9, 11, 12, 13, 19, 23, 41, 46, 54, 62, 63, 65, 69, 72, 77, 78, 92, 93, 103, 109, 113, 114, 132, 133, 135, 173, 177, 178, 179, 187, 188, 189, 207, 208, 209, 210, 214, 219, 225,, 237, 247, 248, 252, 273, 274, 275, 276, 278
Arabic ....xv, 2, 46, 51, 94, 104, 106, 107, 110, 111, 113, 143, 163, 180, 183, 188, 189, 231, 233, 232, 235, 234, 236, 237, 238, 239, 263, 267, 273, 274, 275
Arabs ...... xvi, xviii, 1, 2, 5, 7, 8, 68, 72, 109, 137, 165, 179, 184, 194, 195, 207, 231, 266, 271, 272
Argumentation .... xx, 113, 114, 116, 117, 119, 122, 123, 245

INDEX

Aristotle 112, 150
Atonement, for oath-breaking..99
Aws, The 60, 61

B

Babylon..208
Badar Valley..63
Bakr, Abu... 18, 64, 261, 262
Battle of Badar 69, 200
Battle of Hunayn...77
Battle of Khaybar..73
Battle of Uhud 66, 68, 78, 166, 200
Battle of Yamāma..261
Bedouin, The 10, 62, 70, 74, 75, 76, 77, 187
Big Bang Theory...241
Bin Abu Balta, Hatib 75
Bin Al-Khattab, 'Umar.. 19, 68, 230
Bin Mughīra, Walīd..235
Binary nature of the world..242
Bir Usfan..71
Buddhism 138, 277
By'at ar-Ridwan...71
Byzantine Empire 1, 6, 7, 11, 78, 108

C

Caliphate.. 153, 262, 264
Caravan routes 2, 76, 77
Caravan trade..4
Charity................................. 28, 110, 137, 167, 173, 201, 246, 257
Children 11, 27, 32, 77, 139, 143, 147, 161, 174, 178, 179, 180, 185, 192, 194, 200, 252, 253
Christians .... x, xiii, xvii, xviii, 1, 4, 6, 7, 11, 12, 14, 16, 17, 18, 20, 38, 41, 46, 52, 62, 69, 78, 121, 122, 124, 125, 131, 136, 137,145, 146,

150, 169, 170, 194, 195, 196, 197, 198, 201, 204, 205, 206, 207, 208, 209, 210, 211, 212, 213, 214, 217, 218, 224, 249, 250, 252, 260, 265, 266, 277

Commanding right...... xx, 130, 131, 132, 133, 135, 137, 138, 139, 144, 146, 147, 159, 174, 201, 244

Commerce ....xvi, 13, 17, 60, 61, 77, 133, 195, 248

Conquest of Mecca..76

Consistency, Qur'ānic 81

Constantinople..7

Contextualism...163

Conversion 168, 230

Cook, Michael 265, 266

Covenant, With God 26, 27, 37, 38, 40, 44, 86, 93, 95, 96, 97, 101, 124, 198, 250, 254

Creation 28, 31, 89, 91, 94, 95, 96, 113, 115, 116, 117, 118, 119, 122, 126, 127, 160, 241, 242, 243

Crone, Patricia..265, 267

Crusades, The 214

D

Damascus..6, 78

Debt...102, 157, 167, 256

Dhu'l Qa'dah 70, 252

Dhu-l-Hijjah 252

Discrimination...93, 108, 176, 177

Divorce 102, 103, 175, 178, 180, 181, 200

Dome of the Rock 266, 267, 268

Domestic violence 177, 182

E

Ecumenism 216

Education...5, 141, 172, 176, 185, 206

Egypt 7, 120

INDEX

Idolatry 6, 12, 18, 19, 31, 60, 103, 118, 119, 122, 123, 124, 172, 194, 195, 196, 214
Imams.. 152, 153, 154
Infanticide.. 178, 179, 194, 206
Inheritance 110, 174, 207
Inimitability .... xv, xx, 33, 107, 117, 224, 227, 229, 231, 232, 237, 238, 240, 276
Isaac 30
Ishmael 4, 30

J

Jacob 30, 221
Jahl, Abu 62, 65
Jerusalem 7, 62, 108, 136, 266
Jesus .... ix, xviii, 30, 31, 49, 85, 100, 123, 124, 125, 194, 208, 209, 210, 211, 212, 213, 226, 238, 266, 267, 268
Jews .... x, xiii, xvii, xviii, 4, 5, 12, 14, 15, 18, 20, 38, 46, 59, 60, 61, 62, 68, 69, 73, 74, 121, 122, 124, 125, 131, 136, 137, 145, 170 , 192, 194, 195, 196, 197, 198, 200, 201, 204, 205, 207, 208, 209, 210, 211, 212, 213, 214, 217, 224, 225, 238, 249, 252, 261, 265, 266, 267, 277
Jihad
    Holy war .... xv, xxi, 146, 201, 244, 245, 246, 247, 248, 249, 255, 256, 257
Job 99
Jonah 194
Joseph 61, 188
Judgement 15, 24, 34, 45, 55, 84, 91, 101, 110, 120, 131, 158, 202, 205, 211, 246,
Justice .... xiv, xx, 13, 17, 29, 39, 44, 94, 119, 130, 133, 137, 149, 150, 151, 152, 153, 154,155, 156, 157, 158, 159, 161

K

Ka'ba, The .... ix, 4, 12, 61, 62, 76, 92, 197, 229
Khadija, Wife of Muhammad 10, 11, 19, 23, 107

Khaybar 73, 74, 200
Khazraj, The 60, 61, 78
Khuza'a, The 74, 75

L

Legislation .... xvi, 119, 162, 163, 164, 165, 183, 190, 227
Leviticus 135, 169
Literacy 5, 46
Lot 32, 222
Luqman 134

M

Madyan 20, 119
Mâlik 153
Manāt 124
Marr al-Zahran 75
Marriage .... .11, 102, 103, 146, 157, 172, 173, 174,
    175, 177, 178, 180, 181, 182, 183, 185, 186, 200, 204, 207, 220, 221,
    155, 157, 158, 159, 160, 161, 162, 163, 164, 177, 182, 194
Mary, Mother of Jesus xvii
Mecca .... xiii, xvi, xvii, xx, 2, 4, 5, 6, 9, 10, 11, 12, 13, 14, 16, 17, 18,
    19, 20, 23, 22, 24, 30, 32, 33, 34, 35, 40, 42, 46, 50, 59, 60, 61, 62,
    63, 64, 65, 66, 67, 68, 70, 71, 72,73, 74, 75, 76, 77, 78, 104, 105, 107,
    108, 114, 132, 133, 164, 166, 169, 187, 191, 192, 193, 194, 195, 196,
    197, 198, 199, 201, 202, 203, 209, 210, 229, 232, 233, 235, 246, 249,
    252, 253, 263, 276
Meccans, The .... xvii, 4, 9, 11, 12, 13, 16, 17, 18, 19, 34, 35, 64,
    65, 66, 67, 68, 71, 72, 73, 74, 75, 76, 77, 108, 132, 133, 169, 191, 193,
    194, 195, 196, 197, 210, 235, 277
Medina .... xiii, xvi, xvii, xviii, xx, 2, 5, 12, 15, 19,
    20, 25, 50, 59, 60, 61, 63, 64, 65, 66, 68, 69, 70, 71, 73, 74, 75, 76, 77,
    78, 100, 104, 105, 114, 164, 170, 187, 191, 192,193, 195, 198, 199, 200,
    201, 203, 205, 208, 248, 249, 253
Mental illness 143, 144

INDEX

Militarism 3, 79, 248, 276
Misogyny 176
Monogamy 178
Monotheism .... xvii, 6, 7, 11, 12, 13, 14, 15, 41, 46, 59, 62, 63, 109, 119, 124, 137, 150, 154, 194,195,197, 201, 202, 205, 218, 267,
Moon, The 12, 95, 243
Moses .... xi, xiii, 20, 30, 31, 32, 49, 61, 119, 120, 123, 196, 208, 209, 222, 226, 238, 261
Muhammad .... ix, x, xiii, xiv, xvi, xvii, xix, xx, 1, 5, 6, 7, 9, 10, 11, 12, 13, 14, 15, 16, 17, 18, 19, 20, 21, 22, 23, 24, 25, 30, 31, 32, 33, 34, 35, 36, 37, 39, 40, 41, 42, 43, 44, 45, 46, 47, 48, 49, 50, 51, 52, 53, 54, 55, 56, 57, 58, 59, 60, 61, 62, 63, 64, 65, 66, 67, 68, 69, 70, 71, 72, 73, 74, 75, 76, 77, 78, 79, 85, 86, 92, 93, 96, 98, 99, 100, 101, 102, 104,105, 106, 107, 108, 110, 111, 112, 114, 117, 120, 122, 123, 124, 125, 126, 127, 128, 131, 132, 133, 136, 137, 138, 140, 144, 150, 151, 152, 153, 157, 158, 159, 160, 163, 164, 165, 166, 169, 170, 172, 173, 174, 175, 176, 179, 180, 181, 182, 183, 185, 190, 192, 193, 194, 196, 197, 198, 199, 200, 202, 203, 205, 207, 208, 209, 210, 214, 215, 217, 219, 221, 223, 224, 225, 227, 229, 230, 231, 232, 233, 234, 235, 236, 237, 238, 240, 241, 244, 246, 247, 248, 249, 251, 253, 255, 256, 257, 258, 259, 260, 261 262, 263, 266, 267, 268, 271, 272, 273, 274, 275, 276, 277, 278
Muharram 252
Muhkam .... ix, 81, 83, 84
Muqatil 85
Muqatta'āt 106
Muslim al-Isfahani, Abu 227
Mutashābih .... x, 81, 83, 86, 87, 88
Mysterious letters .... xx, 104, 105, 106, 107, 108, 109,111
N
Nadir, The 61, 68, 73
Najd, The 68

Noah 20, 32, 194
Nomadism 1, 2, 3, 4, 5, 6, 14, 62, 187

O

Oasis of Hunayn 76
Oath-breaking 28, 99, 100
Oaths .... xx, 28, 59, 92, 93, 94, 95, 96, 97, 98, 99, 100, 101, 102, 103, 105, 181, 194, 197, 239
Oratory 6, 39, 134, 232, 235, 236, 238, 273, 278
Orphans 10, 17, 184, 185, 186, 194, 207, 256

P

Paganism .... xvi, xviii, 5, 7, 11, 12, 16, 24, 33, 35, 40, 60, 65, 66, 68, 72, 92, 117, 118, 119, 120, 122, 123, 124, 137, 160, 166, 169, 179, 194, 196, 206, 210, 217, 246, 253, 272
Palmyra 2
Pastoralism 1, 4, 5, 8, 14
Penance 102, 185
People of the Book .... x, xvii, 39, 122, 124, 125, 201, 204, 205, 208, 209, 212, 213, 217, 240, 249
Perfection, Qur'ānic 46, 54, 85, 224, 229, 238, 259
Persecution, of Muslims 16, 17, 19, 31, 50, 59, 60, 65, 198, 201, 213, 247, 251, 254
Petra 2
Philosophy .... xv, 51, 154
Pilgrimage .... ix, 12, 13, 18, 70, 74, 162, 191, 196, 202, 203, 214, 240
Plato 28
Poetry 39, 92, 125, 126, 134, 233, 234, 236, 237, 272, 273, 274, 275, 278
Politics .... xvii, 17, 26, 79
Pollination 241
Polygamy 177, 178, 206
Polytheism ... xvii, 5, 6, 11, 12, 16, 17, 28, 53, 59, 119, 123, 144, 193, 194, 196, 210, 236, 272

INDEX

Poor, The ......xvii, 4, 13, 14, 17, 18, 19, 100, 149, 152, 162, 163, 164, 178, 184, 185, 186, 207
Pope Gelasius 268
Poverty 102, 157, 179, 188
Prayer 25, 42, 44, 62, 127, 135, 144, 162, 171, 172, 174, 201, 203, 246
Prisoners of war 255, 256
Psalms 200, 204

Q

Qaynuqa', The 61
Quraysh dialect 163
Quraysh, The ... 4, 9, 15, 18, 19, 60, 61, 62, 63, 64, 65, 67, 68, 70, 71, 72, 74, 75, 78, 132, 153, 191, 195, 246, 263, 275, 277
Qurayza, The 61, 68, 70
Qutayba 86

R

Rabbani al-Tabari, 'Ali 231
Rajab 252
Ramadan .... x, 30, 64, 102, 202
Razi 259
Resurrection 27, 36, 84, 98, 120, 128, 195
Revelation .... x, xiii, xiv, xv, xviii, xix, xx, 7, 11, 13, 14, 16, 17, 18, 21, 22, 23, 24, 29, 31, 34, 37, 39, 41, 42, 43, 44, 46, 47, 48, 49, 50, 51, 53, 54, 55, 56, 57, 58, 85, 93, 98, 99, 100, 105, 106, 107, 108, 111, 112, 113, 122, 125, 126, 131, 133, 135, 136, 137, 138, 139, 150, 151, 154, 158, 163, 164, 166, 169, 170, 171, 172, 173, 179, 187, 192, 193, 195, 197, 199, 200, 202, 203, 204, 205, 207, 208, 209, 210, 211, 212, 213, 217, 223, 224, 225, 226, 229, 232, 234, 235, 239, 243, 247, 248, 253, 258, 259, 260, 261, 262, 263, 265, 270, 271, 272, 276, 277, 278
Rhetoric 37, 114, 115, 169, 200, 278
Rida, Rashid 231
Roman Empire 2, 3, 248

S

Sacrifice, Human 206
Sadiq al-Rafi'I, Mustafa 201
Sarah, Wife of Abraham 222
Sassanid Empire 1, 6, 7
Satan 22, 128, 145, 172, 245, 272, 273
Science 51, 240, 241, 242, 243
Self-defence 78, 201, 203, 245, 251, 252, 254, 255, 256, 257
Shadows 241
Shari'ah law (Shari'a) .... x, 98, 150, 151, 152, 214
Shī'ī 153, 154
Shu'ayb (Shu'aib) 119, 222
Slander 200
Slavery 69, 100, 176, 183, 184, 199, 227
Slaves .... xvii, 17, 74, 139, 146, 172, 183, 184, 185, 191, 253
Socrates 28
Stoning 181, 221
Sufyan, Abu 62, 63, 64, 66, 72, 75, 76
Sun, The 12, 89, 95, 118, 243
Sunnah 153, 221
Sunnī .... x, 153, 154
Syria 1, 6, 7, 9, 12, 60, 78

T

Ta'if 76, 77, 78
Tabari 259
Tabuk 78, 200
Talib, Abu 10, 18, 19
Talmud, The 208
Theft .... xvi, 38, 187, 188, 189, 190, 200
Theology .... xiii, xvii, 6, 41, 87, 97, 112, 114, 121, 127, 133, 136, 160, 191, 203, 209, 231, 233, 234, 265

INDEX

Tolerance .... xv, 158, 170
Torah, The ..... xi, xiv, xx, 23, 58, 74, 99, 131, 204, 205, 206, 208, 212, 213, 224, 225, 260, 261
Torture 169
Torture, of Muslims 17, 198
Tribalism 2, 3, 4, 5, 6, 9, 13, 27, 40, 53, 154, 160, 195, 236, 248, 248, 273, 275
Trinity, Christian concept of the 16, 210, 211
Truce of Hudaybiyyah 71, 72, 73, 74, 75

U
Umm Habibah 72
Umm Salama 173
Ummah, The .... xi, 59, 138
Umrah, The 70, 71
Unambiguous verses .... xx, 81, 82, 83
Usury 14, 17, 110, 164, 165, 166, 167, 173
Uthman 262, 263, 264
Uthman Codex 264, 267, 268

V
Valley of Hunayn 76
Violence ..... xv, 5, 12, 74, 79, 142, 146, 170, 177, 182, 191, 245, 248, 250, 251, 252, 254, 255, 256, 257

W
Wansbrough, John 265, 266, 267, 268, 269
War .... xiv, xv, 5, 63, 64, 66, 67, 68, 69, 70, 71, 74, 76, 77, 78, 141, 146, 182, 184, 186, 200, 201, 213, 216, 237, 244, 245, 246, 248, 249, 250, 251, 252, 254, 255, 256, 273
War of the Trench 68, 69
Water 1, 4, 5, 9, 12, 60, 69, 73, 89, 115, 222, 239, 240, 241, 242, 247
Watt, Montgomery 265
Widows 17

Women............xvi, xvii, 3, 48, 51, 77, 90, 98, 102, 121, 139, 140, 143, 146, 147, 157, 172, 173, 174, 175, 176, 177, 178, 179, 180, 181, 182, 185, 188, 192, 207, 253
Women, Oppression of..92
Y
Yathrib oasis 4
Z
Zachariah..127
ZamZam well 4, 9
Zoroastrianism 1, 108

www.ingramcontent.com/pod-product-compliance
Lightning Source LLC
LaVergne TN
LVHW051543070426
835507LV00021B/2375